Imagined Olympians

SPORT AND CULTURE SERIES
TOBY MILLER AND M. ANN HALL, EDITORS

Volume 3
*Imagined Olympians: Body Culture and
Colonial Representation in Rwanda*
JOHN BALE

Volume 2
*To Show What an Indian Can Do: Sports at
Native American Boarding Schools*
JOHN BLOOM

Volume 1
*Pretty Good for a Girl:
An Athlete's Story*
LESLIE HEYWOOD

Imagined Olympians

Body Culture and Colonial Representation in Rwanda

John Bale

Sport and Culture Series, Volume 3

University of Minnesota Press
Minneapolis • London

Earlier versions of portions of chapters 3 and 4 previously appeared in the following publications by
John Bale: "Rhetorical Modes, Imaginative Geographies, and Body Culture in Early Twentieth
Century Rwanda," *Area* 28, no. 3 (1996): 289–97; "Capturing 'the African' Body? Visual Images and
'Imaginative Sports,'" *Journal of Sport History* 25, no. 2 (Summer 1998): 234–51; "Foreign Bodies:
Representing the African and the European in an Early Twentieth Century 'Contact Zone,'"
Geography 84, no. 362 (January 1999): 25–33; and "Imaginative Sports and African Athleticism:
Colonial Representation of a Rwandan Corporeality," *Kunapipi* 23, no. 1 (June 2001): 11–26.

Published by the University of Minnesota Press
111 Third Avenue South, Suite 290
Minneapolis, MN 55401-2520
http://www.upress.umn.edu

Printed in the United States of America on acid-free paper.

Library of Congress Cataloging-in-Publication Data

Bale, John.
   Imagined Olympians : body culture and colonial representation in Rwanda / John Bale.
     p. cm. — (Sport and culture series ; v. 3)
  Includes bibliographical references and index.
   ISBN 0-8166-3385-1 (hard : alk. paper) — ISBN 0-8166-3386-X (pbk. : alk. paper)
   1. Sports—Social aspects—Rwanda—History. 2. Imperialism—
Psychological aspects. 3. Human geography—History. 4. Jumping—
Rwanda—History.   I. Title. II. Series
   GV673.R95 B35 2002
   306.4'83—dc21
                         2001005770

For Ruth, Roderick, and Anthony

Terra cognita and terra incognita inhabit exactly the same coordinates of time and space. The closest we come to knowing the location of what's unknown is when it melts through the map like a watermark, a stain transparent as a drop of rain.

—Anne Michaels, *Fugitive Pieces* (1997)

. . . there is no use in pretending that all we know about time and space, or rather history and geography, is more than anything else imaginative. There is no such thing as positive history and positive geography.

—Edward Said, *Orientalism* (1985)

The similar and the same are similar, not same.

—Gunnar Olsson, *Lines of Power/Limits of Language* (1992)

Contents

Preface

This book essays two problems. One takes up most of the book—about 95 percent—and is about *representation*, or the problem of how colonial image makers represented an African physicality. The remaining 5 percent is concerned with the question of *complicity*. In 1995, I submitted for publication a short paper on the subject of this book. One of the readers appointed by the journal's editor suggested that, in a paper about the European representation of Rwandan physicality, I should consider mentioning the 1994 Rwandan genocide. At the time I was not sure how European representations of an extinct athletic practice could, in the slightest way, have any relevance to the horrendous events of the mid-1990s, and I rejected the suggestion. Now I think (though I am not certain) that the reader had a point. So in the spirit of an early definition of the essay, I will try, at the end of the book and in a preliminary way, to make the connection.

My main concern, that of representation, has taken me into the murky waters—or, perhaps, maelstrom—of interdisciplinarity. Having said that, it would not have been possible to write this book from a single disciplinary perspective. In the spirit of the essayist, and taking my interpretation of the essay from Yi-Fu Tuan in *Dominance and Affection*, I have ventured forth and made some "trials or experiments" in as responsible a way as I can.

Acknowledgments

For help in various ways with the researching and writing of this book I would like to thank Martin Gren, Roy Hay, Malcolm MacLean, Simon Naylor, Niels Kayser Nielsen, Tuija Kilpelainen, and Jean-Baptiste Nkulikiyinka. While on various research visits to Belgium, I have benefited greatly from the help of especially Roland Renson, Jeroen Scheerder, and Joseph Ghesquiere. For help in Namur and Tervuren, Belgium, I must thank Gus Beeckmans, Philippe Marechal, and Françoise Morimont. A large number of people who helped greatly by alerting me to particular references or allowing me to interview them are acknowledged in the notes that appear at the back of this work. I am particularly grateful to Anthony Bale, Victoria Berry, Susan Brownell, Paul Dimeo, Henning Eichberg, Verner Møller, and Bea Vidacs for offering many helpful suggestions and comments on various drafts of the text. For translations from French and German works I would like to thank Ruth Bale, Olivier Bellon, Clare Slater-Mamlouk, and Colin Wringe. I must add that the editors of the Sport and Culture series, Ann Hall and Toby Miller, have been exemplary in their support for this project.

Parts of chapters 3 and 4 originally appeared in *Area*, *Geography*, the *Journal of Sport History*, and *Kunapipi*. I would like to thank the editors of these journals for permission to reproduce material from them. Various parts of the book have been presented at a number of conferences. I am grateful, therefore, for participants' comments on my presentations at meetings of the British Society of Sports History (Keele, 1997), the Australian Society of Sports History (Perth, 1997), the Association of American Geographers (Boston, 1998), and at the following conferences: "Cultural Turns/Geographical Turns" (Oxford, 1997), "Citius, Altius, Fortius" (Göteborg, 1998), "Postcolonial Geographies" (Southampton, 1998), and "Sport and Cultural Distinctiveness" (Iowa City, 1999). I also presented ideas that are central to the book at a number of departmental seminars. Especially useful were those that occurred at an early stage of the project at the University of Tennessee, Knoxville (1996); the Katholieke Universiteit, Leuven, Belgium (1996); Moray House, Edinburgh University (1997); and Deakin University, Geelong, Australia (1997). Equally memorable were those seminars where I presented what I had mistakenly thought was the finished draft of the book—at Odense University, Denmark (1998); Karlstad University, Sweden (1998); the University of Stirling, Scotland (1999); the University of British Columbia (2000); and the University of Western Ontario (2001).

In Minneapolis, Jennifer Moore must be thanked for her guidance, patience, and help. Robin Moir, Mike Stoffel, and copy editor Ricardo Medeiros steered the book from submission to publication. An anonymous reader for the University of Minnesota Press provided unusually helpful comments on some very early drafts. I am very grateful to Keele University for granting me a semester's sabbatical to complete this book and to the Research Committee of the Department of Education at that institution for grants to cover various travel, translation, and copyright costs. The library staff at Keele University, England; Bibliothèque Africaine, Brussels; the University of Birmingham, England; the Bodleian Library, University of Oxford; the Catholic Documentation Center (KADOC) of the Katholieke Universiteit, Leuven; the Mid-Africa Ministry of the Church Missionary Society, London; the Royal Geographical Society, London; the Koninklijk Museum voor Midden-Afrika, Tervuren, Belgium; and the School of Oriental and African Studies, London, also deserve thanks for help of various kinds. At Keele,

Terry Bolam, Mike Daniels, and members of the interlibrary loans team helped with photographs and books.

For those named above, and for others whom I may have unwittingly omitted, I must add that, in the end, I have to take full responsibility for what follows.

An Imaginary World of Sport

It would be unfortunate if the study of bodily experiences were
reduced to sexual politics alone.

—Felix Driver, "Histories of the Present"

In November 1995 the (London) *Times* published an article about a
British scheme, supported vigorously by the sports-loving then prime
minister, John Major, to send "sporting missionaries" to Africa. A spectacular photograph illustrated the belief that the "Dark Continent" har-
bored a rich supply of athletic talent which could be used as sports labor
in the global sport-economy (see Figure 4.1). The photograph was taken
in Rwanda, a small country lying in east central Africa and the home of
the Banyarwanda. According to its caption, it showed a young man from
the Tutsi people (one of the three groups—Hutu, Tutsi, and Twa—that
make up the Banyarwanda) leaping over the heads of two European visitors.[1] The photograph represented part of what the author described as
"plenty of treasure [that was] to be found" in late twentieth-century
Africa.[2] It communicated an image of African athleticism, and it was
taken in 1907. The late twentieth-century article that accompanied the
photo implied the need for the more civilized Europe to rescue African
athletes from their primitive conditions by giving them the gift of Western sports. In this way they could be taken to places where their skills
would be appreciated and used.

The photograph and the article presented an ambiguous view of
African corporeality. During the nineteenth and early twentieth centuries, it had been widely felt that Africans lacked physical prowess.

"The African"—essentialized and embracing a huge variety of peoples—was written as idle and lazy and often was seen as a victim of what was perceived as the negative environment of the tropical and equatorial regions.[3] Photographs taken by British explorers during the nineteenth century "tended to reinforce the established image of the African interior as a place of disease, death, and barbarism."[4] These views have not been fully discarded at the start of the twenty-first century.

Yet the photograph from Rwanda depicted anything but idleness, sickness, or barbarity. Here was the African as athlete, the primitive as performer, perhaps a variation on the theme of the noble savage. Here was an image of a potential Olympian. The ways in which European observers grappled with, and made sense of, these different perceptions and their resulting modes of representation form the focal points of *Imagined Olympians*. In what follows I do not explore colonialism as a general phenomenon, but instead examine images created by the particular conditions of place and time. Colonial Rwanda was not colonial Africa, and the geographical specificity of its body culture, in its own way, exemplified and contributed to that difference.

This book might appear to be the first to integrate many allusions to an African body culture, hitherto described in a variety of scattered and often obscure sources. It certainly provides the largest (though far from comprehensive) collection yet assembled of visual and written descriptions of *gusimbuka-urukiramende*, Rwandan—or Kinyarwanda—for the kind of high jumping noted above. But I must stress that I have not written a sports history of a Rwandan form of high jumping. Indeed, this work is only indirectly about Rwanda and I prefer to regard it as an exploration and interrogation of European representations (mainly writings and photographs) of an indigenous form of Rwandan athleticism. Specifically, I want to illustrate the ways in which colonial representations of *gusimbuka-urukiramende* during the first half of the twentieth century were ambivalent and contradictory. At the same time, I want to show how colonial writing, photography, and other forms of visual representation could contribute to the construction of a positive stereotype of Tutsi corporeality.

These are my main aims. Much more tentatively—and marginal to the main theme of the book—I hint at how representations of *gusimbuka*, apparently a small detail of Rwandan culture, may be linked to a mindset that contributed to the massacres and genocide of postindependence Rwanda. I emphasize, however, that this is not a book about the genocide.

Where This Book Is Coming From

This introduction seeks to clarify a small number of terms and starts with a consideration of the idea of an imaginative geography of sports. From the outset, however, I must note that because I have undertaken this exploration of a set of colonial texts, this book must be a partial record; I cannot present it as universal knowledge. The book emerges from my own social and academic placing. But in positioning myself in the text and in reflecting self-consciously about its specificity, I acknowledge that I have had a long-standing interest and involvement in sport from the perspectives of both a participant and a researcher. In the past two decades, I have written quite extensively about modern, achievement-oriented sports through the lens of a cultural geographer. This is where I am coming from to write this work. Does this admission reflect an anxiety to justify it as a geographical study, or does it signal the need to emphasize a distinctive take on the imagined Olympians who form its title?[5] In what ways is the book a geography? In the pages that follow, there is the centrality of imaginative geographies (pace Edward Said),[6] meaning those writings about parts of the world that reflected a European imagination. Explorations of imaginative geographies might be "*best characterised* by a heightened reflexivity toward the role of language, meaning, and representations in the constitution of 'reality' and knowledge of reality."[7] Representation—central to geography, or "earth writing"—can be viewed as interpretation, communication, visualization, translation, and advocacy.[8] I touch on each of these meanings in the following chapters.

In much written work, language has been thought to say what things meant; it was regarded as unproblematic, considered transparent. This view reflects a form of naïve realism or, as the geographer Michael

Curry puts it, "traditional common sense."[9] It is now widely felt that the notion of representation (or re-presentation) is disputable and cannot be taken for granted. Nor is representation about "making copies," but is something that is always constructed by an observer.[10] All representations can be read as deformations, in the sense that all words or pictures are metaphors. They cannot be the same as the things they represent. A reaction against naïve realism has resulted in the recognition that representations carry many meanings, as demonstrated in the chapters that follow. Curry argues that the conservative view—that one person can offer a comprehensive, authoritative view of anything—is impossible. This is in large part so because those who write, like those who are written about and those who read what has been written, are *emplaced*—that is, situated in particular social and academic spaces. In each of these spaces, certain ways of reading, talking, seeing, and citing take place so that particular ways of writing/seeing are acceptable to some people, but not to others.[11] However, this is not to say that one interpretation of an image might not be privileged over another—on ethical grounds, for example— since "to engage in representation is not an ethically neutral practice."[12]

Gunnar Olsson argues that language limits one's world, that many writers have been "driven by a desire for the words they do not possess [and that] conventional language did not furnish the words they most urgently wanted to express."[13] His response is to destabilize representation and to engage in the creation of Joycean neologisms and "dazzling wor(l)dplay."[14] In this book I do not go so far as to play with linguistic conventions, but limit myself to exploring the problem of an accurate and unambiguous form of representation of an African (pre)colonial corporeality. This I undertake by the deconstruction (meaning the way in which the instability of meaning in a text is revealed) of written and photographic texts.

The visual and written representations of the Rwandan high jumper described in my opening paragraph invite many questions. In this book, I will focus on how images produce particular representations of the world, but without an emphasis on how accurately images replicate the real world; what the significance of images are, but without assessing or overemphasizing the representativeness of them; and how particular power relations structure the meanings of images, but without worrying too much about the bias in them.[15]

So I will not be overly concerned, for example, with whether the negative of a photograph has been retouched before publication, whether the various actors have been posed or not, or even if the written word is true. Instead, I will try to focus on the key words of meaning, significance, and power.

The notion of imaginative sports geographies—the colonial textual creation of sports out of regionally specific body cultures—is almost synonymous with what might be termed postcolonial sports geography, and at this point I think a minor digression on postcolonialism is required. The "turn" toward postcolonialism as a major theme in academic studies was stimulated mainly by Edward Said's *Orientalism* (see chapter 3).[16] Drawing on that work, I shall use the term *Africanism* to refer to a Western style that makes statements about Africa, authorizing views of it, describing it by teaching it, speaking for Africa—in short, representing Africa in a style for dominating, restructuring, and, often, having authority over it. This style assumed that effective conquest needed knowledge of conquered peoples. Like geography, the term postcolonialism is centrally concerned with representation and can be interpreted in various ways—as epoch, as object, and as method. As epoch, it refers not only to postcolonization, but also to the period following the commencement of colonialism. It therefore includes aspects of colonial relations between the colonizer and the colonized. It has also been argued that, given the widespread presence of neocolonialism, postcolonialism is an anticipatory discourse, describing something that does not yet exist.[17] The objects of postcolonialism include the corporeal practices of indigenous people that were changed on contact with the colonizer. The body also becomes postcolonial, however, through the methods by which it is researched and recorded in written texts and photographs. Indeed, it has been argued that it is in the struggle for dominance within the processes that represent the body that postcolonial corporeality is constructed.[18]

The methods of postcolonialism can be encapsulated in what is some-times called postcolonial theory. This includes a concern with colonial representation—the rewriting of colonial texts and attempts at alter-native readings and excavations of conventional (or commonsense) colo-nial wisdoms and dominant meanings. Consider, for example, my use of the term *gusimbuka-urukiramende* in preference to "high jumping." I have left these words untranslated—an example of "selective lexical fidelity"—in order to convey the sense of cultural distinctiveness and difference.[19] It also avoids the connotative problems of using Western terms, a subject I will return to in chapter 3. In addition, postcolonial methods seek to raise awareness of resistance to colonization in texts written during and after the generally accepted period of colonialism, and exhibit a willingness to seek out "the density, contradiction and ambiguity of colonial discourses."[20] For example, the ambivalence of colonialism itself is reflected in its contradictory aims of civilizing the colonies, on the one hand, and of subjugating their peoples, on the other. Colonial discourse thus can be said to

> refer to that collection of symbolic practices, including textual codes and conventions of implied meanings, which Europe deployed in the process of its colonial expansion and, in particular, in understanding the bizarre and apparently unintelligible strangenesses with which it came into contact.[21]

In recent years it has been widely recognized that dominance over Africa (for example) can come from writing and photography as much as from settling and ruling over it. The reading and writing of texts can make worlds—often, by stating what they *ought* to be rather than what they are—as much as represent them.[22] Postcolonialism, as a method, also seeks to dissect and destabilize the peculiarities of Euro-American modes of thought as reflected in colonial representations.[23] As a result, the work of some researchers has been to shift the research emphasis away from, say, a fascination with other cultures per se to an interest in "their own culture and its problematic relationship with the cultures over which it has representational power."[24] It is the focus on colonial representation, I believe, that makes this a new contribution, adding both methodologically and substantively to written work in sports studies (including sports geography), the field to which it is primarily addressed. The athlete described in the *Times* photograph alluded to earlier was far from being a "sports"-man. But, as I shall show, it was easy—through the sport-geographic imagination—to see him as one.

Other geographies are implied in the chapters that follow. The images of Rwandan bodies were transported from Africa to different Western destinations, the markets for travel writing and sports science. Writing about *gusimbuka-urukiramende* and taking photographs of it involved not only writers and photographers; it also included a wide range of people involved in different activities, from porters carrying equipment from place to place to booksellers in New York City. So there is also an economic geography, markets for images, lurking in the interstices of the representations of Rwandan corporeality. Today, Rwanda is part of a global system of modern sport. Some Rwandan athletes compete in the middle- and long-distance events at world championships and the Olympic Games, and Chinese investment financed the building of the Amahoro Stadium in Kigali.[25] In the early twentieth century, Rwandan body culture was internationalized—if not globalized—by its representation.

But it is arguable that it was at the local level, rather than at the global—in the zone where Europeans and Africans exchanged images—where entangled geographies of power, uncertainty, and resistance were experienced and recorded in words and pictures. The Rwandan practice of *gusimbuka* was juxtaposed to the European image of high jumping, leading to a kind of "common ground"; the recording of *gusimbuka* revealed connections and interactions, even hybridities. In the longer term, however, it was more a story of disconnection, separation, and the eventual erasure of a form of Rwandan corporeality. It is the microspaces of the jumping performances, where representations of *gusimbuka* were consumed as texts, I will suggest, that the ambitions, fears, and fantasies of Europeans, Tutsi, and Hutu were played out.

A final thought on the geography in all this is that geography, like sport, was central to imperial and colonial endeavors.[26] It was crucial to the mapping of empires, which, in turn, contributed to the development and status of the discipline itself. At one level, the academic discipline of geography provided the cartographic details that enabled such activities as imperial militarism, plunder, and genocide. At another level, organizations such as the National Institute of Geography in Belgium, the Society for the Exploration of Central Africa in Germany, and the Royal Geographical Society in England assisted with the funding of visits to Africa and acted as forums for the subsequent communication and dissemination, via their journals and lectures, of explorers' images of empire. Nor should I ignore the role of two seemingly contrary groups, missionaries and sports scientists, who, as I will show, helped in the creation of such imaginations. However, irrespective of the notional disciplines to which they may have been attached, those who recorded these stories and produced the representations of empires and their peoples were geographers. Among them was a variety of "geographical types" ranging from the dilettante to the scholar.[27] They were all "earth writers," but formed a heterogeneous group. Some wrote for financial gain in popular magazines or books that they hoped would reach the masses. Others sought academic kudos through scholarly journals and learned tomes. Not surprisingly, a variety of inconsistent and contradictory messages was communicated.

To summarize, a postcolonial geography of sport might include, first, the examination of the representation of sport and body culture in colonial discourse, including an interrogation or excavation of the practices of authors, photographers, and others engaged in such discourse; second, the unveiling of sport's complicity in the spatial and environmental domination of colonialism; third, the delinking of the place of sport from metropolitan theory and its totalizing systems of generalizations; and fourth, the recovery of the hidden spaces for body culture that are occupied and invested with their own meanings by colonized peoples.[28] In this book I focus mainly on the first of these four aims. However, this is not to say that the others—including certain "hidden spaces"—are totally ignored.

Body Culture and the Place of Sport

Although I use the word *sport* quite frequently in this book, its use is usually qualified in some way. I prefer the term *body culture* because it places the body at the center of sports studies and avoids many of the connotations carried by sport. Body culture, as used by Henning Eichberg, stresses the body as cultural and places emphasis on the various roles of the body in social processes and historical change.[29] The use of this term also encourages a critical perspective. It sees sport as only one configuration of, say, running, kicking, throwing, or jumping. Susan Brownell has taken the term body culture further and uses it to refer to a system of meanings and symbols, hence recognizing particular ideological, philosophical, or even political underpinnings in particular configurations of body cultural forms.[30] Brownell's system of meanings can be exemplified by colonial writing in which the body of the primitive was the major sign by which she or he was represented: "the body, rather than speech, law or history, is the essential defining characteristic of primitive people."[31] It has also been averred that the body of the African has been rendered as visibly different, confirming the perfection of the Western subject by this "self-evident" difference of race.[32] And many descriptions in travel writing have traditionally been those of manners and customs, which begin with the body as "seen/scene."[33] From such representations of individuals, it is a short step to fit them into body classes or groups and to end up with stereotypes that sometimes serve political ends.

Subsumed within the representations of Africa was the African body. Travel writers and sports scientists were surely well aware of the significance of the African body for their respective readers. *National Geographic* seems to have been a willing provider of bare-breasted African women for the great American male public—for entirely "scientific" reasons, of course.[34] Moreover, in the body of the African male the sports physiologists and anthropologists anticipated the "supposedly scientific ideas about the supernormal physiologies of African athletes that (are said to) haunt white athletes around the world today."[35] Ashcroft suggests that the postcolonial body emerged not only as a physical being or object made of flesh and blood, but as a "discursive site, a grammar, marked by contending processes of representation."[36] In other words, it is socially constructed. Gregory suggests that central to any critical inquiry of colonial discourse should be the recovery and rereading of textual practices that were marked by physicalities and performances.[37] Such observations are especially appropriate in the context of the present work, since the body and its physique was a particularly important theme in the European reading and construction of the different groups of people in Rwanda. Yet, with notable exceptions, students of postcolonialism have tended to ignore sport-oriented body cultures and the writing and imagery generated by them.[38] And although a number of works exist that do discuss sport and empire, they are characterized by an unwillingness to attempt an excavation of colonial representations of precolonial movement cultures. This has resulted in scholarly histories of sport in the imperial and colonial world unwittingly adopting many of the Africanist modes of rhetoric to which I refer in the following chapters. Typically, the word *sport* is applied uncritically.[39] Such works also often employ nontheoretical approaches and fail to critique commonsense views of their subject of study.

The taking of control of Rwanda by Europe (see chapter 1) occurred in the same period as several body cultural developments in Europe that are important to the contents of this book. The gymnastics movement had been developing in Europe from the sixteenth century, and later physical culture, with its emphasis on bodybuilding, also attracted wide attention.[40] Of arguably greater significance was the modern sports movement that also paralleled (and was often part of) the colonial policies of the great powers of the Western world. Moreover, the colonial project and sport were linked through a discourse that displayed an infatuation with achievement and victory. This was a discourse of modernity. Several late nineteenth- and early twentieth-century writers referred to the imperial project itself—especially spying—as "the Great Game."[41] The language of Sir Richard Burton reflected this. Following his ascent of one of the highest peaks in Cameroon, he stated that "to be first in such matters is everything, to be second is nothing."[42]

Mountaineering was the imperial sport par excellence. In it the race, the record, and training were central ingredients.[43]

Modern achievement sport possesses many different characteristics, from superficially similar folk practices that preceded it and, in some cases, continue to exist in parallel with it. Allen Guttmann has suggested that seven qualities serve to characterize modern achievement sport: secularism, equality of opportunity to compete and in the conditions of competition, specialization of roles, rationalization, bureaucratic organization, quantification, and the quest for records.[44] During the course of the late nineteenth and twentieth centuries, these characteristics gradually came to typify Western sport, ranging from baseball to bowling and from football to fencing. Although the sport/nonsport dualism can be seen as a somewhat essentialized and Eurocentric view, it may nevertheless provide a point of departure from which to consider the non-Western practice of *gusimbuka*.[45] As I explore *gusimbuka*, it will become clear that it possessed qualities different from those attributed by Guttmann to achievement sport. Even so, it appeared easy to textually construct it as one.

By the middle of the nineteenth century, national governing bureaucracies were being established in England to oversee the organization of games such as cricket and football. English sports were adopted in other countries of Europe and North America. New sports were "invented" in former colonies (such as Ireland and Australia), and the internationalization of sport was further stimulated by the impetus of the first modern Olympic Games, held in Athens in 1896. The central focus of the early and present-day Olympics is track-and-field athletics involving competitive running, jumping, and throwing events. Mental images of the high jump and of the Olympic Games would return to some of the Europeans who journeyed to Rwanda during the first half of the twentieth century.

The Plan of This Book

The first half of this book (Introduction through chapter 2) is mainly concerned with providing a context for the second half (chapter 3

onwards), which is, for the most part, an interpretation of European representations. I have already implied that the book is a postcolonial geography of sport, a melding of ideas from studies of the body, postcolonialism, and the academic discipline of geography itself. There remains
the need, however, to sketch the context within which the imagined
Olympians of Rwanda were written and recorded. In chapter 1, therefore, I briefly trace the background to Tutsi and Hutu "ethnicity" and the
somewhat complex social (and political) situations in which *gusimbuka-
urukiramende* was practiced. I will stress that, despite popular perception, Hutu and Tutsi were not true ethnicities, just as the Tutsi high
jumpers were not sportsmen—and may not even have been Tutsi.

   I interpret the various representations of *gusimbuka* as being multi-
layered, progressively revealing different layers of meaning or "unspo-
ken tropes beneath the surface."[46] I obtain these by insights from the
analysis of written texts, the visual analysis of photographs and diagrams,
and by exposing the hidden presence of history and politics. In chapter
2, I provide some background to *gusimbuka-urukiramende*. I examine the
first layer of meaning that is visible to the naked eye, barely going
beyond reading *gusimbuka* as a man jumping over a bar. This is the
taken-for-granted or status quo view, and hardly scratches the surface.
The interpretations that are made are of *gusimbuka* itself rather than
representations of it (though such a distinction is questionable, since
gusimbuka is essentially a Western representation). And in providing
some background to Rwandan body culture, I am anxious to dispel the
notion that there is an easy way (perhaps, any way at all) of writing with
certainty about such a precolonial—or even colonial—form of physicality. Given this caveat, I conclude that *gusimbuka* was a folk-like activity that never became sportized. It contrasted, therefore, with other,
Western forms of high jumping (see the Appendix), the images of which
Europeans took with them to Rwanda.

   Chapters 3 and 4 make up what I regard as the core of the book.
The second layer of meaning is found in chapter 3, in which the problems faced by Europeans in the writing of difference are explored. I do
this by excavating textual representations of *gusimbuka* found in colonial

travel writing and other literary genres, thereby illustrating the ambivalence found within and between them. Here I am thinking about the categories and words (the rhetorical modes) used in descriptions of *gusimbuka*. Chapter 4 likewise explores representation through visual analysis, and thus provides a third layer of meaning. I excavate a number of photographic and diagrammatic representations of *gusimbuka* and, in so doing, reveal different ways of reading such representations. In particular, I focus on the ambivalence of a European presence in photographs that tacitly claimed to describe an authentic Africa. I tend to restrict chapters 3 and 4 to what is visible in written text and photograph, respectively. However, I interpret both the written accounts and the photographic records as being much more than images of high jumping.

The excavation of the fourth layer of meaning takes place in the final chapter, in which my much briefer and less detailed readings are derived from a regional, politico-historical context, and therefore connect to processes other than the narrowly representational. Here I see *gusimbuka*, and especially images of it, as representing the Tutsi per se. The written and photographic works that represent *gusimbuka* may appear quite innocent and nonpolitical. They may also appear to be solely Western constructions. However, by recalling the contextual background outlined in chapter 1, a further reading acknowledges that, while ambiguous and fractured, the athletic representations of the Tutsi and their body culture are consistent with (or can be situated within) what Liisa Malkki calls "mythico-histories,"[47] the germs of which had been sown before the end of the nineteenth century. I therefore associate what might, at first sight, appear to be a minor aspect of Rwandan life (that is, representations of *gusimbuka*) with a broader context, and in so doing unearth hidden meanings. Without wanting to exaggerate their significance, I believe that it is possible to show that the images of one form of Rwandan corporeality are, in their own (small) way, part of the multifaceted trajectory that ultimately led to the genocide of thousands of Tutsi people during the 1990s. In order to make this point, I relate the basic findings of chapters 3 and 4 to the stereotyping of the Tutsi and the

Hutu between 1900 and 1960. In doing so, I heed Terry Eagleton's counsel that postcolonialism often tends to inflate the significance of culture (in this case, body culture) in human affairs at the expense of the political.[48] In dealing with a politicized notion of body culture, I conclude that European representations of *gusimbuka* are imbued with political meaning. I also seek to avoid dislocating a postcolonial approach from the study of race and racism, which, some observers believe, has occurred in recent debates.[49] In the context of twentieth-century Rwanda, however, it would be difficult to exclude any discussion of the racialization of Tutsi and Hutu, which was central to the kind of mythico-history to which Malkki alludes.

In this book, I try to put the words and photographs representing a kind of Rwandan athleticism in their place in the wider world. This may have been put differently in the preface to *Beyond a Boundary*, by the Trinidadian Marxist and cricket writer C. L. R. James. In it he poses the question, "What do they know of cricket who only cricket know?"[50] Likewise, we cannot know *gusimbuka* by looking at it alone.

CHAPTER 1

Writing Rwanda

> ... historical falsification is not the result of an accident but of
> a strategy.
>
> —André Sibomana, *Hope for Rwanda*

Who reifies (i.e., makes real) particular cultural meanings? How are these reifications solidified and enforced? Whom do they benefit and harm? In what ways are they contested? And (arguably most importantly) under what conditions are these reifications made and produced? It can be argued that these questions are central to cultural enquiry.[1] It needed certain conditions for Tutsi people to be concretized as an ethnic group, a race, or "the Tutsi." Likewise, it needed certain conditions for a Rwandan body culture to be represented as a form of sport, or "high jumping," that was strongly identified by Europeans with the Tutsi. In the Rwandan context, however, the writing of the conditions under which cultural meaning was attributed to both Tutsi and their body culture is an unusually difficult task. The historiography of Rwanda is substantial—remarkably so, for a country of its size and in view of its oral traditions, which were written down only from the start of the twentieth century—but there are major differences of opinion about its precolonial history. Rwanda scholars preface their studies by noting that "with an intensity that surpasses the normal clichés, there is no single history; rather there are competing histories," that "no true historical interpretation [of Rwanda] exists," that "Rwandan history is a minefield" or "treacherous waters," and that its ethnicity, ethnography, and history are "fictions."[2] Not surprisingly, I have resisted the temptation to provide a broad historical overview. Yet I think it is important, in order to answer the questions posed above, to provide some kind of background to the conditions under which *gusimbuka* was represented by European observers. After all, texts and contexts constitute each other.

For the purposes of this book, what I want to stress is that a precolonial flexibility in the categorization of identity of Tutsi and Hutu was, during the period covered by this study, reified as a set of racial or ethnic categories. It is today widely agreed that in most of precolonial Rwanda, notions of Tutsi and Hutu were different from what they had become by the mid–twentieth century. This is particularly important when it comes to exploring the European representations of Rwandan body culture. Similarly, I need to stress how *gusimbuka* differed from the modern sport of high jumping as practiced in Rwanda today. This I undertake in chapter 2.

Derek Gregory has asked, "By what right and on whose authority does one claim to speak for those 'others,' to call them into presence and to display them as the world-as-exhibition?"[3] What is the relevance of Western paradigms of interpretation to local (Rwandan) situations?[4] And without the complete language skills of an indigenous speaker, it is always necessary to question the authenticity and validity of information produced at the point of contact at which transcultural exchanges took place.[5] I am wary about "recovering" *gusimbuka* for the twenty-first century, and doubt how far I could go toward countering "sets of culturally produced images . . . with more 'authentic' or more 'human' representations."[6] However, written and photographic depictions that constructed and represented *gusimbuka*, and the uses to which those depictions have been put, cannot begin to be appreciated outside their social and historical contexts—their situatedness.[7] The reading of a photograph "is always historical; it depends on the reader's "knowledge" just as though it were a matter of a real language."[8] Representations cut across time, but "the appearances of the event photographed [or written about] implicate other events."[9] And it is not just history that forms the context in which a representation may be (re)defined; "society, language, or the unconscious which are beyond the individual's control or even knowledge" also have to be recognized.[10] Writing "neutral" histories are problematic operations. Indeed, "many today would have it that the greater the appearance of neutrality, the more there is to suspect," whereas traditionally the reader trusted the author(ity); today, "facts" are often seen as attempts to persuade.[11] Hence, it is the images and traces, rather than the realities of Rwanda and its body culture, that I cover in this and the following chapter. Perhaps I provide evocations or impressions, rather than histories of *gusimbuka* and its regional context.[12] This is writing that appears evident without full evidence. But whatever way it is read, I am more concerned with European inscriptions than with indigenous histories, and with advancing interpretations and readings than with disseminating information. Hence, my impressions of the contested history of both Rwanda and its body cultures are brief, but my readings of how the European imagination represented it, and what these representations might mean, take up the entire second half of the book. I recognize that such representations will often say more about the concerns of the European than about the African people who they claimed to describe.

Precolonial Rwanda

Precolonial and colonial Rwanda was commonly represented as a kingdom in which Twa, Tutsi, and Hutu were characterized by rigid social stratification and ethnic cleavage. Today, this is widely regarded as myth. Likewise, colonial writing about Rwanda placed considerable emphasis on protection via a clientage system in which Tutsi pastoralist patrons provided the majority of the population, the Hutu, with access to cattle and protection.[13] But the question of whether the patron-client relationship was equitable or exploitative has been the subject of much debate.[14] Additionally, the traditional view that quite distinct waves of settlement by three different peoples occurred at different points in time has become discredited. In particular, the Hamitic hypothesis (discussed later)— that the ruling Tutsi originated in the far north of Africa (even Asia) and were in some way superior to the other groups; that they introduced the cow, the system of royalty, and some aspects of monotheism; and that they were born to rule—is today regarded as lacking any foundation.

An alternative view, more widely held today, is that the forerunners of Banyarwanda settled the region over a period of two thousand years. Originally organized in small groups based on lineage or on loyalty to an outstanding leader, they built the complex state of Rwanda. It is not necessary to review here the details of the emergence of the Rwandan state; they are not central to this book's purpose. However, an awareness of who Hutu, Tutsi, and Twa were is of importance and will aid an appreciation of the chapters that follow. Various categories (race, ethnic group, caste, social class) have been used to describe the three groups, and in this section I want to consider the utility of such categorizations. To do this, I emphasize the country's regional differences and try to show that in precolonial times Rwanda was far from being a homogeneous country, politically or socially.[15]

Consider first the early colonial writing that described each of the groups in Rwanda as a race. The word *race* cannot be used in the Rwandan context simply because the majority of scientists no longer accept that it has any scientific validity when applied to human beings per se. It is widely regarded that no such biological characteristic as race exists. Skin color can be read as a way of categorizing bodies as a historically specific system of "dermo-politics."[16] In brief, "what no biologist, eugenicist, geneticist, supremacist, or polemicist has been able to show is that there is any coherent way to define similarities *within* groups and differences *between* groups on the basis of physical and genetic variation."[17] This is not to deny, however, that race became reified and was regarded as a fact in many of the Western writings about precolonial and colonial Rwanda.

A second designation given to Hutu, Tutsi, and Twa is *ethnic groups*. But the existence of a single and highly sophisticated language, Kinyarwanda, created a common set of religious and philosophical beliefs. Additionally, the three groups lived amongst each other and shared a common culture that valued music, poetry, rhetoric, and body cultures such as dance and *gusimbuka-urukiramende*. Furthermore, Hutu, Tutsi, and Twa were divided between eighteen clans, all of which mixed the three categories of ethnicity and all of which claimed descent from the same mythical ancestor. As with race, however, nothing in the above seemed to prevent the ethnicization of Tutsi and Hutu in the twentieth century.

A third term sometimes applied by Europeans to each group is *caste*.[18] This implies a strict separation of economic activities and a degree of ritual purity/impurity. A widespread and popular view holds that the Tutsi were cattle herders, the Hutu farmers, and the Twa hunters and gatherers. In early times, as now, most people in the region were cultivators who also raised small stock and occasionally a few cattle. A far smaller number of people scorned cultivation and depended on large herds of cattle for their livelihood. Cultivators and pastoralists lived interspersed in most areas. When Rwanda emerged as a major state in the eighteenth century, its Tutsi rulers measured their power by the number of their subjects and counted their wealth in the number of their cattle. The two were usually related. Giving, or temporarily granting, cattle was a way of winning supporters, and a large number of supporters helped to win cattle, both in conflicts with other members of the elite and in adventures abroad. There was some specialization, with Tutsi breeding cows and Hutu tilling the land, but all groups revered the cow. What early Europeans visitors saw was a specialization that reflected the *regional* balance of power. Still, "many Hutu (but not all) in precolonial Rwanda owned cattle, and many Tutsi (but not all) practiced agriculture."[19] In the north, Tutsi did not possess cattle and Hutu had large herds. There is also a tendency to forget that towards the end of the nineteenth century a serious epidemic decimated a huge number of cattle. In the central region where the court (see chapter 2) was dominant, Tutsi chiefs were powerful enough to confiscate cattle that survived from both other Tutsi and Hutu. The idea of caste also requires endogenous marriages. In precolonial Rwanda these were not strictly adhered to, and intermarriage between Tutsis and Hutus was far from unknown. It has been estimated that "tracing back over three generations alone for Rwanda as a whole, 25 percent of Rwandans today would have representatives of both Hutu and Tutsi among their eight grand-parents," with much higher percentages in some regions.[20] Though endogamy did tend to characterize the small number of Twa, they were not regarded as "untouchables" nor were they economically specialized. In addition to hunting and gathering, some were potters, others servants of Tutsi chiefs or clowns and jesters at the court. Caste is clearly an unsuitable term to apply to the people of precolonial Rwanda.

A fourth term that might be applied to the Tutsi, Hutu, and Twa is *social class*, but regional differences make any generalization implausible. The idea of say, a Tutsi social class can hardly be applied to precolonial Rwanda. In the central region, where Tutsi power was strongest, one may have been able to speak of a Tutsi class since those who exercised power belonged to the royal clans. But while the *mwami* ("king" or "sultan") and the royal lineage were Tutsi, not all Tutsi were aristocrats, and lesser Tutsi occupied a place in society little different from that of Hutu. And in the north, most Tutsi owned nothing, while Hutu cultivators possessed large amounts of land and cattle.

Social identity was passed on from the father, but changes in category could occur as a result of social recognition. Hence, a Hutu owning a large number of cattle could marry a Tutsi, and their descendants—usually carried over more than one generation—would be considered Tutsi, the result of his wealth, not their mother's origin. Similarly, a Tutsi who became poorer could come to be considered a Hutu. Exceptional bravery could also lead to a change of category, and an adopted child (common in times of famine) would always take the identity of the adoptive father. It would therefore appear that it was not possible to ascribe the notion of class to the groups in precolonial Rwanda. The meaning of group identity varied both within Rwanda and over time, and no uniform definition of ethnicity existed.

Rather than races, classes, castes, or ethnic groups, what seems to have existed in precolonial Rwanda were categories of identity that varied geographically. To belong to the category Hutu, Tutsi, or Twa was only one element of social identity. There were also regional attachments, occupation, and clan membership or lineage, depending on the region. These could be of equal importance. All of these characteristics corresponded to *ubwoko*, a Kinyarwanda word that could be translated as "category," "species," "type," or "class" (in its most neutral sense). Hence, if asked what his or her *ubwoko* was, the reply of an individual in precolonial Rwanda would depend on the context (e.g., profession, class, or region of residence). There is no word in Kinyarwanda for "ethnic group" that refers exclusively to Hutu, Tutsi, or Twa. Clearly, the word *ubwoko* is vitally important in understanding what the terms Tutsi and Hutu meant before the arrival of the Europeans. If more attention had been paid to problems of translation (i.e., representation), many mistakes—even bloodshed—might have been avoided.[21] To claim to be—or to be given the label of—Hutu, Tutsi, or Twa prior to colonization was a reflection of a mobile social reality. A Hutu could become a Tutsi, and vice versa.

It is important to note that as the precolonial period neared its end, the main form of opposition was not between Tutsi and Hutu, but between the Rwandan court and the powerful notables and lineages who ruled in its name.[22] The *mwami* had traditionally been primus inter pares, exercising little power but having a sacred function. There was a centuries-old struggle between Tutsi who recognized the sovereignty of the *mwami* and the royal court (along with the Hutu and Twa who served them) and those lineage heads and neighborhood groups who refused to accept the authority of the *mwami* authority and his Tutsi chiefs. This group included some Hutu, Tutsi, and Twa from the east and west, but especially from the northern monarchies, which were controlled by Hutu who assimilated all Tutsi to the royal lineage, including lowly Tutsi who lived in poverty. Clearly, the Tutsi *mwami* could not be called "absolute." By the late nineteenth century, it is thought that while the terms Tutsi and Hutu did exist, it may have been common for people to identify themselves by clan affiliation first. The terms Hutu and Tutsi did not have the same significance as they came to assume during the colonial period.[23]

It was under Mwami Rwabugiri, who reigned from about 1860 to 1895, that Rwanda experienced a period of great social upheaval. Rwabugiri created a more centralized state based on power of the throne, in the process smashing the power of the lineages and incorporating smaller Hutu "statelets" in eastern and western Rwanda under his control, but not those in the north. Hereditary power held by old Tutsi families was eroded, and new officials were appointed who were directly dependent on the *mwami*. He also refined the patron-client relationship and introduced onerous clientage ties that were restricted to Hutu. A new centralized system had hardened the distinction between Tutsi and Hutu and made the terms political labels. The relationship between lords and peasants thus took on an ethnic flavor.[24] This is an important point to bear in mind, because it is sometimes argued that the cementing of the Tutsi-Hutu dualism was solely a colonial construct.[25] However, despite these centralizing tendencies, the *mwami*'s power and that of Tutsi chiefs was still often limited to recognizing some form of tribute. To maintain this, frequent raids were required into peripheral regions. As noted earlier, smaller Hutu kingdoms also existed within Rwanda, and while their leaders recognized the authority of the *mwami*, the respect was reciprocated because of the Hutu monarch's supposed ability to make it rain. At least one is known to have received tithes from his Tutsi counterpart.[26]

The importance of cattle as wealth meant that Tutsi were able to dominate much of Rwanda, especially the central region. The aristocrats assumed a sense of superiority that was linked to what they owned rather than their "racial" characteristics. A Tutsi sense of superiority is said to have been based on elitism rather than racism.[27] Part of this elitism was reflected in attitudes that stressed military skill, martial ability, and athletic prowess. In its drive to expand, Rwanda attacked neighboring peoples regardless of whether they were pastoralists or cultivators, and regardless of whether they were organized in lineages or in states. Capital to organize an army came from the livestock controlled mainly by Tutsi. By the end of the nineteenth century, the court was asserting that all Rwandans who held land or cattle held them by its discretion and enjoyed their produce as royal favors.[28] The *mwami* justified these and other extravagant claims through the assertion of five myths which, according to the Belgian anthropologist Marcel d'Hertefeld, were: (1) the Tutsi had heavenly origins, (2) "natural" basic differences existed between Tutsi and Hutu, (3) Tutsi brought with them a superior form of civilization, (4) divine sanctions existed against those who would rebel against the established regime, and (5) the *mwami* was divinely appointed by God.[29] The role of the central court had led to the internalization of an inegalitarian ideology founded on these various myths of origin.

However, again there is a need to emphasize regional differences. The northern part of the country virtually escaped domination. When the *mwami*'s representatives sought to collect tithes from these regions they were apparently greeted with clods of earth, if not spears or at least jeers.[30] Even in the center and south, some enclaves refused to submit to the *mwami*'s power. The notion of an absolute Tutsi monarchy is contradicted by the geographical divisions of Rwandan society. It has been concluded that the interpretation of a nation made up of a people conscious of its unity and wishing to live together is not applicable to precolonial Rwanda.[31]

The word *tutsi* was apparently first used to describe the status of an individual—a person rich in cattle—but became the term used to refer to a superior group as a whole. The word *hutu*—meaning originally someone subordinate to a more powerful person—came to refer to the mass of the ordinary people. The identification of Tutsi pastoralists as those in power and of Hutu cultivators as subjects was becoming general when Europeans first arrived in Rwanda at the turn of the century. At this time, Hutu accounted for about 84 percent of a population that totaled between one and two million. Tutsi made up about 15 percent, and Twa only about 1 percent.[32] However, as I have tried to indicate, these groups and population statistics were far from being completely fixed throughout the country. For example, in the western region of Kyanaga in 1954, Tutsi accounted for over 46 percent of the population with higher percentages in intraregional areas.[33]

The Colonial Period

The Rwanda that was witnessed by the first Europeans to visit the region was formed during the reign of Rwabugiri. On the eve of European colonization, the *mwami* and his Tutsi elite were already the dominant group in Rwanda though, as I have noted, some northern Hutu principalities remained independent. In most of central Rwanda the *mwami* owned all the land and cattle and ruled despotically. He was traditionally the supreme judge. The army was "multiethnic," but the highest officials were Tutsi. Chiefs who administered provincial areas were Tutsi, and where Hutu did participate in political power it was in the middle echelons of state organization. It has been estimated that Rwanda was ruled by about 5 percent of the Tutsi population, the overwhelming majority of whom were poor.[34]

Certain physical and moral stereotypes were attached to the two main groups of people before the colonial period, but it was the decades after 1900 that the transformation of a fairly complex status hierarchy into the more essentialized ethnic pyramid of Tutsi, Hutu, and Twa was solidified. The Europeans dealt mainly with the *mwami* and his court. Because the *mwami* was descended from Tutsi lineage, Europeans tended to conclude that all Tutsi were "masters" of the country, thus ignoring the majority of Tutsi and the northern Hutu kingdoms. At the court, the Tutsi construction of what was to become the perceived norm in terms of corporeality had already started, but would be further refined in conjunction with often unwitting European representations of them.

Rwabugiri's reign was followed by that of Mwami Musinga, under whom the rivalries between the court (and powerful chiefs) and the ordinary people continued. Musinga's ascension to *mwami* more or less coincided with the start of European colonization in Rwanda. The first European incursions into the region today known as Rwanda and Burundi occurred in the 1860s. In 1885 the Berlin Conference dictated that the region should become the responsibility of the German Empire, though it was an Austrian Oskar Bauman, in 1892 who is regarded as the first European to have set foot in Rwanda. In the following decades a number of German expeditions entered the region, notably those led by Count von Götzen, whose report was published in 1895; Richard Kandt, arguably the first European interested in developing closer contact with Rwanda, in the late 1890s; Parish von Senftenberg in 1902; and in 1907 by the sportsman-anthropologist Adolf Friedrich, Duke of Mecklenburg, who features significantly in the chapters that follow.[35] Other aristocratic "explorers" followed, including the Belgian diplomat Eugène, Prince de Ligne; Baron Greindl, the Belgian consul in Berlin; Sir Alfred Sharpe; and the Comte de Briey.[36] Each of these had varying degrees of contact with Banyarwanda. Subjects, formerly separated by geographical and historical disjunctures, found their trajectories intersecting in a "contact zone."[37] It was not simply a question of the Europeans affecting the lives of Africans; interaction also took place in the opposite direction. For many Europeans, the initial impressions of Rwanda were positive. In the early years of the twentieth century it was looked upon by some as an equatorial idyll—"the Switzerland of Africa"—lying as it does in the Great Lakes (or interlacustrine) region of East Africa. With an element of hyperbole, Louis noted that the "aura of romanticism about Ruanda and Urundi"—picturesque mountain countries inhabited by Tutsi, Hutu, and Twa—"explains in large part the importance which the imperial powers attached to them."[38]

In situating the representations of *gusimbuka* within the political and social contexts, it should be noted that the travels of Mecklenburg, his antecedents, and other Europeans who followed him were part of the near completion of the major phase of the colonial project in Africa. In many ways, colonialism in Rwanda was similar to that in other parts of Africa. It was administered from Europe, valorized in various ways, and viewed, reported, and represented through European eyes. This was common to all colonized regions. But Africa was not homogeneous and Rwanda was substantially different from other colonial territories. The colonial writing of Rwanda took place under specific conditions. More significantly for this book, colonial interference in the running of the country, especially before the 1930s, was limited. The country was administered from Berlin in the most cursory way. Although a German military command was installed in Kigali in 1908, power was left in the hands of Mwami Musinga, who continued to exert administrative control over much of Rwanda on behalf of the colonial power. In addition, the number of colonial settlers in the region was small. For these reasons, indigenous cultural activities continued to be practiced during the first third of the twentieth century, at least, and during that period the Tutsi elite could hardly be regarded as having been subservient. Indeed, they claimed for themselves the apex of racial and cultural development and, as I will show, their corporeality frequently spoke for them. Rwanda could, to a degree, be distinguished from its African neighbors (by Europeans who journeyed there) by the corporeal specificity of its body cultures.

The Tutsi elite are thought to have scorned the first European visitors, whose eating habits and odor they found disgusting, as inferiors.[39] As late as the 1940s, their attitude toward Europeans was said to be one of "well-bred indifference."[40] Hutu, on the other hand, welcomed them, and initially saw them as liberators. And though the Germans from the first period of contact found much to disapprove of in Tutsi, many were "enchanted with their physical appearance and their style and manners."[41] The Tutsi monarchy, with its "king," Musinga, mirrored the monarchies of Europe and resonated with European's infatuation with racial hierarchies, and thus convinced the Europeans of Tutsi legitimacy. As a result of indirect rule, in 1914 only twenty-four German military officers resided in Rwanda at a time when the total number of Europeans there was only ninety-six (over half being missionaries).[42] The Tutsi leadership under Musinga exploited both the limited European presence and the availability of their weapons by strengthening the control of the central court over the northern and eastern peripheral areas. When local insurrections took place, the Germans were happy to subcontract control to Tutsi chiefs.

In 1916, the Belgians occupied the region as a result of the East Africa campaign in the First World War. After the war, Belgium was mandated by the League of Nations to administer Rwanda (or, to be historically accurate, Ruanda-Urundi, which in 1946 became a Belgian trust territory under the United Nations). Like the Germans before them, the Belgians discovered that Musinga led a full-fledged nation and hence favored a policy of indirect rule. The need for large numbers of Europeans to oversee the administration of the country seemed unnecessary. For the combined areas of Rwanda and Burundi, the European population in 1923 was 236.[43] Full use was made of the existing political system. In actively supporting the *mwami* as ruler, the European nations had aligned themselves with the Tutsi.

Belgian influence became dominant following the removal of Mwami Musinga in 1931. His replacement, his son Rudahigwa, was chosen by the Belgians. Musinga was anti-Belgian, a non-Christian often regarded as ugly and perverse. He was photographed at events featuring *gusimbuka*, usually pictured wearing African clothes (see chapter 4). Rudahigwa, on the other hand, became a Christian and combined the wearing of Rwandan and Western garb, though this did not necessarily signify an overly pro-Belgian position. His own Christianization was followed by a massive number of Tutsi conversions. Rudahigwa's adoption of Christianity may have possessed social and political motives, and alignment with the Belgians was, of course, far from inconsistent with Tutsi self-interest. Ian Linden neatly summarized Rudahigwa's position as representing "a happy marriage between the old and the new."[44] This was symbolized by the fact that Rudahigwa, while being more than happy to encourage and embrace Western sports and be photographed playing tennis, could continue to show pride in *gusimbuka* and other Rwandan traditions (see Figures 2.5 and 2.6). There remained an emotional attachment to the symbols and traditions of the past.

The colonialists had been fascinated by, and often enthusiastic about, the division of the Banyarwanda into what they read as three clearly defined groups, each with their own essentialized traits. It fitted perfectly, not only with their divide-and-rule policy, but also with the scientific categorizing of peoples (into hierarchical classifications such as races) which was typical of the ideas of the late nineteenth and early twentieth centuries. Such categories were based largely on the external appearance of a minority of the population, which reinforced the rank attributed to each group (see below). The emphasis placed on what were seen as different physical traits is particularly significant for the representations of what were read as Tutsi "athleticism." The Europeans were also very keen to apportion moral characteristics to each of the three groups of people in Rwanda. Physical and moral "traits" became "conflated into a kind of Lamarckian evolutionary code."[45] In order to reinforce these categories, the Belgians and the Tutsi aristocracy combined to focus especially on Tutsi, for whom "traditions," which at times bordered on fantasy, were established.[46] These traditions built on ideas whose foundations went back to well before the nineteenth century. Hutu and Tutsi were defined according to their degree of beauty, intelligence, political organization, and what were viewed as their respective body cultural practices. Tutsi were not seen as conforming to the negative Negro stereotype. The extent to which the European representations of Rwandan body culture can be said to have contributed to these traditions, and the extent to which such images served the interests of Europe (or, more precisely, of Belgium) and the Tutsi elite, will be considered in chapters 3 and 4.

The Hamitic Hypothesis

The divisions noted above were explained and exacerbated by the widespread acceptance during the colonial period of the so-called "Hamitic hypothesis."[47] From the mid–nineteenth century, the Tutsi had been viewed by many European observers as migrants or "invaders" from as far north as Egypt and, originally, Europe. Africanist discourse saw them as being of a different ethnic origin from other Africans in eastern central Africa. The French racial theorist, Aryanist, and believer in the inequality of races, Joseph Arthur, Comte de Gobineau (1816–82), had argued that a race of Hamitic (or even Semitic) people had settled in the Great Lakes area of central Africa, an idea adopted and publicized by the British geographer-explorer, John Hanning Speke.[48] It continued to be accepted without criticism well into the twentieth century. Parish von Senftenberg believed the Tutsi to be of Semitic origin, though he was careful to note that they were not of the "Jewish type."[49] Other Western travel writers believed that the Tutsi were descended from the pharaohs. Attilio and Ellen Gatti happily accepted this view, and observed that these are the tallest, handsomest, keenest of all Africans, undoubtedly the purest "surviving Pharaohs" on earth. . . . The incontrovertible fact is that the giant Watussi are, in the middle of a vast mass of bantu natives, like a small unique island of thoroughbred Hamites.[50]

The Hamitic hypothesis, it has been argued, was applied in Rwanda because of the need to solve the "problem" of who had created the civilizations (and, it could be added, the corporeal prowess of the people) in this part of black Africa. According to Gobineau, it could not have been the "pure black African." A non-Negro solution was needed, and was provided by the migrant, but mythical, Hamites.[51] I use the word "mythical" because no hard evidence of migration actually exists. There is no evidence of any northern linguistic traits, and it has been claimed that the interlacustrine peoples themselves possess no records of immigration from the north.[52] Physical differences between groups may imply former migration, but such differences in appearance between Hutu, Tutsi, and Twa are grossly exaggerated.[53] However, it is hardly surprising that none of these reservations prevented the reification of the Hamitic hypothesis by Tutsi intellectuals themselves. Indeed, hard-liners in both Tutsi and Hutu groups came to accept the myth, and it became part of the generally accepted history of Rwanda.

I have already alluded to the concept of the stereotype, and at this stage it may be appropriate to elaborate on that term. I have implied, and I will explicate below, that in Rwanda there existed both negative and positive stereotypes. Hutu and Tutsi respectively seem to perfectly illustrate the notion that "*the* most negative *stereotype* always has an overtly positive counterweight."[54] And "idealization only serves to emphasize the negative qualities of those actually encountered"[55]—in this case, the overwhelming majority of the population, the lumpen Tutsi, the mass of Hutu, and the Twa. Rwanda is also illustrative of the fact that stereotypes arise when self-integration is threatened. Drawing on the work of Sander Gilman, it can be argued that our images of the world are altered by our interactions with reality. We may see someone as aggressive, but without a recurring pattern of aggression we can resolve the conflict between a bad image and a complex reality, hence seeing the individual as being both good *and* bad. But when the sense of order and control undergoes stress, an anxiety appears which is projected on to the Other, thereby externalizing our loss of control.[56] The Other is therefore stereotyped, that is to say, labeled with a set of signs mirroring that loss of control. The Other is invested with qualities of the "bad" or the "good." The good Other becomes the positive stereotype—that which we fear we cannot achieve.[57]

Central to the Hamitic hypothesis was the positive Tutsi stereotype—tall, straight-nosed, thin, and less dark-skinned than the Hutu. At the same time, the "Hamites" were seen as members of a superior race, as born leaders. The Hamitic Tutsi was said to "resemble the Negro only in the color of his skin"; or, "he is a European who happens to have black skin."[58] The Europeans seemed happy to construct the Tutsi-Hutu difference on the model of France in the Middle Ages, invoking Franks and Gauls as medieval analogs.[59] Even in the late 1950s, it was possible for a Belgian observer to note that "almost everyone is susceptible to the Tutsi physique and manners for a certain time."[60] In an extreme rhetorical appropriation of Tutsi people, the claim was made that they are

> tall, slightly built men of graceful, nonchalant carriage, and their features are delicate and refined. I noticed many faces that, bleached and set in a white collar, would have been conspicuous for a character in a London drawing room. The legal type was specially pronounced.[61]

Likewise, through the use of the rhetorical mode of idealization, it was recorded that

> [t]hese natives present a most graceful and dignified appearance and moreover posses the rare qualities of honesty and truthfulness, so seldom found among the inhabitants of Africa today, with high foreheads, oval faces, and clean-cut features of Egyptian cast. We never tired of watching them. To see a group of these fine fellows talking and laughing together was a real pleasure, which could never be the case of the snub-nosed Bantu.[62]

If it were a case of the Tutsi being virtual Europeans it would be easy (almost natural) for the Belgians to work with them and to entrust them with the administration of the territory. The attraction of the hypothesis for the Europeans was that it allowed Tutsi physical characteristics to be correlated with mental ability. It was also typical of Africanist rhetoric that certain peoples and cultures were closer to the European than others.[63] Indeed, in Nazi Germany the notion of the *Volk* had even encouraged the constructions of nostalgic anthropologies in which the Hamitic Tutsi were freely thought of as Aryans.[64]

If Tutsi were stereotyped as tall, stately, and thin, then Hutu were short, stocky, plain peasants. They conformed to the negative Negro stereotype. Typical representations of them included the following:

> It is not surprising that those good Bahutu, less intelligent, more simple, more spontaneous, more trusting, have let themselves be enslaved without ever daring to revolt.[65]
>
> The Bahutu display very typical Bantu features … They are generally short and thick-set with a big head, jovial expression, a wide nose and enormous lips. They are extroverts who like to laugh and lead a simple life.[66]

Such judgments were supported by the results of what are today regarded as dubious anthropometricism. The measurements of the so-called "giants" of Africa varied considerably between individual observers. Lionel Decle stated that they stood between 5 feet 6 inches and 5 feet 8 inches; others suggested an average height of 5 feet 8 inches or nearly 5 feet 11 inches (1.80 meters), while an extreme estimate by Attilio Gatti (an Italian millionaire-traveler) placed the Tutsis' "*average* height at above seven feet."[67] Often, it was only measurements above the average that were cited in order to stress a "giant" or "freak" image. Hence, "heights of 1.80, 2.00, and even 2.20 meters are of quite common occurrence, " noted Mecklenburg.[68] What sometimes turned out to be a selected sample of monarchical Tutsis who had intermarried and shared the same gene pool was hardly typical of the group as a whole.[69] The Hutu and Twa were recorded as smaller in stature. A study of the two main groups showed the average Tutsi to be 1.74 meters tall in contrast to the Hutu average of 1.69 meters.[70] Such differentiation, based on average heights, has been described as nonsense, not simply because of the problem of the representativeness of the arithmetic mean, but also because of the substantial number of people of mixed origins.[71] And while the data noted above were used to identify two "races," the greater difference between samples of French senators and lords (1.70 meters) and conscripts (1.61 meters) was never used to suggest racial differences.[72] Differences in diet, exercise, and choice of partner are widely used to explain such variations in the West but not, it seems, in the case of Rwanda. It has been pointed out that in the case of Tutsi and Hutu, "the difference in physical stature between the groups has been wildly exaggerated: it is rarely possible to tell whether an individual is a Twa, Hutu or Tutsi from his or her height."[73] However, "the fact that these distinctions were quite obviously heavily elaborated cultural constructs—ideal types confounded by the reality of physical diversity and variation—did not in the least detract from their power as classificatory tools.[74] Indeed, "otherwise incidental physical differences came to bear the weight of an entire history of state formation."[75]

The European promotion of Tutsi was undertaken by the Germans, the Belgians, and, initially at least, by European missionaries, notably the Roman Catholic Society of the Missionaries of our Lady of Africa, also known as the White Fathers.[76] Members of the Church Missionary Society (CMS) of the Church of England also promoted Tutsi people through their writings during the 1920s and 1930s, and in doing so often alluded to Tutsi athletic skills. Among the missionaries were a small number of Europeans who had a working knowledge of African languages. Others who promoted the Tutsi included a number of bourgeois travelers from various nations of western Europe and the United States who were attracted to the eastern Congo and Rwanda during the second quarter of the twentieth century. The works of these writers was literary rather than scholarly—examples of popular ethnography—and rejected the discipline of anthropological fieldwork. The time spent by travel writers in particular locales was limited, compared with that of the modern ethnologist and anthropologist. Mecklenburg—the first European known to have witnessed *gusimbuka*—studied anthropology at Dresden but wrote for the popular end of the travel writing market.[77] He appeared to make a traveler's passing observations rather than the considered thoughts of a scientist, though *how* considered some of the scientist's thoughts were should not be exaggerated.[78] Among the more prolific writers on the Banyarwanda and their lifestyle were the popular works of Attilio and Ellen Gatti. Between them, they authored more than a half dozen books and several journal articles that made at least some mention of local athletic pursuits. Such writers often included photographic evidence of Tutsi corporeality, though their written accounts of *gusimbuka* rarely extended beyond a page of text. Even Mecklenburg's account, which seemed to become definitive during the course of the first half of the twentieth century, did not exceed a single page. Most descriptions were not published in scientific journals but in books and magazines that found their way into public libraries and the homes of the upper and middle classes as much as—if not more than—on university library shelves. *Ruanda Notes*, newsletter of the Rwanda Mission of the CMS, made several brief allusions to Rwandan athleticism during the 1920s, but had a limited circulation. Other writers to focus on *gusimbuka-urukiramende* included a variety of "scientific" authorities that included geographers, anthropologists, physical educators, and sports scientists. It seems likely that several of these never actually witnessed a *gusimbuka* event or even visited Rwanda, but instead drew on secondary material—often, from Mecklenburg's account.[79] Geographical journals made passing reference to Tutsi physicality, based on his account.[80] In the construction of a Rwandan—or, more precisely, a Tutsi—athleticism, it did not matter that *gusimbuka* had not been witnessed personally. It was not what was seen that mattered as much as the dreams and fantasies of those who presumed authority. While allusions to dancing were common in anthropological works, there have been few serious aca-demic discussions of *gusimbuka*. One huge compendium on culture in Rwanda includes only a single reference to the Rwandan form of "high jumping."[81] The first detailed analysis of it was published only in 1941 by the German-born polymath and Tutsi eulogist, Ernst Jokl (see chapters 4 and 5).[82]

The colonial powers may not have invented the categories of Tutsi, Hutu, and Twa, but the activities of the Europeans hardened them. The Catholic Church believed that the best hope for the future of Rwanda lay in the Tutsi as "born leaders." Subsequently, Tutsi were favored by the education system, came to dominate the educated class, and assumed a disproportionately significant place within the nation's administration. The Hutu also absorbed the Hamitic thesis. They had been taught it in schools by Catholic missionaries and read about it in the work of Father Albert Pagès or the more popular two-volume book, *Ruanda*, by Canon Louis de Lacger.[83] Many Hutu, having been continually told that they were naturally inferior, came to believe it. The extent to which the written and photographic representations of Tutsi contributed to this image of superiority can be judged from the contents of the following chapters.

The ethnic division of the Banyarwanda was institutionalized in 1933 with the issue of mandatory identity cards by which different peoples could be "officially" identified. Asked which group they were affiliated with, about 84 percent said they were Hutu.[84] The possibility of a Hutu moving from the peasant class to the aristocracy was finally removed. It has been argued that forty years of Belgian administration included the "disintegration, distortion and bastardization of indigenous social and political structures and their consequences."[85] Race and social identity—a single element of the *ubwoko*—were in this way isolated. Differences had been reified (or "thing"ified) into solidified groups, and the Rwandans now began to define themselves according to European labels—a legacy of Tutsi power, Africanism, and the "crushing philosophy" of the Christian dictum of each according to his station.[86] At the danger of oversimplifying, it can be said that, for the first half of the twentieth century, it was in the interests of the Belgians to support the Tutsi and it was in the interests of Tutsi to be seen as allied with the Belgians. For the Belgians, Tutsi were born and traditional leaders; for an elite minority of Tutsi, Belgium was the colonial power that would guarantee their continued political dominance.

Amplified Traditions

By the 1930s, and arguably much earlier, the Tutsi elite were far from being bystanders in their image making. As colonialism proceeded, it was in the interests of the Tutsi hierarchy to reinforce European images of their own superiority and to claim that their superiority was rooted in history and culture. It has been suggested that "Rwanda is unique in the sheer abundance of traditions purporting to show the superiority of the Tutsi over the other castes, and in the cumulative impact of these traditions on society as a whole."[87] Before 1900, Tutsi nobility (though not, as noted earlier, all Tutsi) had become a well-defined social class whose "eating habits, deportment, culture and ideology" were designed to instill what Maquet termed a "premise of inequality."[88] The variety of folktales from Rwanda "were supplemented by court historians whose task was to hand down to posterity the glorious traditions of the realm— not as history might have it but, rather, as royal ordinance prescribed."[89] The pre-eminent Rwandan historian is widely regarded to have been Alexis Kagame (1912–81), a seminarist at Kabgayi between 1929 and 1941 who subsequently obtained a doctorate from the Gregorian University in Rome. Authorized by Mwami Rudahigwa to reassemble various ritual traditions in order to conserve the "natural inheritance" of the Tutsi, he published two volumes of his dynastic history during the 1940s and authored a lengthy poem that glorified both Rwandan royalty and the nation's Christianization. In these publications Kagame consistently defended the preeminence of the Tutsi and their Hamitic status and virtually ignored the Hutu. His work is regarded as central to Rwanda's historiography and to generations of Rwandan youth.[90] With Father Pagès, he erected a "traditional" kingdom and a "traditional" aristocracy that were hybrid constructions. In so doing, he "borrow[ed] some traits from European historical stereotypes and others from the Rwandan nobility as it had been re-engineered by colonial policies."[91] This involved what has been termed "a chilling traffic back and forth between the essentialist construction of historians, anthropologists, and colonial administrators, and those of Hutu and Tutsi ethnic nationalists."[92] According to the 1990s Rwandan civil rights activist, André Sibomana, Kagame's account of the history of Rwanda "consists of nothing but falsehoods from the first page to the last."[93] More benignly, Kagame has been described as having played "the exceptional role of intermediary" in the history of Rwanda—"at the same time a dignitary close to Rudahigwa, a priest trained for the purpose by Canon de Lacger and a genuine investigator seeking information."[94] But Rwanda scholar Jan Vansina has summarized Kagame as "a mass of contradictions . . . a humanist, and yet a racist who firmly believed in the superior talents of the Hamites and the lesser ones of Negroes, although everyone was equal in the eyes of God."[95]

Gusimbuka-urukiramende and its representations by European writers and photographers should be read in the light of these comments. In their works both Kagame and Pagès alluded to *gusimbuka*, but the extent to which Sibomana would have regarded such body cultural practices as falsehoods is unclear. It is impossible to assess the extent to which *gusimbuka* and its European-constructed images were part of a reconstructed "traditional Rwanda." After all, "local assertions of what is traditional are just that—assertions."[96] However, there is every reason to believe that sports (or, as I would say, body cultures) were included, along with attire and the arts, among the aspects of culture which, under Rudahigwa, were reinvented to crystallize Tutsi ideology.[97] But reinvented from what, in the case of *gusimbuka*, is unclear. The origins of such body cultural practices is simply not known, but I stress that European texts, explored in later chapters, contributed to both Tutsiness and Tutsidom. I also consider the extent to which the Tutsi elite may have sought to depict Tutsi athletes (a small minority of Tutsi, let alone Banyarwanda) as an image to outsiders that depended on their perception of the outsiders' perception of them.[98]

Although by 1950 differences in income and animal ownership between Hutu and Tutsi were not great,[99] the politically dominant group was still a small Tutsi elite that provided the monarch and the majority of chiefs and that owned cattle and land. Open opposition to Tutsi dominance in Rwanda came in 1957 when a manifesto, written by Hutu intellectuals who had been educated in Catholic seminaries and been introduced to Christian socialism, made pleas for democracy. By the 1950s, the winds of change were blowing through Africa, and with greater Hutu political awareness the Belgian administration and the Catholic Church decided to switch their support to the educated Hutu. Hutu militancy increased, as did opposition to the monarchy. The existing system of Tutsi advantage was challenged. It was now Hutu who increasingly felt that they could rewrite history and, having learned about the Hamitic thesis in their school texts, now turn it to their advantage. They represented Tutsi as Aryan "immigrants" or "invaders." The Hamitic hypothesis was no longer a Tutsi advantage but a stigma, and the Hutu had begun to believe that they alone were the native people and masters of Rwanda. In 1959, the Belgians failed to prevent the escalation of a series of riots against the authority of Tutsi chiefs. Several hundred Tutsi were killed, and many were exiled or fled to neighboring states. The power base had shifted to the Hutu elite. This was a turning point in the political history of Rwanda. In 1961, the monarchy was abolished and the *mwami* fled, following seizure of power by the Hutu and more Tutsi deaths and migrations. Independence was declared in 1962, and Hutu monopolized power. Whereas in 1952 Tutsi had accounted for 17.5 percent of the population, by 1991 the corresponding figure was only 8.4 percent.[100] One can thus view the subsequent ethnic cleansing and genocide as horrendous extensions of the trend that began in the 1950s. The perceived descendants of "Aryans" had become the target of official government policy.[101] The Rwanda genocide claimed the lives of between 500,000 and one million people; some estimates claim that among these were 80 percent of Rwanda's Tutsi population.[102]

Conclusion

This chapter has set the scene for both an introduction to *gusimbuka-urukiramende* and to my excavation of its European representations. Rather than collectively labeling the people as Banyarwanda, Europeans most commonly represented Rwanda's population as the Twa, the Hutu, and the Tutsi—the definite article assuming definite boundaries. I have stressed, however, that this trichotomization resulted from the reification of the categories of race and ethnicity. They were not ethnic groups, but they became ethnicized. Ethnicity became conflated with race as "a nineteenth-century category of spurious biological worth."[103]

In what follows, therefore, it would be unwise to read the Tutsi as a clearly recognizable group of people, though they were frequently represented as such. The European reading of the groups making up the Banyarwanda had a very significant corporeal dimension. Tutsi were homogenized into a more "European-looking" race than their Hutu neighbors. This did not prevent them from retaining many Rwandan body cultural traditions, notably dancing and the practice of *gusimbuka-urukiramende*, to which I now turn.

CHAPTER 2

Gusimbuka-Urukiramende:
A European Record

> We have witnessed a transformation of jumping techniques. We
> all jumped from a springboard and, once again, full-faced. I am
> glad to say that this has stopped. Now people jump, fortunately,
> from one side. Jumping lengthways, sideways, up and down.
>
> —Marcel Mauss, "Techniques of the Body"

At the time of the early European expeditions to Rwanda, track and
field in Europe and North America was experiencing growing popularity and visibility. The sport had evolved from of a number of diffuse
forms of local body cultures that became standardized in the form of
recognizably modern events. The (English) Amateur Athletics Association was formed in Oxford in 1866, and by 1910 most of the nations of
western Europe and North America had adopted the sport and established national governing bodies. The Olympic Games at Athens in
1896 and the next two celebrations (held at four-year intervals at Paris
and St. Louis) were relatively low-key. The games of 1908, held in
London, and what many regard as the first modern Olympics, held in
Stockholm in 1912, substantially raised the profile of track and field.
Mecklenburg and other explorers and missionaries, journeying in central Africa, would have almost certainly been aware of these developments, including the fascination with achieving world records. 1912 was
also the year of the formation of the International Amateur [*sic*]
Athletics Federation (IAAF), the bureaucracy that governs the sport and
which, during the course of the twentieth century, was to embrace over
two hundred nations. Africa witnessed the growth of track and field in
the 1920s and 1930s though the seeds of the sport were sown earlier.[1]
The IAAF continues to colonize the so-called Third World, and in so

doing erodes indigenous body cultures. Track and field, like other sports, was essentially a European project which, with its secular, bureaucratic, rational, quantified, standardized, and record-oriented qualities, had no real parallel in the world of the premodern.[2]

The modern spectacle of competitive sports was, in many ways, an isomorph of the growing world political system.[3] But the growing popular awareness of international sports events was, in a sense, similar to the news of the Tutsi high jumpers reaching Europe and North America; each included representations of faraway places with strange-sounding names. Sport provided a form of popular ethnography or cross-cultural voyeurism which paralleled the academic ethnography of the anthropological and geographical records of African peoples and places.[4] In this sense, the stadium—where peoples from foreign lands were exhibited—was a metaphor for the world exhibition and the world itself. However, the growing seriousness of sports was not lost on some late Victorians, who felt that the removal of play (or a "pure" element) had led to sport becoming too serious and, consequently, degrading. Some even yearned for other forms of body culture, divorced by time and space from the age of machines.

Although the first modern Olympic Games contained no indigenous Africans, those of Paris and St. Louis provided the opportunity to display various "native" groups in the world exhibitions that were held alongside the sports events (see chapter 3). By the 1920s, however, black athletes were becoming increasingly visible in the serious world of sports. The decades following the First World War witnessed a growing scientific and popular interest in the athletic potential of African athletes, among them the high jumpers of Rwanda, fuelled by the emergence of sports journalism.[5] In the African athlete the gazes of the negrophile and the sports scientist intersected. As Western sports became introduced to parts of Africa, the rhetoric and iconography found in sports publishing predicted how the indigenous African—the raw material for an increasingly global sports system—would be processed by the machine of colonial sport development. A cartoon in a 1923 edition of the French sports magazine *L'Auto* showed a seminaked native who, in 1922, was carrying a spear and shield and surrounded by a landscape of palm trees. By 1925, it showed how he would be transformed into a uniformed and shod sports athlete bedecked with a victor's garland, carrying a cup and standing in what was unmistakably the sportscape of the athletic arena.[6] Although, as I will show, the European image of the African was riven with ambiguity, it was often the essentialized nature of black athletes—that blacks were in some way *fundamentally* different—that carried over into the twentieth century.[7] From the 1920s, black athletes, including high jumpers from Africa, were representing France, and later Britain, in the Olympic Games.

The kind of track-and-field events that were developing in Europe placed an emphasis on achievement, recording, and technology. It involved the recording of precise and detailed measurements (see appendix). Its measured time and space enabled a kind of a global currency that attracted mass interest—the record. From the IAAF's global database, one can discover the high jump record for each of the affiliated nations. At the time of this writing, the Rwandan national men's high-jump record is 1.90 meters (about 6 feet 2¾ inches), held by Côme Habingabwa, achieved in Kigali in 1983. The respective women's record, reflecting modern sport's ideology of equal opportunity, is 1.40 meters (4 feet 7¼ inches), achieved by Immaculée Mukambuguje in 1976.[8]

Achievement sport provided the cultural lens through which most Europeans witnessed *gusimbuka-urukiramende*. But it was only one form of high jumping body culture that could be found in the newly expanding world of images. High jumping, for example, was also practiced as welfare sport, as an element of gymnastics and physical education. This often reflected a concern with the maintenance of an appropriate body in which form, posture, or style was important—a kind of high jumping which was founded on a different principle and ideology from that of achievement-based jumping. From the work of Renaissance writers on education, it seems that jumping was practiced from the perspectives of physical education, or military training. It could not be sportized because of the local nature of the various forms of measurement.[9]

During the nineteenth century, when gymnastic high jumping was at its most popular, performance continued to be prioritized over results, and form was more highly regarded than effort. At this time much of Europe was experiencing the growth of a welfare-oriented form of body culture associated with the German and Nordic traditions of gymnastics rather than with the British idiom of sport which was often vigorously opposed by proponents of the German and Nordic models (see appendix). High jumping formed a part of such gymnastics, but its base was welfare and fitness rather than achievement. In some cases, it also carried with it the ideological baggage of nationalism. Indeed, it has been argued that the performance of a group of gymnasts refers to a number of distinctive values that must be decoded by the spectators, such codes referring to deeper cultural values than is the case in sports.[10] The gymnastic model of jumping, as well as the achievement model, would have been in the minds of many of those—especially those from mainland Europe—who ventured to Rwanda in the early twentieth century.

Gusimbuka-Urukiramende

In addition to the achievement and welfare models, folk forms of vertical jumping existed in parts of the world still relatively untouched by European colonialism and imperialism at the beginning of the twentieth century (see appendix). Such traditions were incompatible with the codification and internationally standardized rules of the global forms of sportized jumping. They may have contained the ingredients of ritual, but they were also entertainment. They possessed characteristics of what we would call fun, the circus, the fete, or the carnival. Such activities were also as much disport as sport, and were often part of social life, not something different, not something that was necessarily held in special places. They may have been related to religious festivals or carnivals, and sometimes attracted crowds that merged with the performance and were not restricted to particular segmented spaces. Some of these qualities may be applied to *gusimbuka-urukiramende*, to which I now turn.

There may be many histories of Rwanda, but, to my knowledge, there are no written histories of *gusimbuka*. When asked about it, some Rwandans may dimly recall their grandparents having mentioned it, but according to Rwanda scholar Danielle de Lame, few Banyarwanda living today would be likely even to have heard of it.[11] The major Rwandan description of it, by Aimable Ndejuru, draws almost entirely on European sources, and in doing so it exemplifies a kind of ethno-Africanism or "the rendering of non-Western alien societies by those societies themselves"[12]—in this case, the fabrication of Rwanda by a Rwandan. However, in the representation of *gusimbuka* it is overwhelmingly a case of the European speaking for the African. It is from this perspective that what follows is mainly constructed.

If any of the Europeans who visited Rwanda before the twentieth century were fascinated by *gusimbuka*,[13] they appear to have left no written or visual records of it. Of course, the fact that it was not recorded in some of the earliest accounts of the region does not mean that it did not exist (or that it did). At the end of the nineteenth century it was not necessarily easy for Europeans to record the traditions of Rwanda and its neighboring areas. Until the mid–nineteenth century, traders had to exchange their goods at the kingdom's frontiers.[14] Europeans had visited neighboring Burundi some years before Rwanda, and Richard Burton, in 1858, had recognized the "inhospitality" of Burundi Tutsi, though he also observed their "well-made limbs and athletic frames."[15] Writing in 1890, Emin Pasha found them still a "mysterious" people.[16] The problems that could be faced in Burundi were outlined a few years later by the French anthropologist, Lionel Decle. He stated, "[D]uring the whole time I travelled through their country [Tutsi] tried to break into my camp every night.... It was with the greatest difficulty that I avoided an open fight with them, and of course under the circumstances a thorough study of the people was out of the question."[17]

But body cultures in Burundi were not ignored. A report from 1901 referred to "jumps of great extravagance," "gigantic leaps" and dancers dashing as if to jump over the heads of the accompanying musician.[18] In 1905, one Father Joseph reported to the journal of the White

Fathers that he had witnessed natives who "jump themselves to death, just like bears at a fairground but without violin music and the grinding of a barrel organ."[19] However, in neither of these quotations is jumping explicitly divorced from dancing, and no written evidence seems to exist of any form of indigenous high jumping ever having been practiced in Burundi.[20] The same cannot be said for neighboring Uganda. Almost certainly in the late nineteenth century, the English missionary John Roscoe recorded high jumping—a "game [that] boys especially love"—among the Banyankole, another ruling aristocracy of "Hamitic" cattle owners living in the Ugandan region of Ankole, which borders Rwanda.[21]

Gusimbuka, however, has been very widely recorded as a Rwandan body cultural activity. In this section I want to confirm that this *was* a precolonial activity, explore how it changed during the first half of the twentieth century, and suggest why it failed to survive into the second half of the century. First, however, why was it not apparently recorded by Europeans in the first decade of their presence in Rwanda? Alison Des Forges suggests that at the turn of the nineteenth century, Europeans were generally indifferent to the learning of Kinyarwanda or about Rwanda itself. In any case, it was only the *mwami* and his elite who were privileged to deal with them.[22] At the same time, while eager to learn about the Germans,

> the Court and notables tried to keep the foreigners ignorant about Rwanda.... When foreigners did manage to ask about the history of the customs of the kingdom, they usually received no answer or answers so vague as to be of no help to them.[23]

Rwandan reliance on "ambiguous language and the employment of ruse" angered the more straightforward Europeans, who were known to read the Rwandan view of communication as a "not ignoble contest between two intelligences."[24] In any case, discussions of native customs were unlikely to be uppermost in either party's mind. And as in Burundi, dancing seemed to most impress the first—and many later—European visitors to the region.[25] The lack of more extensive early recording of native high jumping in Rwanda may have simply reflected both the modest scope of initial anthropological and geographical surveys and the ways in which mainly upper-middle-class male travelers had been trained to look at Africa and the African. Additionally, they may not have been able to gain access to the sites where *gusimbuka* was practiced and performed. It was found mainly at the court and practiced by a minority of the population. In the early days of a European presence in Rwanda, the court was often avoided because of the demands that it would have placed upon them.[26] And given the variety of things that were waiting to be recorded, the lack of time, and the particular priorities of ethnographic convention, many minority customs may have been excluded from examination. Johannes Fabian has suggested that many explorers may have been drunk, sick, under the influence of drugs, or consumed by sexual passion rather than with "rationalized frames of exploration."[27] Other visitors to the region simply may have lacked interest.

The expeditions of the early 1900s were modest, compared with that led by Adolf Friedrich, Duke of Mecklenburg (1873–1969), in 1907.[28] This was the first major anthropological survey of Rwanda. Including ten Europeans and five-hundred African bearers, it covered a vast number of aspects of local life which his expedition recorded in minute detail.[29] It is therefore not surprising that it was his party that is thought to have been the first Europeans to witness and photograph a performance of *gusimbuka-urukiramende*. Mecklenburg observed and photographed a jump, the height of which he claimed to be 2.50 meters. He explicated that it was by a Tutsi athlete and alerted his readers to the fact that this performance was a substantial improvement on the world's record of achievement sport.[30] Given his interest in sports, it is not surprising that Mecklenburg drew attention to sport-like pursuits. In a letter to H. Kna in 1928 he recounted his 1907 visit and observed that the sport of high jumping was "native to the Tutsi" and that they "must have always been excellent jumpers"[31] It is not clear, however, if Mecklenburg inferred or assumed the indigenousness of *gusimbuka*, or whether it was explicated for him by native informants. Nor is it clear how distinctive it was as part of Tutsi, as opposed to Banyarwanda, body culture.

Because precolonial Rwanda possesses no art or sculpture that represents human or animal figures, no visual evidence of *gusimbuka* exists.[32] The strongest evidence to support Mecklenburg's statement that (some form of) high jumping was practiced in precolonial times comes from the oral records of former recruits to the court (see below). Additionally, stories from the precolonial oral traditions of Rwanda include one that refers to a young girl who was able to outperform boys at jumping and other physical activities.[33] *Gusimbuka* translates into English as "jumping," and *urukiramende* as "the installation for the high jump" (i.e., a crossbar resting on two vertical supports).[34] *Gusimbuka-urukiramende* refers to jumping *over* such an installation. That these words are precolonial in origin, and that they were applied to a form of vertical jumping, is unequivocally supported by the global expert on Rwandan linguistics, Professor André Coupez, whose view is based on their etymology.[35] Professor Ernst Jokl asserted that Tutsi had been known as excellent high jumpers "*long before* the emergence of the modern sports movement," a view supported by Maquet's recognition of it as a recreational activity in his study of "the period *immediately preceding* the time when Ruanda was submitted to the influence of western culture"—that is, before about 1910.[36] It is highly unlikely that leaps as high as those described and photographed by Mecklenburg and others could have been achieved by untutored athletes. At the same time, it is impossible to state when the practice actually started in the form shown in Figure 2.1, a photograph from 1926.[37]

Musinga seemed to be of no assistance to Europeans in matters concerning Rwanda's cultural history. Mecklenburg's ethnographer, Jan Czekanowski, received no cooperation from either him or his notables in his research, and despite Czekanowski's "persistent inquiries they refused to recount to him the history of the kingdom [and] refused to allow themselves to be measured for his charts."[38] Nevertheless, Mecklenburg's widely published record of Tutsi high jumping became

Figure 2.1

the defining reality and was to be cited as the authoritative account, without closer inspection, for many subsequent decades. The account perpetuated itself: Writers on Rwanda would sometimes acknowledge *gusimbuka* with reference to Mecklenburg's report and then move on to their more pressing interests, such as big-game hunting.[39] Missionaries might devote a few lines to the high jump, but then turn attention to prayers that would save the African for Jesus.[40]

In 1908, Dr. Weidenfeld of the University of Cologne also witnessed a form of high jumping, but unlike Mecklenburg (and perhaps lacking his sporting interests), he felt that time was much too short for any personal researches in this field.[41] During the second and third decades of the twentieth century the number of European travelers to Rwanda increased. Many (though not all) witnessed and wrote about *gusimbuka* in varying degrees of detail, often appearing in awe of what they invariably regarded as Tutsi body cultural practices. The English missionary Algernon C. Stanley Smith was clearly impressed. Anxious to inform his Anglican sponsors of the news from Africa, he commenced his first epistle from the Ruanda Mission to England in 1920 by introducing the Tutsi and their high-jumping skills. Only having done that did he get down to the business of writing about saving heathen souls for the glory of God.[42]

In order to appreciate *gusimbuka* more fully, I now want to try to place it in some sort of social context. A central feature of pre- and early colonial Rwandan society was the court (which might be described as a capital or center of government that periodically moved from province to province) of the *mwami*, who, as noted in the previous chapter, was thought of as a sacred being. Around 1920, the court included the homes of 10,000 or more notables and servants.[43] The *mwami* was God's representative on earth and all court traditions were magical, even if they might have appeared to an outsider to be purely utilitarian. It was arguably the exclusivity of the court that is represented in much *gusimbuka* activity. A group of young men known as *intore*—collectively, the group was known as the *itorero*—was periodically recruited to the court to undertake "manly" and military training. It is thought that this practice originated in the early sixteenth century when Mwami Mukobanya called on leading chiefs to send their sons to court. The aim was to not only enhance the legitimacy of royal authority but also to build up an army following defeats from armies of northern kingdoms.[44] The court became the diffusion center for the model elite Tutsi and the site that forged Rwandan culture and mentality.[45] Each *intore* recruited to the 'court'—of both the *mwami* and of local chiefs who personally selected them—was trained in a variety of manly arts and corporeal skills. At the court they totaled several hundred and sought to win the favor of important notables or even the *mwami*.[46] It is implied by Ian Linden that the *intore* were "turned into competent soldiers *and athletes*" well before the start of the nineteenth century.[47] Though the *intore* are almost invariably identified (in popular European travel writing, at least) as being Tutsi, it would be erroneous to assume that Hutu and Twa boys were totally excluded.[48] Indeed, in precolonial Rwanda, it is unlikely that participation in most body cultural activities were drawn along group or ethnic lines.[49] This means that for the precolonial period, and for much of the colonial period, it may be best to think of *gusimbuka* as a courtly, rather than a Tutsi, practice undertaken by a select minority of the population. Indeed, in the most detailed work on traditional Rwandan body culture—written by a European-educated Rwandan, Aimable Ndejuru—the word Tutsi is mentioned in the section of his dissertation that addresses high jumping only when he is quoting from German descriptions.[50] And it was probably embedded in what was the fundamentally Hutu nature of much of the ritual and many of the institutions of the central state.[51]

The training of the *intore* included poetry, panegyrics, dancing, self-defense, self-control, fighting, spear throwing, running, and *gusimbuka*. They were also said to be schooled in manliness and fidelity, military prowess, and self-mastery.[52] Achieving the "triumph of the will" might not be an overly extreme way of expressing it. It should be clear that the qualities required of the *intore* were well served by *gusimbuka-urukiramende*—a body cultural practice that was more than simply part of military training, an interpretation sometimes placed on it in European representations. An *intore* was a "chosen one," a title to which boys of around twelve years of age aspired. It has been said that physique was crucial in the selection of *intore* dancers, and it seems reasonable to assume that the same criterion was applied in the selection of high jumpers.[53] Those found to be best suited to *gusimbuka* therefore may have been above average height, a physical characteristic that I have already shown to be frequently—but misleadingly—attributed to Tutsi people per se. The preparation required of the *intore* seems to have been both intensive and time-consuming and lasted many years.

Helen Codere has recorded a description of life as an *intore* in her oral histories of traditional Rwandan life in the early years of the twentieth century. I quote from her work at some length in order to provide the flavor of the life of a former *intore*, Ruhamiriza, who from a young age had experienced many years of training.

When we were little we liked to shoot with bows and arrows. Each of us had a little bow and arrows made from sorgho stalks. We shot at everything we saw, even relatives and other people. Later a target was made for us and we tried to hit it from as far away as we could. We threw things at one another, small fruits of different sorts and such things. That was to teach us to dodge projectiles in battle. We jumped a high jump. Of course, it was only a jump of a few centimetres, but it gave us good exercise. Then they would put something we liked off at a distance and we would race to get it. Sometimes we were given stalks which we threw like lances as far as we could. And we played hide and seek. . . .

When I was twelve I was enrolled in the *itorero* which means "the place where one is chosen." The itorero of chief Rwamanywa were divided into two corps or armies. . . . At that time the *intore* were not settled in one place. They moved about to stay in distant places for a certain period. It was a sort of military maneuver, in order for us to have been in different parts of the country. . . . When we came to Kinyana the sous-chief had a plot of land cleared for us. It was like a football-field. . . . There were one hundred and fifty of us, almost all Tutsi. There were a few Hutu but not more than ten. In any case the Hutu children were at one side in the dances; they were in separate quarters, and we did not eat or drink milk together with them. The one exception was the drinking of other drinks with them, but that did not go against the etiquette of the nobility in any way. We had two houses for our quarters. It was necessary to lodge together, or very near to one another, because there were activities that required our attendance day and night.[54]

Ruhamiriza went on to describe the day's activities. In summary, these included morning activities such as forming a circle and reciting the introduction of a panegyric, making a "very rhythmic cry," stretching their arms straight up to the sky and moving to a certain cadence while chanting in a high note and then reciting a very long panegyric, performing various dances, and, at noon, returned to lodgings and drinking milk and "liquor like sorho and banana beer." In the afternoon, the *intore*

> returned to the field and took up other activities such as practising to shoot at a distance, *gutebanwa*, [and] shooting at a target, *kumasha*. An example of the kind of target we shot at was a lance. After that we ran races and jumped and had contests of strength like *gukiranagukayana*, wrestling done with the hands, and *gukashurana*, ordinary wrestling. We also threw lances and projectiles. We were divided into two sides and we shot at one another with arrows without their iron points. Afterwards we formed small groups of four or five and composed songs and autopanegyrics, or made up new dances. Then it was nighttime and we went back to our lodging to eat and drink and wait for the hour of *igitaramo*, spending the evening in company.[55]

As noted above, one of the skills learned by the *intore* was high jumping. Ruhamiriza states that he practiced it *before* entering the *itorero*, but he in no way prioritizes it over other elements in the overall repertoire of training. The Rwandan historian Alexis Kagame also seems to give high jumping equal status among the corporeal activities in the training of the precolonial *intore*, citing it along with spear throwing, foot racing, archery, and dancing.[56]

At important celebrations the *mwami* would order a series of body cultural activities to be performed at the court. These were commonly described in European reports. The terms given by Europeans to such events varied considerably, but included "entertainment," "exhibition," "fete," and even "pantomime," though, as I will show, sport-related metaphors were also often used. *Gusimbuka* was one of the activities included at such events. It was also performed at important weddings and outside the court at local gatherings of importance. Although allusions are made to contests between different corps,[57] it seems to have been as much, if not more, an exhibition than a competition, held on cleared land adjacent to the *mwami*'s court and attended by huge crowds, said to number several thousands. Its noncompetitive nature is suggestive of ritual, the idea of winning being irrelevant to most ritual events.

European records of these fetes are not consistent in their reporting of the place of *gusimbuka* in the overall program of events. Some witnesses give the impression that it was not performed as frequently as dancing, and this may be reflected in the substantially greater numbers of references to, and coverage in greater detail of, Rwandan dances.[58] In some cases the dancers were also high jumpers. The master of the dance troupe of Chief Rubarakambu was claimed as the "champion high jumper" of Rwanda, while Butera, the *mwami*'s leading dancer in the 1930s, was also said to be celebrated as a high jumper.[59] Ellen and Attilio Gatti suggest in one account that jumping formed a kind of warm-up before the same performers took part in the *intore* dance.[60] But in another account, Gatti saw the high jump as the climax of the entire event.[61]

Gusimbuka may well have been an activity that was concentrated at the court, but beyond being both manly training and a courtly entertainment for the *mwami* and various chiefs, it seems to have been practiced at the community level as part of what Europeans described as recreational gatherings. The forms of poetry, music, and dance that were practiced at the court "were universally admired and imitated by the people of the central kingdom."[62] It is plausible, therefore, that the diffusion and imitation of *gusimbuka* resulted in what Maquet described as a traditional form of popular recreation, which he termed "jumping

competitions."[63] Bourgeois observed that it was an exercise for supple-
ness, without specifying membership of the *intore*.[64] In the late 1920s
Pagès claimed it was a "popular amusement," but identified it as Tutsi.[65]
In the early 1930s its lack of exclusivity was implied by Dr. J. E. Church
of the mission hospital at Gahani, who casually observed that one of his
"boys" (assistants) was able to jump over his head with ease.[66] Some
years later it was claimed that boys of twelve and thirteen years of age
frequently amused themselves by practicing *gusimbuka* and clearing over
one meter in height by using oil cans to assist takeoff.[67] This kind of
observation suggests that while *gusimbuka* may never have been the quo-
tidian of Rwandan life, it was a form of popular amusement. Some of
the photographs in this and subsequent chapters support this view. It is
equally clear, however, that others represent events of a much more
choreographed, organized, and spectacular nature.

Gusimbuka is likely to have been witnessed by a sizeable proportion of the population of the regions in which it was mainly practiced
(probably the central region), if one is to judge by the crowds shown
in some of the photographs in chapter 4. The names of the best high
jumpers were known to at least some of the population. The most
famous high jumper during the reign of Mwami Musinga (1897–1931)
was said to be Kanyamuhungu, while under Rudahigwa (1931–59) the
most renowned jumpers were Kanyemera, Gashiramanga, Mwunvaneza,
and Ngoga.[68] That these names could be recalled during the late 1970s
suggests that *gusimbuka* was, at that time, still well known among at least
some Rwandan people.[69]

What emerges from descriptions and photographs of *gusimbuka-
urukiramende* is the heterogeneity of its context. The variation in the
equipment used and in the kinds of sites at which it took place make it
fundamentally different from any sportized model of high jumping. So,
too, did the fact that different varieties of *gusimbuka* apparently existed.
Shortly after the end of the First World War, a British visitor to Rwanda
observed that "a jump was made over three natives in a row, one in front
of the other."[70] And in addition to the running high jump, it appears that
a standing high jump was also practiced. Mecklenburg's adjutant, von

Weise, reported that without the assistance of any run-up, a number of Tutsi jumped over the heads of a party of German explorers.[71] This may have been what Dr. Weidenfeld was describing in 1908. He noted that from a position with the knees bent and both feet solidly stamped on the ground, men would jump vertically and land on the same spot. Their body heights were marked on branches stuck in the ground, and their aim was said to be to jump higher than the appropriate mark, though the athlete is not mentioned clearing any bar.[72] It is not clear, therefore, if Mecklenburg and Weidenfeld were describing the same kind of practice.

As noted above, *gusimbuka-urukiramende* is thought by some to have been of ritual significance originally, though this aspect of Rwandan body culture has not been thoroughly explored and what has been written is invariably Eurocentric. One can only speculate about the meaning of *gusimbuka* for those who practiced it. The vertical axis is of considerable historical importance in Banyarwanda society. According to Gasarabwe-Laroche, reaching toward heaven, as opposed to plunging down to the lethal forces of the subterranean world, is one way of reading the leaping of the high jumpers and dancers—an "appeal for the heaven-sent blessings of life, strength, joy, and victory."[73] It is plausible, then, that the upright reeds supporting the crossbar were stereotypical emblems of Tutsi identity.[74] It is also popularly thought of as part of the *intore*'s rite of passage: The *intore* would be a man when he could clear his own height. Ndejuru reaches this conclusion after an elaborate discussion in which he argues that originally two upright poles placed in front of huts had a crossbeam (*Igifashi*) placed across them. Women who had experienced frequent miscarriages were placed on this crossbeam in order to prevent any future child's premature withdrawal from the uterus. *Igifashi* freed (or liberated) the child from being stillborn. It is from this that Ndejuru seems to extrapolate *gusimbuka-urukiramende* as a symbolic liberation from childhood.[75] In addition, several theories suggest that it originally had other symbolic significance. It has been suggested that the vertical leap (leaping over things was said to be a form of liberation in a wide range of contexts) symbolized both the

transcendence of evil, the healing of a defect or illness, and the acquisi-
tion by the *intore* of the power of the place that was straddled.[76] This
may be related to the pervasive concepts of flow and blockage in
Rwandan life. Derived from bodily flows such as water, blood, and
semen, which can, during illness or injury, be "blocked," Taylor suggests
that analogies of such body flows/blockages are often drawn between
them and social life—for example, "by analogical extension the concern
with unobstructed connection and unimpeded movement characterizes
earlier Rwandan symbolic thought about the topography of the land, its
rivers, roads and pathways in general."[77] Flow implies openness and continuity, and is regarded as something positive; blockage implies inter-
ruption and closure and is considered negative. *Gusimbuka* can, I think,
be read as a symbol of flow in which the athlete approaches the potential blockage of *urukiramende*, but, successfully clearing it, maintains the
flow. This seems especially appropriate as the Kinyarwanda word for
"flow" (*isibo*) was also used for "force," "élan," and "flight."[78] The dialectics of flow/blockage appear to persist in some realms of Rwandan symbolic thought.[79]

There may also be a political dimension to *intore* body culture. It
has been suggested that the court etiquette of the *intore* dancers—and, it
could be added, of high jumpers—was not of the type that displayed
potential strength and power, but were exhibitions "of finesse that sealed
their boundary and kept them above the arena of competition. It was a
demonstration of the *immutability* of their superiority."[80] As I will suggest in the final chapter, it may have been one of a repertoire of body
cultural practices which, as perceived by Europeans, maintained the distance of the Tutsi elite from the majority of the kingdom's population
and, at the same time, can be read as confirming their feeling of superiority over Occidentals.

The microgeography of *gusimbuka-urukiramende* was fundamentally different from that of other configurations of high jumping.
Throughout the history of *gusimbuka*, a stone, a termite mound, a ridge,
or, on occasion, an improvisation such as a large log[81] was used to aid
the athlete's takeoff, and an unprepared surface was used for landing.

These conditions were quite unlike the plane surface and soft landing area which characterize the space of the sportized high jumper. In the case of *gusimbuka*, the vertical supports and the crossbar that delicately rested on them appear to have been made of relatively rigid reeds. In early photographs, the uprights rarely appear to be vertical but at an angle, facing away from the jumper, though Western-style equipment was used in many performances from the 1930s to the 1950s.

A photograph from about 1917, shown in Figure 2.2, provides an exemplary representation of *gusimbuka* as it appeared in colonial images from the late 1910s to the early 1930s. The athlete is jumping off an uneven surface and seemingly taking a downhill run, though other accounts refer to an uphill approach.[82] The athlete appears to be taking off from a small (natural?) ridge rather than the more frequently shown stone or mound. He is wearing a loincloth, which he holds with one hand. He is carrying a "pipe" in the other, as shown in some of the other photographs in this book. Ndejuru suggests that this is a sign that he had achieved high status as a performer.[83] Several accounts refer to a line

Figure 2.2

of jumpers—it could also be termed a *team* of jumpers—following each other in rapid succession toward the takeoff point.[84] This is quite different from the studied concentration adopted by modern Western high jumpers, where, as individuals, they compose themselves for the optimal moment to make their attempt. There appears to have been little consistency in the arrangement of the high-jumping equipment. The size of the takeoff mound varied considerably between events, as did the closeness of the spectators and the kind of surface from which the jump occurred. All these features serve to distinguish *gusimbuka* from sportized high jumping. From European reports, however, it is not fully clear how competitive *gusimbuka* was. It does not appear to have been competitive in a Western, sportized sense. At some events, athletes were happy to stop participating when they were tired,[85] performance being clearly prioritized over the Western concept of the result. This is not to say, however, that a competitive dimension never formed part of such jumping. Bourgeois notes that the reed was raised following the elimination of competitors.[86] And competition was sometimes taken seriously enough for scatological language to be directed at athletes who failed to clear the bar.[87] That it could, at different times and in different places, be both a competition and a performance makes it as ambiguous, from a Western perspective, as the representations the West made of it.

With the growing number of European travelers, missionaries, and explorers in Rwanda from the mid-1920s, distinguished visitors were sometimes treated as honored guests of the *mwami* and other chiefs. At courtly exhibitions of athleticism they were therefore able to witness—and record in writing, film, and photograph—the corporeal skills of the Banyarwanda, as the many descriptions and illustrations in subsequent chapters will show. But spectatorship occurred in a variety of situations. For example, a short item in *Ruanda Notes* described how, at Nyanza in August 1925, two members of the CMS, Captain (later Reverend) Geoffrey Holmes (a British Military Cross recipient, member of the British Olympic team, and captain of the Army ice hockey team) and William Roome, were visited by Mwami Musinga. Holmes wrote:

After a chat in the guest house I asked Musinga if he had any good runners and said I'd like to try one out. So he picked out two and we ran 100. Unfortunately one of them beat me by about a foot; and I beat the other about the same.

Musinga was very bucked, so I asked him to show me some jumping, and we went down to the football field, and he put a few men over the tape. The chap who beat me running did about 6 ft. 2 in. Roome got a very good snap of this. I did not compete!!![88]

In the one hundred–yard dash bicultural participation was considered workable, but *gusimbuka* and the Western high jump, on this occasion, at least, seemed sufficiently different to put the European well and truly in his place. I am unaware of any reports that describe colonials participating in it, apart from their role as spectators.

Reporting the events of Christmas Day 1930 at the CMS mission at Gahini, Dr. J. E. Church—an enthusiastic sportsman while at Cambridge University—noted that following a "topping service" in the morning some "jolly good sports" were held in the afternoon. Neighboring chiefs attended with some of their *intore*. Flat races, long jumping, and "sack bumping" were organized for the British, and high jumping, archery, and spear throwing "for chiefs and the Batutsi."[89] Later, in the 1930s, the American visitor Negley Farson witnessed a rather less jovial demonstration. He described how a Belgian administrator "sent for" the son of a local chief and "made him" jump over his head. "Then, when the native failed to clear a bar that was about 6 feet 6 inches from the ground, the *Administrateur* turned to him angrily. 'You're not trying!' he said."[90] Ellen Gatti witnessed one competition that was arranged for a Belgian movie-making expedition by the local Belgian administrator.[91] Professor Joseph Ghesquiere has described how, during a visit to Kigali in about 1958, the *mwami* had asked (or told) a high jumper to travel a considerable distance to the arena that had been built near his palace in order to demonstrate his high-jumping skills to the European guest.[92] European involvement, and in some cases hegemony, in the organization of *gusimbuka* also seems to have included schools.[93] As in other colonies, indigenous body cultures—provided that they were not overly erotic—could be retained in the mission school curriculum to be practiced alongside newly imported Western body cultures such as gymnastics and soccer. It would appear, nevertheless, that it was as a sort of tourist attraction that most Europeans encountered high jumping, albeit for selected and favored visitors only.

Despite the relative visibility of *gusimbuka*, its significance should be kept in perspective. Into the 1940s and 1950s the European popular imagination continued to most frequently associate Rwandan athleticism and artistry with dancers. The best of these were seen as "national heroes," and during the colonial period it was Butera as a dancer, not a high jumper, whose image was printed on the Congolese ten-franc banknote.[94] Likewise, in an advertisement to promote tourist flights to equatorial Africa in the early 1950s, the Belgian airline Sabena constructed its image of the Belgian Congo (with which, at the time, Rwanda and Burundi were invariably grouped) by adopting an *intore* dancer as the icon to represent the primitive (Figure 2.3). This was, perhaps, a sufficiently "African" image, one that fed and reflected the longtime European fascination with African dance. It was different enough from the (as perceived) commonplace high jumper who could be readily witnessed in every high school track-and-field meet between Boston and Los Angeles. The dancers, on the other hand, were *obviously* "primitive." Dancers and drums—but not *gusimbuka*—were also prominent in the fairly lengthy, though stereotypical, portrayal of Tutsi in the Hollywood movie *King Solomon's Mines*. Made in 1950, this film probably brought the Tutsi to the attention of as many people as the material that was written about them did.[95]

In the early 1920s many of the *intore* had come to trust the Europeans and admire things European while, at the same time retaining a respect of the Rwandan court. French and history at school in the morning was combined with the conventional *intore* training at the court in afternoons.[96] But unity and discipline began to decline, and heavy drinking and rape assumed part of an increasingly unruly lifestyle. Their conduct was regarded as depraved, and a military education was hardly appropriate in a colonial setting. As a result, the *intore* were disbanded in 1923, under Belgian orders on religious and strategic grounds as part of a "massive onslaught on the traditional prerogatives of king and court."[97] When the *intore* elite performed at court for the last time, Musinga wept openly.[98] *Intore* leaders were dispersed to distant locations, and those who remained at court were disorganized. Gradually, the company disintegrated. By the end of the 1920s, the Rwandan court traditions increasingly seemed irrelevant and anachronistic in the face of both political opposition and incipient social and economic transformation.[99] When, in 1935, Mwami Rudahigwa succeeded in regaining the *intore*, it was conditional on their attendance at the White Fathers school at Nyanza.[100] The name *intore* came to refer to something quite different from the product of the *itorero* as described by Ruhamiriza

Figure 2.3

earlier in this chapter. What was said to be "the pride of [Musinga's] entourage fell under European influence."[101] The onset of modernity in Rwanda is often associated with the further reduction of traditions following the death of Musinga in 1931 and the subsequent widespread adoption by Rwandans of Roman Catholicism. Mwami Rudahigwa, symbolically moved from his court which was constructed of traditional materials, into a brick-built detached house, "rejected a vast body of court tradition."[102]

Gusimbuka-urukiramende (in its precolonial and early colonial form) was in decline, as were many other indigenous customs. They seem to have become quasi-folkloric when performed at the *mwami's* arena or other such sites. From the early 1930s, even the corps de ballet made fewer and less frequent appearances.[103] It is in this context that it might be concluded that the tradition of *gusimbuka* had been modified, even sanitized, if one is to judge from some of the filmed performances of it (see chapter 4). A sign that by the 1940s and 1950s the Banyarwanda were abandoning their traditional ways was shown by their "infatuation with tennis shoes, berets, bicycles and radios," an article in an American geographical magazine rather patronizingly observed.[104] Missionaries and administrators gradually came to ignore indigenous corporeal activities, and only the royal drum and the multiethnic dancers were conserved as folklore and exotica.[105] It seems likely that *gusimbuka* had become too strongly identified with Tutsi at a time when Hutu political awareness was being more forcefully articulated.

The decline of *gusimbuka* also appears to have coincided with the growing adoption of European sports. In the early 1920s, the representative of the Belgian Resident in Nyanza was convinced that European ways of training the body were superior to those of Rwanda. Teaching at the school there, he insisted that students should learn to swim and took them to practice regularly in a local stream.[106] "Football is the great game here," Dr. Leonard Sharp had reported from the first British mission school in Rwanda as early as 1922.[107] Missives home often requested second-hand soccer balls and other sports equipment. A Fédération de Football au Ruanda-Urundi was formed in 1935, and by the 1950s soccer had become the nation's most popular sport.[108] Even the former *intore* Ruhamiriza claimed soccer as one of his favorite sports, and in the Christianization of Rwanda the soccer field was a significant site for proselytizing.[109] By the 1950s soccer matches were arranged between royal teams in addition to the customary activities at celebrations held at the *mwami's* arena.[110] In mission schools, European gymnastics and sports had become central to the curriculum. By mid-century the *itorero* had become known solely as a dance troupe. This was particularly so of the *intore* at the *mwami's* residence in Nyanza, who were now called the Royal Watussi Dancers and overshadowed the other nondancing practices of the former *intore*.[111] The title *intore* had become virtually synonymous with dancer.[112] The Belgian anthropologist Marcel d'Hertefelt, when living in Rwanda from 1957 to 1973, never witnessed *gusimbuka-urukiramende*, and the linguist André Coupez who was a resident there from 1952 to 1989, only saw it performed once.[113] Tourists visiting Rwanda in the 1950s were aware of *gusimbuka*—an indication of its broader visibility—but their expectations of witnessing it were not necessarily fulfilled.[114] Among three hundred photographs in a mid-1950s photographic essay of Rwandan life—including "the Rwandan heritage" as evidenced in dance, music, arts, crafts, and sacred objects—no mention, let alone a photograph, of *gusimbuka* was included.[115]

A question often facing historians is the extent to which cultural phenomena exhibit continuity or change. Do native traditions, in a relatively seamless way, become sportized in a European sense, or are Western body cultures superimposed unconformably upon the traditional? *Gusimbuka* never seems to have assumed the characteristics of a modern sport. It is impossible to state the effect, if any, that early German-Rwandan contact had on the nature and meaning of *gusimbuka*, but it seems clear from visual evidence that many of its early twentieth-century characteristics remained intact fifty years later. Figure 2.4 shows a bare-footed jumper demonstrating his skills to an accompanying Belgian visitor (complete with camera, signifying the cultural distance between him and the native athlete) at Kigali in about 1958. There can be few more recent photographs of *gusimbuka* than this. The performance is taking place on a running track rather than the grass infield of the *mwami*'s arena, symbolically emphasizing the difference between it and the achievement sport model. The equipment being used shows signs of European modernity. Western-style apparatus (with the graduated high-jump stands and the crossbar resting on moveable pegs) was used in many performances from the 1930s. This contrasts with the two reeds with a third carefully placed across the top, as shown in earlier representations. And the athlete in this photo is wearing Western-style sports clothing, having dispensed with the long robes of the early years of the century. But this also shows the selectivity of the adoption of Western innovations and how characteristics of the older jumping

Figure 2.4

genre were still present. The use of the foot-first technique, the right-angled run at the bar (as opposed to the diagonal run in the Western style), the stone takeoff, and the lack of any specialized landing facilities such as a dug soil or sand surface all reflect its Africanness. Rather than being repressed by colonial control, *gusimbuka-urukiramende* had become something of a hybrid. Use could be made of standardized Western equipment—clothing and, on occasions, footwear—but indigenous elements in the overall performance remained.

By 1950, the *mwami* was considering the possibilities of Westernizing the body cultures of Rwanda, of having his nation adopt Western sports, in order to take part in international competitions. To some extent this had already happened with the introduction of soccer and other sports. At the same time, the Rwandan elite wished to retain aspects of its own corporeality.[116] It seems clear, therefore, that the Tutsi elite was in a position to determine what to absorb from the Europeans into their own body culture and what to reject. During the period of its existence, *gusimbuka* never became a sport in the modern sense of the word. It existed nowhere else but in Rwanda and appears to have resisted the forces and pressures of Western modernity. During the first half of the twentieth century, it could all too easily be read as existing between the premodern and the modern. On the other hand, it could be read as having reached modernity in a form different from that expected by Western observers. There is no indication that the Rwandan jumpers transferred their skills from *gusimbuka* to the Western sportized model of high jumping. But why should they have been expected to? Theirs was no more an expression of the Western model of high jumping than the *intore* dancers were members of the Bolshoi Ballet. Their form of jumping may have superficially resembled the Western models, but its function did not. Nor can it be said that *gusimbuka* ever became fully folkloric. It did not possess the exotic capital of dancing and, unlike *intore* dancing, it did not assume any kind of "staged authenticity."[117] Only rarely, as it did during the 1940s and 1950s, did it seem to become alien to how it was performed in its local setting.[118]

Another way of reading *gusimbuka* is as a form of resistance or, at least, transgression. The distinction between these two terms has been suggested by Tim Cresswell:

> [T]ransgression, in distinction to resistance, does not rest on the intentions of the actors but on the *results*—on the "being noticed"—of a particular action. It is those who react to it who judge transgression; resistance rests on the *intentions* of the actors.[119]

Indigenous native body cultures and their hybrid forms have often been presented as forms of resistance against the forces of colonialism.[120] During the colonial period, however, it can be argued that the ability of the African to engage in any kind of body culture was "licensed in the double sense of being allowed, but remaining under the control of the licensor."[121] More accurately, in such situations athletes from colonized nations can be said to have transgressed boundaries. By simply (being read as) clearing heights beyond those achieved in the West, the Rwandan high jumpers can be viewed as transgressive—they were "out of place" in what was perceived to be a sport dominated by the Occident. Some critics would recognize true resistance as the simple lack of participation in, or discontinuation of, Western sports and a return to indigenous body cultures.[122] That few nations have undertaken such an uncoupling may simply reveal the strength of neocolonial sport hegemony. However, the mere knowledge of the master's sports system by outsiders invades the totality of control—a control that can never be absolute.[123] This was the situation that seemed to exist in colonial Rwanda from the 1920s. Western body cultures co-existed with indigenous ones, as shown in Figures 2.5 and 2.6, with Rudahigwa taking part in, respectively, a game of tennis and assisting with the organization of *gusimbuka*. A refusal to accept the categories of the colonial power is revealed in the representations of *gusimbuka*. Perhaps it was uncolonizable; in it the African appeared to be more than equal to the European.

Usually, resistance is interpreted in postcolonial studies as being against the powers of colonialism and imperialism. But things are rarely as simple as this. It is surely plausible that, while the Tutsi favored

Figure 2.5

Belgian support, they also wished to avoid appearing in any way inferior to the European. Hence, references in the chapters that follow to the representation of black people performing apparently significant athletic feats could be unsettling for certain occidental mind-sets. Such performances may be seen as even more resistant when they occurred in the body cultural activities (e.g., sports) of the imperial realm. The fact that many Western observers read *gusimbuka* as a sport (see chapter 3) means that it can be seen in a similar light.

I have already noted that soccer was popularly adopted in Rwanda, and it can be argued that the Western model of high-jumping posed no real threat to *gusimbuka* because it was simply something quite different.

Figure 2.6

The pride of the Tutsi elite could have been dented had *gusimbuka* become transformed into "high jumping," despite the *mwami*'s undoubted interest in European versions of physical education, Western sports, and even Olympism. But when, in the early 1950s, overtures were made for Ruanda-Urundi to join the Congo Sports Federation, they were rejected because the Tutsi leadership regarded itself as different from and independent of the Congo.[124] Into the 1950s, *gusimbuka* coexisted alongside the pressures for the introduction of Western sports. But its demise resulted less from the introduction of Western high jumping than from the demise of the monarchy, the emergence of a Hutu-dominated independence movement, and the events that followed these developments. What I am suggesting is that the practice of *gusimbuka-urukiramende* fitted into the broader context of Tutsi power and into the process of Tutsi status enhancement over the Hutu. The situation in Rwanda was far more complex than simply being one of Western colonial hegemony.

Resistance can finally be read through the lens of Homi Bhabha's notion of mimicry. He writes that "mimicry is the desire for a reformed, recognizable Other, *as a subject of a difference that is almost the same, but not quite.*"[125] In other words, it requires similarity and difference at the same time, in which the colonized is like the colonizer, yet always remains different. From the perspective of colonized peoples, in order to act as an oppositional strategy, mimicry must "continually produce its slippage, its excess, its difference.... Mimicry emerges as the representation of a difference that is itself a process of disavowal."[126] The ambivalence of mimicry leads to an "incomplete" colonial subject— "almost the same, *but not quite*/not quite-not white." Therefore, mimicry is at the same time a resemblance and a potential menace.[127] Through mimicry, the colonizer comes to see traces of himself in the colonized. Hence, in posing a challenge to the European, mimicry is often seen as a form of resistance.

Gusimbuka could be read as mimicking the high jumping of the European. For the European observing *gusimbuka-urukiramende*, it could be seen as a case of a "white presence and its black *semblance*."[128] The

Rwandan jumper was a colonized subject who, through *gusimbuka*, was recognizably the same as the colonizer (in his practice of high jumping), but still different—familiar, yet threatening. Rwandan athletes were not actually mimickers who slavishly copied Western athletics, but their apparent high jumping skills still seemed to communicate to the colonials a disoriented image of Europe. As Bhabha might say, he was almost a high jumper, but not quite one—or, he appeared to be a sportsman, but he was not sportized. The mimicry of the high jumper can be disturbing to the European because, as noted above, mimicry is simultaneously similarity and menace. *Gusimbuka* resembled the Western high jump and, as a result of the European's way of seeing, it threatened them at their own sport. The African high jumper, because of his perceived superiority, subverted the identity ("the African") of that which was being represented. The Rwandan high jumper no more needed sportizing than the Tutsi stereotype needed Europeanizing. To those from the Occident, the Tutsi was already practicing sport, and was therefore an honorary European. As Bhabha would say, the relation of power, if not totally reversed, at least seemed to vacillate. The surveilling eye is confronted by the other's returning gaze and finds its mastery undone.[129] It could also be argued that following the widespread publicity afforded *gusimbuka* by Mecklenburg's report and its inclusion in *National Geographic* and elsewhere, European travelers to Rwanda expected to find the Tutsi high jump. Rwandans obliged, illustrating the ambiguity of colonial power.

During the 1950s, Tutsi began to be regarded as scapegoats for Rwanda's political and economic ills. It became less in their interests to be identified as representatives of the nobility. The association of *gusimbuka* with the Tutsi elite would seem to have made it less attractive than dancing—which explicitly included Hutu and Twa—as a form of Banyarwanda representation. In 1958 it was declared that ethnic designations should disappear from official government documents as the Tutsi leadership, facing increasing threat, sought to placate political insurgency and make abortive gestures toward national unity.[130] The Hutu revolt and the start of the massacres of the Tutsi began in 1959, the monarchy was abolished in 1961 and from 1962 the Hutu-dominated government promoted a more violent Rwandan politics that led to the 1994 genocide.

A somewhat arcane physical activity undertaken mainly by a small number of athletes in a small central African nation had long lost its raison d'être. In 1960, a guide to the social achievements of Ruanda-Urundi confirmed that soccer was the most popular sport and that track-and-field athletics, with which many Europeans had assumed *gusimbuka* would seamlessly merge, was practiced "on a very small scale." There was no mention of any kind of high jumping.[131] *Gusimbuka*—projected by popular media as the "sport of the Tutsi"—had died out following the Hutu-led revolution.

Rather than being read as a presporting practice, *gusimbuka* might be better rendered as a nonsportized body culture. Although having certain welfare (physical training) and achievement elements (oral records of famous athletes), the Rwandan form of high jumping does not fit neatly into either the achievement or the welfare ideology. Instead, it was one of a large number of unstandardized forms of jumping found throughout the world. In the early twentieth century, there was some debate, notably in Germany, about whether "sport" was a term that could be meaningfully applied to "primitive" peoples. To an extent, it mirrored the same kind of debate going on about "primitive" art.[132] However, whereas African sculpture was artized and found its way into the galleries of Europe and North America, an equivalent sportization of African body cultures such as *gusimbuka-urukiramende* never occurred. It remained a distinctive form of local culture and never became part of either international sports or traveling shows of folklore. Even before the technologization of sportized high jumping and the associated expense of inflatable landing surfaces, no Rwandan high jumpers were featured at an international level, in contrast to those from other African countries (see chapter 3). This reveals that no simple shift of corporeal allegiance took place between *gusimbuka* and modern sport. The widely held assumption that this shift could take place is based, of course, on a typically Western way of thinking—and writing.

Conclusion

The three configurations of high jumping noted at the start of this chapter show how different underlying philosophies or ideologies help explain the different elements of what Eichberg has termed a body cultural trialectic.[133] In this way I have begun to clarify the character of *gusimbuka* by contrasting it with other configurations of high jumping that, in their ideal types, are typifed by achievement and welfare ideologies. The concept of body culture is helpful, I think, because it implicitly recognizes the problems of using the term sport. This can be said to have a fragmenting effect that leads to dichotomies such as elite versus mass sport, professional versus amateur, performance versus health, etc.[134] I have preferred to preface the term sport by adjectives such as *achievement*, *welfare* or *folk*. Rather than fragmenting sport, this sees three quite different body cultural models. But while these three configurations of body culture are, in their ideal types, distinguished by different underlying ideologies, the rigidity of the schema can be relaxed to accept that elements of one mode of body culture may enter another. For example, achievement dimensions may enter the folk mode.

Although *gusimbuka-urukiramende* can be read as being ideologically different from the sportized and welfare-inspired jumping cultures of early twentieth-century Europe, it was not so visibly different that it failed to cause problems for those who sought to record and represent it. For example, was it the same as, or different from, the achievement model with which most Europeans were familiar? It appears that *gusimbuka* was a sort of folk jumping which never became sportized. It neither sought records nor attempted, in any social-democratic fashion, to improve the welfare of the national population. It was hardly egalitarian, shunning as it did women. In the following chapters, I explore its representations by colonial writers and photographers.

CHAPTER 3

Imagined Olympians

Faced with anything foreign, the Established Order knows only
two types of behaviour, which are both mutilating: either to
acknowledge it as a Punch and Judy show, or to defuse it as a pure
reflection of the West.

—Roland Barthes, *Mythologies*

With increasing frequency, in recent years students from a variety of
disciplines have addressed the ways in which pictorial and literary representations of place carry multiple meanings.[1] This concern arises
from what has been termed a "crisis of representation" which recognizes
that problems of description become problems of representation.[2] As a
result, scholars in fields ranging from literary studies and photography
to anthropology and geography have been forced to explore and grapple
with the problem of what constitutes an adequate account of another
culture in the face of contrasting representations of it. Even adequate
accounts, however, will not be perfect representations. As Gunnar Olsson has noted, "[K]nowledge by definition is an exercise in translation
[and] a translation can never be perfect."[3] His compatriot, Martin Gren,
adds that "there is always a gap between 'reality' and our representations
of 'it.'"[4] This gap would seem likely to be at its widest when the cultural
distance between two societies is at its greatest. In essence, therefore, all
ethnographies, histories, and geographies can be viewed as fictions, in
the literal sense of *fictio*—"something made." And, as Derek Gregory
notes "[T]here are no end of ways in which they can be 'made.'"[5] Being
fictions, such writing generates a new, imaginative geography that can
only be discovered via a sensitivity to "the particular way it writes people and place, society and space."[6] A postmodern perspective, which presents a more culturally relativistic view of the world, has paralleled these

kinds of observations. According to this relativistic position, all representations are caught up in the constraints of language, culture, and politics and can, therefore, be said to always be *mis*representations.[7] Such a view would argue that no one representation of people and place should be privileged over any other, a subject I return to in the final chapter.

An imaginative geography is quite different from the mental map Europeans may have had of Africa and "the African." An imaginative geography is much more active and fantastical, stressing the lack of innocence in representation. Imagination has the power to construct geographies rather than simply express perceptions of them. Imaginative geography is an idea that may help "the mind to intensify its own sense of itself by dramatizing the distance and difference between what is close to it and what is far away."[8] In particular, it "legitimates a vocabulary, a universe of representative discourse peculiar to the discussion and understanding of [Africa]." The drama and the distance result in the inhabitants of imaginative geography being figures that are, to actual Africans, "as stylized costumes are to the characters in a play."[9] Said's imaginative geography serves to legitimate a European view, often in the interests of Europe. At his most uncompromising, he notes that

> we need not look for correspondence between language used to depict [the African] and [Africa] itself, not so much because the language is inaccurate but because it is not even trying to be accurate. What it is trying to do … is at one and the same time to characterize [Africa] as alien and to incorporate it schematically on a theatrical stage whose audience, manager, and actors are *for* Europe, and only for Europe. Hence the vacillation between the familiar and the alien.[10]

Said's claim of the deliberate inaccuracy of all colonial accounts might well be questioned, as may his assertion that colonial writing inevitably emphasizes difference and inferiority. Surely, every single piece of knowledge produced in and by the West was not necessarily contaminated with fiction or malice.[11] Other critiques—especially of *Orientalism*—illustrate the essentializing nature of much of Said's early work, which reinforces the binary opposition between East and West and lacks historical vision. He also tends to ignore the complicity of colonized peoples with the forms of knowledge that are produced about them.[12] Yet it is hard to deny that "all cultures impose corrections upon raw reality" and that very often other cultures are received, "not as they are but as, for the benefit of the receiver, they ought to be."[13] In this normative mode the westerner (as I will show) often seemed to be converting "the native" into something else, making it difficult to make any sense of things except in the way they are represented. Ways of seeing the African athlete, for example, became obvious through such representations. A recurring theme in the European representation of Africa was the familiarity of the symbolic language that was employed; "known rhetorical figures were used to translate the inarticulate."[14] In producing their texts, the Europeans "took their pre-texts with them" in which their "dreams of the fantastic were captured."[15] And having been captured, they were, by means of metaphor, transported from one place to another.

Said's notion of imaginative geography, which he initially applied to the Orient, is also applicable to Africa. However, black Africa, as opposed to the oriental North Africa, was thought, at least since Gobineau, to be incapable of civilization.[16] Africa, as a colonial space, differed from the Orient insofar as it tended to be reduced to "the forest" and "violent nature…without tenderness and feeling"—Conrad's infamous *Heart of Darkness*; the Orient, on the other hand, was recognized more through cultural institutions such as temples and mosques.[17] More than this, Africa has been read as "the Other's Other, the Orient's Other."[18] The term Other is widely used in postcolonial writing to define something (or somebody) against which we compare ourselves, that is, something we have to construct. It is understood, not on its own terms, but is given qualities believed to be the opposite of those that define it. It is often the different and distant negative against which an authority is defined, against which home is defined, the antithesis of civilization. As I will show, *gusimbuka-urukiramende* was usually seen as a Rwandan version of Western sportized high jumping, being different but the same—the Occident's Other. The writing of *gusimbuka* was a disciplined one, undertaken via academic disciplines, in popular and scholarly journals, writing and photographs, usually underpinned by the cultural and political norms of the West. Often, however, what was represented in the books and journals was not the direct result of having visited the place or people, but rather the result of having seen a representation of it, in print, in a photograph, or on film. Therefore, some of the images that I will be writing about here are representations of representations.[19] Such writing is progressively distanced from the events it claims to communicate. But I will not be overly concerned in this and the following chapter with the lack of correspondence of colonial writing with reality. Instead, I wish to emphasize what particular colonial images and statements might mean.

I do not want to present Rwanda as simply another example of a general model such as that shown in Figure 3.1. This summarizes a traditional European approach that represented the African Other as "natural" and "living in the past."[20] Other binaries included time extending from the present to the past—from the modern to the premodern, from places with history to those without history. Space went from north to

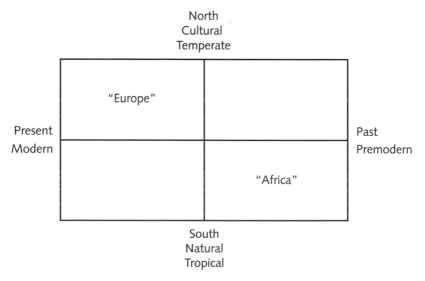

Figure 3.1

south, from the temperate to the tropical and torrid, from the cultural to the natural. This suggests the simple grid in Figure 3.1, through which a reading of colonial texts could take place and which can be illustrated by a specific piece of writing about Rwandan body culture, in this case, dancing. By the end of the nineteenth century, native dancing had "become a leitmotif in the western image of non-Christian or primitive behavior."[21] Much of African dancing, including, as it did, seminaked men and women, was often perceived and projected by Europeans to be savage, exotic, or overly erotic—and hence inferior to purified Western forms of dance. In describing such a body culture, the language used by Attilio Gatti is exemplary. In Rwandan dancing he observed "such a *riot* of *savage* rhythms, of *violent* colours, of *barbaric* motions, that we felt *wrenched* away from the present."[22] From such descriptions, it is clear that Africa was at the end of a Europe-Africa spectrum of time and space. Here the native body culture was something to be seen and confirms the "generalised codes constitutive of savagery."[23]

However, such polarities as those implied in Figure 3.1 obscure the fact that African populations (e.g., Tutsi and Hutu, with the Hutu as the Tutsi's Other) and body cultures were as complex and varied as those of the Occident.[24] And so, too, were the occidental readings of them. The present study is, of course, a more localized and focused exploration than was Said's in *Orientalism*, and I feel that it benefits from his insights without having to necessarily accept the difficulties of his totalizing tendencies. What I try to demonstrate is that within the discourse on the tiny nation of Rwanda and one of its body cultures, there were heterogeneities, inconsistencies, and slippages that the Africa-Occident binary (which Said's early work encourages) tends to suppress.[25]

It is widely felt that European readers enjoyed the supply of representations of alien customs, provided that such customs could be read as preserving a sense of moral, physical, and racial superiority.[26] As a result, it has been concluded that "*[a]lways* with reference to the superiority of an expanding Europe, colonized peoples are represented as *lesser*, *less* human, *less* civilized."[27] But it can be argued—in the context of the colonial world, especially—that one should never say "always" because specific situations may reveal conditions that are at odds with the generalities of homogenizing models and theories. This is crucial to the subject of this book. As I shall show, while widely applied to much of Africa, modes of negation were often more difficult to apply to *gusimbuka*—which included men only—than to dancing and other "primitive" body cultural practices. In any case, where live subjects were on display and performing, there was the possibility that the performers "would offer unexpected visions and unscripted meanings."[28] If the civilizing mission of the colonists was to erase difference (the Other as same), representational problems could still result when Europeans encountered "unconverted" body cultures that appeared, at the same time, different from and similar to those of Europe. The problems may have been exacerbated if such body cultures could, apparently, produce superior performances—placed (quite literally, in this case) above the physical body of the European—that belied European expectations of racial superiority. Martial race theory (Others differentiated through their martialism or athleticism) represents a challenge to Said's critique of colonial discourse because the Others—in this case, invariably represented as Tutsi—were not necessarily considered antithetical to the Western self.[29] As a result, conflicting rhetorics were employed. Contradictory ways of seeing people and places, and the messages communicated by those images, are frequently found in the early twentieth-century travel writing and photography that was associated with European colonialism and empire. The German and Belgian colonial presence in east equatorial Africa was no exception. In what follows, I will try to show how both distance and difference from the African were stressed but, at the same time, how some modes of rhetoric were able to bring the African and the European closer together.

In addition to Othering, a further set of strategies has been termed "ordering." This involved the reduction of diversity and chaos into categories and sets that could be transported back to the colonial power. Ordering was achieved by recording, measuring, ranking, classifying, and generalizing. Texts per se can be regarded as ordering techniques. These tactics made order out of the previously unrecorded and uncategorized materialities of Africa. It has been suggested that by stressing strategies of ordering, it may have been possible to avoid applying the implicit violence of Othering to what was often an ambiguous setting.[30]

Ambiguity was often a reflection of the fact that class, gender, and nation served to differentiate colonial discourse, but generally, though not universally, the world of travel writing was one of upper-middle-class men. In the context of this book, it was mainly men recording male corporeality. There is considerable debate surrounding the question of whether men's writing about Africa differed from that of women. After all, many women were as imperialistic as men.[31] At the same time, I should repeat that these masculinities were not homogeneous, and for this reason we should expect varied readings of Rwandan corporeality. Yet much colonial writing did appear to code the European empires as places where "extreme forms of masculine behaviors were expected."[32] There were no women in Mecklenburg's expedition. William Roome, a fellow of the Royal Geographical Society who traveled in Rwanda as part of his missionary duties in the 1930s, was probably typical. His book, *Tramping through Africa*, was "dedicated to Grace, my dear wife who made these journeys possible by keeping the home fires burning."[33] Some husband-and-wife teams did travel into the region, Ellen and Attilio Gatti and Mr. and Mrs. Alexander Barns being examples. Indeed, Ellen Gatti summarized her African experiences in a book of her own.[34] Yet the women seem to have played the lesser role both in organizing things and in representing the results in print and pictures. The American author of *Behind God's Back*, Negley Farson, dedicated his book to his wife in somewhat ambiguous terms noting that she was "my sole companion on this drive from coast to coast across Africa; she was better than any man."[35] But by and large, the European representations found in the present book were the result of men looking at, and often idealizing, other men. And they were masculinist in the sense that, while claiming to be comprehensive, tended to forget that women existed.

I stress the masculinity of the representations discussed in this and subsequent chapters because it has been increasingly recognized that the kind of geography being undertaken by the European travelers in their fieldwork in Africa, as elsewhere, was centrally a masculine practice.[36] Indeed, Gillian Rose has argued that fieldwork per se is a masculine gaze: "Geographers become stronger men by challenging nature ... tough heroism establishes fieldwork as a particular kind of masculine endeavour."[37] This resonates particularly strongly with colonial fieldwork, from which the resulting writing often reads like an adventure story—the result of male encounters.[38] After all, the empires in Africa were sources of eye-catching collections of physical exhibitionism and rituals, hence satisfying the European male's "wildest imaginings."[39] Rose's comments also relate to the commercial interests of the male bourgeoisie and of the scientists from the "new" disciplines of anthropology and geography, which in England were often supported by the masculine bastion of the Royal Geographical Society.[40] Other masculine gazes on the subject of what follows came from the highly gendered fields of physiology and sports science.

Daniel Bivona avers that Lewis Carroll's heroine in *Alice in Wonderland* was trapped by an "ethnocentric net from which she is powerless to free herself," and Thomas Richards also alludes to *Alice* and "the problem of positive knowledge" of disordered nature in mid-Victorian writing.[41] This leads to the basic question of how Western writers (and, I should add, photographers) construct representations of the "strange and (to the writer) often incomprehensible realities confronted in the non-Western world. What are the cultural, ideological or literary presuppositions upon which such a construct is based?"[42] Or, alternately, "[W]hat happens when one deposits a representative of [European culture] in a foreign country populated by beings who live by unfamiliar rules?"[43] Clearly, what would have been normal in a European setting would be inappropriate in the "wonderland" of Rwanda simply because most of the Europeans did not *know* what they were talking (and writing) about.

Rather than being exposed to a single colonialist gaze, early twentieth-century Rwanda was part of an image world of African corporeality composed of complex and multiple images that were circulated around Europe and North America.[44] David Spurr has suggested that this "profusion of different voices" assumed a number of widely divergent forms, with twelve rhetorical modes (basic tropes, or a kind of repertoire for colonial discourse) being used in colonial writing to describe non-Western people.[45] These ways of writing about the Banyarwanda and *gusimbuka-urukiramende* operated across a range of contexts, among them the anthropological and the athletic. They may have sometimes clashed with one another, yet all contributed to the matrix of power relations that characterized the colonial situation.[46] In this and the following chapter I employ four of Spurr's modes: *surveillance, appropriation, idealization*, and *negation*. Each of these I apply to the representation of the physicality and athleticism of Tutsi men, though because they overlap considerably, they should not be interpreted as mutually exclusive. Of the four categories on which I concentrate, surveillance merges with classification; idealization merges with three other categories—aestheticization, naturalization, and eroticism; and negation merges with debasement. The strength of Spurr's approach is its ability to show that the process of essentialization is much more than pejorative stereotyping. Instead, different rhetorics are seen as being juxtaposed.[47] In this chapter I want to concentrate on a number of written texts in order to illustrate how Tutsi corporeality was (and, to some extent, continues to be) constructed for, and communicated to, the West. In addition, and specifically, I want to show how the body culture of the male Tutsi was transformed by a Western imagination into familiar and reductive cultural forms. In this way I seek to add to the relatively small number of geographical studies of ways of seeing indigenous people as part of colonial discourse, in the specific context of *gusimbuka-urukiramende*.[48]

For purposes of convenience, this chapter is organized in four sections, each focusing on the application of one of the rhetorical modes.

Surveillance: Rhetoric of the Record

Visual observation—the European gaze or examination—is widely regarded as the essential starting point of the Western record of the

African. The commanding view of the colonizer provides the source of both information (and with it, authority) and aesthetic pleasure. Although photographic and other visual records (see chapter 4) might be assumed to represent the most obvious forms of surveillance of Rwandan body culture, the written and quantified record of the African body were also essential parts of the modernist project of bringing order to Africa. The quantified record of *gusimbuka-urukiramende* was a form of surveillance. Just as countries could be "reduced to a litany of great cities, and great cities were reduced to a checklist of prominent buildings, historic monuments and scenic viewpoints,"[49] so geographical variations in the human body and its performance genres could be categorized into racial types, specimens, and tribes.[50] This was especially appropriate in the case of Rwanda, with its three apparently recognizable "types" or even "races." Through the use of quantification and measurement, the European could codify differences in customs that would be represented as fixed and normalized.

The contact zone in which both sides of the colonial divide absorbed and inscribed aspects of each other's culture has alternatively been called the "theater of contact."[51] The theatrical metaphor encourages several possible readings of both contact and surveillance. Quantification and measurement could only be undertaken by observation, and this was sometimes claimed to have resulted from the privileged perspective of the European observer. Rather than being members of an audience, some travelers felt themselves to have been privy to local knowledge and therefore able to function as behind-the-scenes observers. Such a focus for representation not only implied a gain in status by association, but also excused the European from trespassing on the African's private domain. Local knowledge can, therefore, be seen as a help rather than, as is often thought, a hindrance.[52] For example, obtaining access to *gusimbuka*, implied Attilio Gatti, was the result of the *mwami* being not only an acquaintance of his[53] but also "a very good friend ... for many years."[54] Even so, in travel writing the indigeneous tended to be written about, not engaged with. And despite Gatti's apparent—if, perhaps, exaggerated—claim of interaction between European and African, the literary, mathematical, and photographic opportunities "set up the locals as exotica ripe for capture."[55] Such capture could become more efficient if it was possible for the explorer/traveler to move beyond playing the role of metaphorical audience or behind-the-scenes observer and become the stage manager, as Gatti claims—and, as I will show—Mecklenburg seems to have claimed for himself. It can be argued, however, that the greater the active interventions of the European observer, the less objective the ensuing recordings.[56]

The Europeans consumed *gusimbuka* as a version of something known already to them; it also encouraged the use of Western models of recording athletic performance. These assumed three forms: (1) measurement of the Rwandan body itself (see chapter 1), (2) quantified recording of the resulting athletic performances, and (3) measurement of incidental but related activities and artifacts. As Simon Ryan has observed "[T]he space of empire is universal, Euclidean and Cartesian, a measurable mathematical web constructed and maintained by positivism."[57] Imperialism involved the quantitative measurement of the imperial realm—a means of recording that was frequently in collision with idealized or naturalized modes. Under the influence of positivism, one sought generalizations—in this case, generalizations about the body and about athletic performance.

Anthropometry was part of the physical anthropological project of body mapping, an imperial analog of the geographical mapping of Africa itself. As I noted in chapter 1, it was often stressed that the Tutsi, as a collectivity, were above average in height—a flawed statement, but one far from lacking value in constructing the Tutsi stereotype. The high-jump performances were measured via a similar ideological lens. The measurement of African athletic performances in Western sports dates from at least 1902,[58] but the most notorious example of such surveillance is arguably that associated with the "anthropology days" at the St. Louis Olympics of 1904. This is germane to the theme of this book, because observations made in the report of those games reveal contemporary attitudes toward the perceived athleticism of "native" peoples. At St. Louis a series of track-and-field events were arranged in which various "savages" who had been "displayed" at the Louisiana Purchase Exposition (around which the 1904 games were organized) took part. The events were said to be a scientific experiment ("the first athletic meeting held anywhere, in which savages were exclusive participants") to demonstrate the rumored athletic prowess of these people. They in fact served to demean them.[59] Filipinos, Ainus from Japan, and "Pygmies" were represented and their performances measured and recorded. The high jump was won by a Sioux American, George Mentz, whose performance was measured at 4 feet 7 inches (1.39 meters), while a Patagonian was photographed clearing a height a good foot lower.[60] To the surprise and disappointment of the organizers, their achievements appeared inferior to the competitors in the "official" Olympics. Dr. W. J. McGee, chief of the department of anthropology at the exposition, attributed the savages' poor performances to a lack of training in Western sports. The writer of the official report, however, simply concluded that the meet had conclusively shown that the savage had been greatly overrated from an athletic point of view.[61] Eichberg suggests that these native groups were able to distinguish themselves "by their laughter and readiness to view the situation as great fun," in contrast to the much more serious disposition of the achievement-oriented athletes.[62] This may have been the case in some events, but more important, in my view, is the fact that the anthropology days illustrated a meeting of cultures. The Olympics may have lost the quality of laughter and popular carnival, but the American assumption that indigenous people could, through the practice of their own corporeal activities, produce outstanding, quantified performances in ideologically different Western sports, is arguably a more important reading of these rather pathetic events. The initial view of the Americans certainly implied the possibility of a seamless transformation from the folk to the achievement model.

Following the debacle of the anthropology days, the report of the 1904 Games insisted that "lecturers and authors will in the future omit all references to the natural athletic ability of the savage, unless they can substantiate their alleged feats."[63] It is unlikely that Mecklenburg read the report, but the measurements of the jumps witnessed in Rwanda would supply the substantiation it required. Providing that the height of a mound or stone forming the takeoff point could be deducted, measurement of the net height jumped could be readily made. Seeking to record sport-like achievements of the Banyarwanda with "exact evidence," Mecklenburg reported a high jump by a Tutsi (*not* named as a Rwandan) of 2.50 meters (about 8 feet 2½ inches), and jumps by "young boys" of 1.50 to 1.60 meters (around 5 feet).[64] But subsequent records of the performance witnessed by Mecklenburg are inconsistent. Over half a century after Mecklenburg's visit, the influential German sports scholar Carl Diem, described the athlete's jump as 2.53 meters, despite having been personally informed by Mecklenburg's anthropologist colleague, Czekanowski, that it was 2.35 meters.[65] Given Mecklenburg's greater fame and his report's more extensive media coverage, his figure of 2.50 meters prevailed as the truth. Selected record(ing)s of later performances include those of Peter Schumacher, who supplied a figure of 2.45 meters; Pauwels, who stated 2.40 meters; and the Belgian cinematographer Gourdinne, who gave a measurement of 2.20 meters (7 feet 2⅝ inches).[66] In the decades between 1910 and 1950, other visitors recorded a wide variety of measurements. "Heights of 7 ft. 2 ins. are said by reliable observers to have been reached by the best" of the Tutsi jumpers, noted Ernst Jokl, though he later stated that the best Tutsi performance was 7 feet 4 inches.[67] At an event witnessed by William Roome at Gatsibu, six athletes were said to have beaten the "world's record" of 6 feet 7 inches. Two of them, one being Kanyamuhungu, "must have cleared a height of eight feet," he reported, a measurement which Roome was "careful to take clear above the stone from which they jumped."[68] The fact that some athletes were remembered by their names led Ndejuru to attribute a kind of achievement orientation to *gusimbuka-urukiramende*.[69] Gatti claimed that he recorded one performance with particular accuracy, measuring the height "*exactly* at 8 feet 3⅛ inches from the ground."[70] Martin Birnbaum claimed that he had witnessed heights of between 7 and 8 feet, though Patrick Balfour estimated more modest performances of 6 feet 6 inches while Felice Belotti was not prepared to go further than to observe that "nearly all jump more than six feet."[71] Merlyn Severn described an event at which jumping started at 5 feet 6 inches, and proceeded to 7 feet 5 inches; Roome witnessed jumping commencing between six and seven feet.[72] These performances were aided by a run-up to the point of takeoff that also encouraged measurement. Its length was variously recorded at about ten yards, thirteen yards, fifteen yards and twenty paces.[73] Standing high jumps, which involved no run-up, were recorded as being between 1.30 and 2.00 meters.[74] A wealth of statistical information was clearly made available.

It was recognized that a complete record of the event would require the measurement of not only the height of the jump, but also the height of the mound or stone from which the athletes took off. For example, Mecklenburg claimed that the one he observed was about a foot in height; Gatti measured one at 2⅛ inches (making his recorded jump 8 feet 1 inch); Jokl provided a measurement of 3–4 inches; Birnbaum of 2 or 3 inches; Severn of about 5 inches; and Catlow of about 6 inches.[75] The consistently reported notion that they could only achieve such heights with the help of the takeoff mound suggests a lurking sense of negation and a refusal to unequivocally acknowledge Tutsi athleticism. Such elevated takeoff points, calculated Jokl, gave a Tutsi jumper an advantage of about six inches.[76] According to Stanley Smith, by taking a "small anthill into account," a clearance of 7 feet 10 inches was reduced to one of 6 feet 4 inches.[77] In both cases the African leap was translated into the terms of the European jump, but, at the same time, negated by alluding to the assistance given by the raised takeoff. Finally, the modern concern with quantifying the number of spectators in attendance was not unknown. Barns estimated that between two thousand and three thousand spectators attended an event at Mwami Musinga's great courtyard.[78]

The concern that everything should be accurately measured reflected the European obsession for detail and the glorification of Western forms of knowledge. In the context of *gusimbuka-urukiramende*, such attention to measured detail constitutes the colonial view as one of power, turning the sacred heaven-earth axis of verticality into a measured space. But it was also the view of the emerging world of sports. Observing the measurement of athletic performance at the 1936 Olympics, Walter Benjamin noted, "Nothing is more typical of the test in its modern form as measuring the human being against an apparatus."[79] While the European examinations were not necessarily aimed at the immediate training of Rwandans in athletic technique, the recording of their athletic performances created "a field of comparison between different individuals [that] allows for the generation of a norm with which to grade the capacity, attributes, or performance of the subjects."[80] Africanism can, therefore, be said to be a discipline of detail and, indeed, a "theory of detail by which every minute aspect of [African] life is testified to [by] an [African] essence it expressed, that [Africanism] had the eminence, the power and the affirmative authority over [Africa] that it had."[81] Everything about *gusimbuka* would be fully visible to the reader.

It may be of interest to compare these performances with the heights reached by contemporary sportized high jumpers, but I am less attracted to the heights that were reported than to the meanings of such measurings and recordings. In other words, the high-jump records are texts to be deconstructed. All this quantification and measuring can be read as "an insertion of a foreign discourse which can only ever construct observations in its own terms" and as a part of the longer-term European project of the systematization of nature.[82] Measurement was central to the European description of the non-European world. It reflected a European way of seeing that was authoritative, powerful, and appropriative despite—or, perhaps, because of—mathematical or quantitative representation in apparently neutral and value-free, "nonideological" terms. Quantification would remove the obfuscation of the written word. As Barnes has shown, however, mathematics is hardly lacking in cultural bias, residing as it does in the classifications and meanings of a particular culture.[83] Quantification and the record were part of the language of modern achievement sport, imposed on the nonsportized oral world of Rwanda via the lens of the achievement orientation of the Western sports enthusiast. Even if those who took such measurements were not track-and-field fans, the urge to measure and record was undeniable.

In its own small way, the measurement of the high-jump performances in Rwanda served the same function as the more literal mapping of broader empires. The athletics statistics of the European were, like the map, an imperial technology of ordering and domesticating that allowed a form of homogeneous recording to appropriate the African for the European realm. To be sure, the application of European statistics of Rwandan high jumping were made out of context. But this did not mean that *gusimbuka* was distanced from sportized high jumping.[84] On the contrary, the Western statistics can be read as bringing the African high jump into the realm of modern sport.

The African body and its performances were as much objects of examination, commentary, and valorization as was the African landscape.[85] It was valued for ethnological and scientific advances; in the case of the Tutsi, it was also valued for its athleticism and its potential Olympism. Its value was best estimated by measuring it—that is, determining its output—in terms of quantified records. In this way it could also be located within the expanding empire of international achievement sport.

Appropriation: Claiming by Naming

Colonial discourse implicitly claims the place surveyed as the colonizer's own. Local culture and space are imaginatively transformed and appropriated for the Occident, a "natural abundance that awaits the creative hand of technology."[86] A basic feature of colonialist discourse was the "*transferability* of empire's organizing metaphors."[87] Like colonial landscapes, the African body was "brought within the horizon of European intelligibility through the multiple practices of naming."[88] The geographer Yi-Fu Tuan has alluded to naming as a form of power—the creative power to import a certain character to things. He observes that the words used by explorers in the naming of things were often inappropriate, and that certain terms evoked a European image that fitted poorly with an African actuality.[89] So, "language is power because words construct reality."[90] Metaphors are graphic transformations of reality, and when widely used and adopted, their metaphorical use is forgotten and a literal meaning is ascribed to the same words. The application of European terms to African body culture revealed the problem of translating something from one culture to another. The very act of naming "was a way of bringing [a Rwandan corporeality] into textual presence, of bringing it within the compass of a European rationality that made it at once familiar to its colonizers and to its native [practitioners]."[91] Rwandan bodies were verbally ordered and domesticated, the strange and menacing becoming domestic and serene.[92] Missionaries and clergy not only introduced European languages, but also helped to standardize native languages. Naming could be termed "linguistic settlement."[93] Banyarwanda were rhetorically dispossessed of their indigenous corporeal culture, and the possibility of an indigenous athleticism was effaced by the widespread application of terms such as *high jump, hoogspringen* (Dutch), *Hochsprung* (German), and *hauteur* (French). The French term makes height rather than the act of jumping explicit. The use of familiar words or terms of reference from sources of the colonial gaze made it possible to view the Europeans in Rwanda as being confronted with nothing so much as an image of themselves.[94] The term high jump connoted competitive, modern sport and, it can be argued, was a far from perfect translation of *gusimbuka*, but naming had acted as norming.[95]

Exactly the same conclusions, of course, could be applied to the widespread use of the term sport in relation to *gusimbuka* and the running and throwing events that were often performed with it. Some observers thought the Banyarwanda were the only people in central Africa who, during the 1920s, practiced sport.[96] Sport could bring the African and the European together. The athletic prowess of the "muscular Christian," according to Captain Geoffrey Holmes (noted in chapter 2), constituted a common bond that united the two worlds of British and Rwandan body culture. Somehow, this bond of itself "enabled him, in such a large measure, to win the friendship of the *sport loving* Batusi."[97] Prince Eugène de Ligne referred to the overall event in which *gusimbuka* occurred as a "fête sportive,"[98] but in the 1920s sport was a slippery term, that continued to carry some of its nineteenth-century disportive connotations and was applied to many disparate activities, from elephant shooting to cricket and from pig-sticking to high jumping. But for most European observers, the Rwandan version of high jumping was unquestionably a sport—frequently, one regarded in the achievement-oriented, Olympian mold. An introductory geography and history textbook from the mid-1920s generalized the Tutsi as practicing sports "avec ardeur." The sports were said to include archery, high jumping (2.20 meters without a "springboard"), and javelin and discus throwing.[99] William Roome appeared confident in describing high jumping as the "favourite sport" in Rwanda;[100] Weule felt it was their "chief sport."[101] The "grassy plot" where jumping took place was "a native representation of a *sports ground*."[102] Jokl could see it as nothing other than a version of the Western model—a modified form of "the Osborn technique," a reference to the style of a well-known American world record holder (see appendix).[103] In seeking to identify sports records among the different races, Lothar Gottlieb Tirala, director of the Institute for Racial Hygiene at the University of Munich during the 1930s, acknowledged the Tutsi as undisputed leaders in the high jump; he ranked North Americans second.[104] In doing so, he implied the existence of a shared basis for comparison and ignored differences in body cultural ideology.

If *gusimbuka* was a sport, it would also need to have its champions. This title was applied by Roome to Kanyamuhungu—"the champion jumper of Ruanda"; Smith, in parentheses, added "possibly the world."[105] The naming of an individual jumper opposed what was typically a totally dispassionate and scientist view. Usually, European representations of the indigene resulted in a reductive construction of colonial subjectivity—a depersonalized type such as "native," "Tutsi," or "savage." The use of the man's name accepted "the necessary cultural and personal individuation that selfhood generally presumes."[106] Yet through his designation as a champion, he was still being appropiated.

With sport and champions came the record. The Tutsi athletes were said to "casually break any known world record."[107] Mecklenburg found it necessary to add a footnote contrasting the Tutsi performance of 2.50 meters with what he believed to be the existing American world record of 1.94 meters.[108] This observation may not be surprising, in view of his considerable interest in sports. Hoberman has claimed that while admiration for black physicality existed during the nineteenth century, in Germany it was not until the 1920s that the African was seen as a potential athlete.[109] Yet in 1907 Mecklenburg was comparing the Tutsi high jump with the world's record, leaving little doubt about the African's Olympic potential. As noted earlier, the measurements used to describe the Rwandan records were often, literally, imperial in nature. Their performances meant something only when compared with the records of the West—a comparison that was itself an appropriation. It was also possible to talk of the Tutsi record as being about 2.20 meters.[110] This kind of observation, where a class of people was awarded a record, exemplified the Western desire to categorize. The reading of the Rwandan athletes went beyond record breakers and Olympians. Ethnicity, sport, and nation could be conflated to typologize a collectivity into a national concept. A Belgian commentator noted that *gusimbuka* was "in someways, the national sport of the Watutsi."[111] This not only appropriated *gusimbuka* as a sport, but also elevated the Tutsi to imagined nationhood, ignoring both Hutu and Twa in the process. The use of other words appeared to appropriate *gusimbuka* for gymnastics rather than sports. The use of the term *springboard* to define the hardened termite mound or stone in a number of descriptions was totally inappropriate and misleading.[112] The likening of the termite mound to a springboard made *gusimbuka* into an analog of the European turner-style gymnastic high jump. Indeed, Rummelt seemed to think that that the mound or stone really did provide a spring rather than an aid to leverage.[113]

All this shows how, to the westerner, Africa was "always *like* some aspect of the West"; the Africanist was converting an African body cultural practice into something else—a Western sport. Said observes that "he does this for himself, for the sake of his culture, in some cases for what he believes is the sake of the [African]."[114] Europeans saw the natural (including human) resources of colonized lands as rightfully belonging to "civilization" and "mankind" rather than to the indigenous peoples. The notion of Africa as the colonizer's inheritance is reflected in the way in which African culture was recorded and perceived. The European view looked forward in time as well as in space.[115] For example, the descriptions of the area around Lake Tanganyika by Sir Richard Burton and Henry Morton Stanley included its transformation into an Anglicized and Edenic landscape inhabited by church spires, pretty cottages, meadows, gardens, and orchards.[116] In the case of *gusimbuka-urukiramende*, the texts of those who witnessed it also transformed it into familiar cultural terrain. The way in which the Rwandan high jumper was seen as resembling the European athlete through preformulated discourses on sport and Olympism can be understood as an attempt to contain the unfamiliar via a comparison with the familiar. But it can also be seen as a way of establishing the Rwandan as being (naturally) suited to the reproduction of a European system of sport.[117] Hence, whereas Stanley's gaze had constructed the English country village out of the East African landscape, those who viewed *gusimbuka* had constructed an imaginative sports landscape made up of the Olympic Games, champions, and world records. At the same time, however, this also suggests the use of the mode of negation, since Rwanda's athletic space was implicitly viewed as a void or a blank space waiting to be filled with European athletic sports.

Frequent allusions were made to the Olympics. The display of physical performances ordered by Mwami Rudahigwa for Attilio Gatti was described as "a sort of Olympic Games."[118] The Tutsi athlete "puts Olympic high jumpers to shame," noted Martin Birnbaum, who in 1938 speculated about the possibility of sending a team from Rwanda to the Olympics.[119] Patrick Balfour reckoned that "they could walk off with the high jump contests at the Olympic Games," while a Belgian bureaucrat, writing what was essentially colonial propaganda, thought that "[o]ne day they will probably win *every* jumping event at the Olympic Games."[120] Ellen Gatti hoped that "some enterprising entrepreneur will bring a bunch of these lads" to the same games, and Mary Akeley, a wildlife photographer from about 1914 and a voracious author and traveler, welcomed the possibility of witnessing the Tutsi athletes competing against the 1948 Olympic 100-meter champion from the

United States, the sprint-hurdler Harrison Dillard.[121] Although Tutsi women did not take part in *gusimbuka*, Jokl saw them as possessing even greater Olympic potential than the men.[122] However, it was the Western model of sport per se, rather than the Olympics that may have provided the dominant image for the European imagination. Such misprision led Dr. J. E. Church to liken a mission hospital event that included Tutsi chiefs and a *gusimbuka* performance of 7 feet 5 inches, to an English seaside sports meeting that he had once attended—"the CSSM [Children's Special Service Mission] sports at Sheringham with Reggie Manwaring."[123]

Jokl was a consistent supporter of the sportization of *gusimbuka*. He recalled that in 1950 he "suggested to Dr. Ralph Bunche, then in charge of the U.N. Trusteeship Council in New York, that a modern system of Physical Education and coaching be introduced to Ruanda and Urundi and that an effort be made to enter a Watusi team" (not, notice, a team from Rwanda) in the Olympic Games.[124] A similar proposition had been made nearly twenty years earlier, when it was suggested in a Belgian sports journal that two jumpers from Rwanda should represent Belgium in the 1932 Los Angeles Olympics.[125] Likewise, at least one U.S. track-and-field coach traveled to Rwanda in the 1950s to consider recruiting Rwandan high jumpers to the American intercollegiate sports system. He observed that, under official conditions and using the occidental technique, they would probably surpass the existing world record.[126] These idealized views, these attempts to read and legitimate an appropriated *gusimbuka* as an Olympic sport, seemed to totally ignore the fact that there was neither a Rwandan track-and-field federation nor a Rwandan Olympic committee. Moreover, Rwanda's status as a Belgian protectorate would have made any participation in any international competition a logistical hazard. But most importantly, *gusimbuka* was simply not a sportized body culture. Yet an Olympian gaze was still present in 1964, when the doyen of track-and-field historians, Dr. Roberto Quercetani, combined appropriation with negation, noting that the athletic "potential" of Tutsi would not be fulfilled until they had taken up high jumping with a "singleness of purpose."[127] Here was an oblique allusion to the stereotype of the lazy native. That the *intore* and the high jumpers who followed them could have possibly possessed such a single-ness of purpose was lost in such observations.

Representing *gusimbuka* as a version of something that was already known—the repetition-across-difference, as Boehmer puts it[128]—would be seen by Said as a way of controlling the threat that it represented.[129] In this case, the threat was to the established view of the world sporting order. But with the Tutsi high jumpers, the threat was seemingly impos-sible to avoid. The fact that the Rwandans appeared as sportsmen meant that they "sidestepped the position of silent object."[130] It was the mis-perceived congruence of *gusimbuka-urukiramende* with the sportized high jump that led a prominent German physician to ask: "What, then, will be left of our world records?"[131] This message was carried to audi-ences beyond sports science, academe, and *National Geographic*. In the context of the radio sports broadcast, a popular Finnish sports journalist of the 1930s, Harri Eljanko, observed to a mass audience that it would not be surprising if future world records for the high jump were held by members of the Tutsi "tribe."[132] The high jumpers of Rwanda were seen as ideal bodies awaiting the body management of Western sport. Given their athletic skills, it was automatically assumed that European sports—and, by implication, the universal space of Olympism—could be easily introduced into the region.[133] Olympism would lead to refined perfor-mance. Hence, despite the fact that the Europeans saw the Tutsi as supe-rior high jumpers, it was felt that they could be further improved within the global—that is, Western—sports system. The Western view of prog-ress, carrying with it more than a hint of negation with respect to the African, was reflected in the words of Stanley Smith who, having wit-nessed a leap of 7 feet 10 inches, insisted that the athlete "could do better than that."[134] If they were trained in the European manner, they would "jump equally well" without the aid of the raised takeoff, noted Roome[135]—another case of the seamless conversion of indigene to ath-lete. Even more dramatically, it was suggested by the German hygienist Lothar Tirala that, with modern jumping techniques, the Tutsi could probably jump 20–30 centimeters (8–12 inches) higher.[136] Like African art, *gusimbuka* reflected simply a stage in the development toward a civilized body culture.[137] The way in which it was read also presumed the continuing vitality of Rwandan culture and its corporeality. Drawing on Christopher Miller's observations on African art, such writings as those noted above "*rewards* Africa for conforming to a European image of [athletics], for acting as a mirror in which the European can contemplate a European idea of [sport]."[138] *Gusimbuka* could not be seen as another, different kind of body culture. The widespread colonial practice of designating "our" space from "theirs," as a way of making geographical distinctions, was less easily applied to its cultural space.[139]

Appropriating *gusimbuka* for the achievement orientation of the Olympic arena was carried furthest by Jokl who, in a detailed kinesiological analysis of the Rwandan jumping technique, argued that they were already modern athletes, having "used the modern technique of high jumping long before western athletes 'discovered' it."[140] Negley Farson was equally impressed by the modernity of their technique which, he claimed, "was just coming into recognition when I was at university." He added, "[A]nd this was 'Darkest Africa!'"[141] Applying observations by Gregory in a quite different context, the European witnesses of the Rwandan high jump found in the corporeality of Africans the possibility of bridging the African past and the global present.[142] While in many situations the differences between African and European were vast, the latter viewed *gusimbuka* as a kind of meeting ground. The athletics statistics and, as I will show, the evidence of the photograph were each seen as providing "the cultural equivalent of a universal currency."[143] It could be argued, therefore, that to some extent "the other was the same [but] all the more unsettling for that."[144]

The ordering which had been carried out by the male European gaze had prepared the bodies of the Tutsi for entry into the spaces of Western sport: "everything is in order; it is a question of simple substitution and supplement rather than true transformation."[145] Richard Phillips sees such a world as liminal in character—"a topsy-turvy *reflection of home*, in which constructions of home and away are temporarily disrupted before being reinscribed or reordered, in either case reconstituted."[146]

The fantasies that projected the Rwandan on to the global sports stage suggest how occidental writing tried to minimize cultural differences through the unifying power of Western cultural institutions such as the Olympic Games and the sports record. The limited compass and the narrowness of vision of the Europeans' conceptual framework was exposed in their misconceptions and in the poverty of their vocabulary and imagery, which led them to see Tutsi high jumpers as nothing other than potential world-record breakers or Olympic athletes.[147] Like Alice in Wonderland, they could be said to have failed in the hermeneutic task of sorting out rituals from records, since the name given to the event, high jumping, misleadingly obscured the distinction between the Rwandan body practice and that bearing the same name in Europe.[148] To an extent, terms such as Olympics, record, and sport, as applied to *gusimbuka*, can be described as "big" metaphors. Unlike the small variety that "pepper individual sentences and … contribute to writing style," they are metaphors of appropriation that shape the way we think about things.[149] They create knowledge that becomes hegemonic. In this case, they shape the way we think what sport is.

It has to be said, however, that to an extent the big metaphors were contested. Occasionally some European explorers seemed to be less certain (or less rash) about the rendering of *gusimbuka*. Czekanowski, Mecklenburg's anthropologist colleague, translated the German *springen* (jump) as *kusimbuka* [sic] but at the same time failed to include coverage of it under his quite detailed descriptive category of *spielen* ("games"). He referred to it only in a short paragraph describing a photograph (Figure 4.2).[150] This is not to ignore the fact that, on rare occasions, alternative signifiers were used in its representation. For example, Meeker described it as a "traditional Watusi *art*."[151] Much more interesting, I think, is the use of the term *Springkünstler* ("spring artist") in the title of a paper on Tutsi athleticism published in 1929.[152] Whereas the term high jump blurred the distinction between "home" and "away," nonsportized representations signified something quite different. The jumper as artist rather than athlete immediately connotes a performance rather than a result, a participant rather than a winner, an entertainer rather than an athlete. *Springkünstler* explicitly acknowledges artistry rather than sport and athleticism. It fits much better into the world of entertainment and display that seems to have formed the context in which *gusimbuka* was most often represented—that is, in its festive rather than its military form. But the term *spring-artistry* was never widely adopted, despite the fact that it was arguably much more suitable.

Nor was it universally believed that *gusimbuka* was associated solely with the Tutsi. Untypically, Robert Borgerhoff noted that it was not only Tutsi who excelled in dancing, archery, javelin throwing and, especially, high jumping, but *equally* Hutu and even Twa. Here, as early as the 1920s, was a colonial voice that refused to recognize the Tutsi as exceptional. Borgerhoff thought it unfair and inaccurate to credit them as better athletes.[153]

Other alternative readings further reflected the malleability and fluidity of the Africanist view. The sport metaphor was not invariably used to describe the repertoire of events that comprised the exhibitions of local body culture. Belotti, for example, used the term *pantomime*[154] while the events were collectively referred to as a *fête* in French language reports.[155] Lewis Catlow recognized implicitly the ambiguous character of the term *sport* and was quite clear that what he was witnessing was a spectacle rather than a contest.[156] And, on occasions it was made explicit that the Tutsi athletes' jumps "cannot be compared against western records."[157] In such cases (as with Kna's use of the word *Springkünstler*), the colonial representations acted less conservatively and refused (or failed) to see *gusimbuka* as (potentially) conforming to Western athletic norms.

But it was the term *high jump* that (while correctly describing what was happening) appropriated *gusimbuka-urukiramende* through its Olympian connotations. In other words, by looking to the world of sport for language to describe what was being observed there is the danger of falling into a trap of simple appearances. Olsson observes that language does not express things but relations, and thus can become an act of creation.[158] *Gusimbuka* became high jumping—a body culture *for* Europe. The application of the term *high jump* brought the Rwandan closer to the European—an example of "*logos* over *mythos*, of writing over oral culture."[159] At the same time, the Western view exemplified a paradox of colonial discourse, with appropriation lying alongside other traditional tropes such as debasement and negation.

Idealization: Noble Athletes

In the introduction to this book, I noted that a common tendency among nineteenth- and early twentieth-century Euro-Americans was to deny African body culture and to see the African as nothing more than a savage. J. A. Mangan summarized his impressive work on *The Games Ethic and Imperialism* by observing that the "overestimation of Western tradition resulted in underestimation of indigenous custom."[160] The rhetoric used to describe *intore* dancing, noted earlier, exemplified this. But I think Mangan overestimates the extent of the Western devaluation of the African. One need only read the extravagant language used to describe the grace of Rwandan high jumpers to see that this was the case. To be sure, it was possible to negate (even) Tutsi athletic performances (as I will show later in this chapter), but it remains very clear that the ambivalence of colonial discourse is reflected in writers' frequent willingness also to describe the physicality of the African in highly idealized terms.[161]

It was possible to represent Tutsi as "primitive people," as the Sabena advertisement had put it (see chapter 2), but the fantastic high-jump performances exhibited self-control rather than frenzy. So while cultural difference could be claimed for the "Tutsi high jumper," cultural retardation and physical inferiority were less easy to adduce and the "natural" categories of Europe and Africa (as shown in Figure 3.1) became blurred. Here the African performed better than the European at something the latter perceived as his own. The Tutsi were also seen as having crossed an unmarked boundary, transgressing the sport-space of the white American and European. In Rwandan body culture, the European may have perceived an unnatural form of African nature. And un-natural nature may have produced a feeling of unease, though not necessarily of dislike.[162]

Mecklenburg described the jumping as "noteworthy," "remarkable," and "wonderful." The athletes had "slender, splendid figures"; the jump of 2.50 meters was "incredible."[163] His colleague, Czekanowski, stated that the high jumping achievements of the young Tutsi "bordered on the unbelievable."[164] Such idealization of Tutsi performance continued in subsequent descriptions. For example, Lewis Catlow described the run-up to the jump as having been made with "*incredibly* long strides."[165] The Comte de Briey observed that Tutsi high jumpers displayed "an impeccable style."[166] Gatti noted, "[W]e saw *slim* figures take a few *easy* steps, *effortlessly* abandon the ground and . . . *soar* high over a thin reed, descending in *graceful* curves, landing *lightly, composedly.*"[167] A jump of more than two meters was said by one observer to have been made "without difficulty," while Barns thought that Tutsi athletes could "easily" break the world record.[168] Mecklenburg implied on at least one occasion that the performances were "natural"—that is, that the athletes had not previously practiced high jumping.[169] These effortless jumps were seen to have been made by natural athletes; the Tutsi were "naturally sport loving" or a "race of natural athletes," which meant that without training they could clear their own heights.[170] This was not the lazy, indolent, "psycho-biologically disadvantaged" native of the environmental determinist's Africa.[171] Presented here, instead, are images of the naturalized and idealized African—physically perfect, naturally gifted, graceful, and able to outperform the best the Occident could offer. It was the fact that the Tutsi could produce "outstanding high jumpers in large numbers" (hundreds of them were said to be able to clear over six feet) that led Jokl to see them as exceptions to the "rule" that the natives of Africa could not excel in athletic exercises requiring the more differentiated skills displayed in the West.[172] According to Said, such vaunting of Tutsi athletes would have been as distorted as its negative counterpart and likewise produced by Western projections onto the African Other.[173]

The philosophy that had explained the slothfulness of the native African—that of environmental determinism—was also used, in large part, to explain how nature had endowed Tutsi with their natural athletic prowess. Kna noted that young cattle herders learned early in life to quickly but effortlessly climb steep slopes. It was the nature of the terrain and topography that was the principal factor contributing to their musculature and their resulting high-jumping abilities. Mecklenburg concurred by observing that the leg muscles and sinews of the mountain dwellers were far better developed than those of people of the plains.[174] Thirty years later the British track coach, ex-soldier in the King's African Rifles, English javelin-throwing champion, and *News of the World* athletics reporter, F. A. M. Webster, recognized "something in the construction of the heel" that gave black athletes "additional springing power which is seldom possessed by a white person."[175] Webster included Tutsi as Negroes—a rare example of them being essentialized along with African Americans and other black Africans. More frequently, in both sporting and nonsporting discourse, they were distanced from the typical Negro because of their alleged Hamitic origins (see chapter 1). Lothar Gottlieb Tirala idealized Tutsi and negated all other black people in the same sentence in his 1936 book *Sport und Rasse*, arguing that although the Tutsi were the best high jumpers in the world, they were not strictly Negroes.[176] Or, put another way, if they were the best high jumpers in the world, they could not possibly be Negroes. Instead, they were probably Ethiopians who had invaded Rwanda from the north.[177] Here, the Tutsi amounted to an honorary Aryan.

In general, however, the descriptions arrayed above seem to see "African natives being collapsed into African animals and mystified ... as some essence of the continent."[178] This follows Karen Blixen's assertion that "the Natives were Africa in flesh and blood."[179] The African—in this case, the Tutsi—could naturally jump 2.50 meters at a time when the European view of the world record was only 1.97 meters. Jokl observed that

> these primitive people carry out a technically complicated athletic movement which modern athletes can only learn to perform gradually during a prolonged and scientifically supervised period of training. The Watussis, on the other hand seem to conceive the control of the movement patterns underlying advanced high jumping rather complexly. They apparently

have found an *autodidactic short cut* which enables them to acquire mastery of the jumping technique without taking recourse to the analytical process of learning which we have to go through in our athletic training.[180]

That indigenous cultural practices could have involved the same degree of training and skill as that required for the European high jump was again unconsidered.

Tutsi athletes were also seen as being what Western athletes could have been, had they not fallen into an implied state of physical degeneracy resulting from the restrictions of modern culture. They were read as being not only different from Western athletes, but, having failed to be overtaken by the machine age, they were also regarded as better athletes who inhabited imaginary geographies of desire and existed harmoniously with nature—effectively, as part of nature. In such a situation, people and place represented something that has been lost by civilization through its separation of culture and nature.[181] This could be seen as a display of sympathy with the African Other or the negrophilic romanticization of "healthy primitivity in the application of what was deemed to be a simple pastoral culture ... [and] the natural masculine outdoor life of sport."[182] In Rwanda, the healthy primitivism of the Tutsi could be viewed as embodying imperial dreams and perhaps even impulses for Western regeneration.[183] F. A. M. Webster also reflected such atavistic tendencies. He referred to "a tribe in the far interior who had been said to be capable of clearing over 7 ft.," adding that the

> efficiency of these native high jumpers probably owes much to the fact that nature and natural environment, without the cramping and distorting engines of civilization in the shape of ill-made and badly fitting footwear, have allowed the feet to full play for development and growth, so that flexibility and spring have been retained unimpaired.[184]

It was more than simply sympathy to black African culture when he added that "what black men are doing today I suppose our own white ancestors were able to achieve when they too enjoyed the freedom of savagery."[185] Like some of the other bourgeois males who traveled to Africa, Webster seems to have been disenchanted with a rational social order and the urban and overdeveloped culture of the machine. In addition, the early twentieth century had witnessed what was seen as a growing degeneracy in Western society, with normative masculinity perceived as being in a state of crisis.[186] Webster's final words appear to be seeking a remaking of the natural body, innocent and premodern, following its cultural depletion. In the Tutsi high jumper he saw a "pure human body, a body innocent of techno-scientific culture."[187] For others, the apparent subordination of the competitive spirit that was observed in *gusimbuka* provided a hint of a kind of primitive communism. For example, Severn noted that in the Rwandan high jump "rivalry has its well-defined limits" and that jumping stopped when the athletes felt tired, "leaving the field with their arms around each other's necks."[188] These were early twentieth-century views that ultimately saw the need for bodily re-creation as much as, if not more than, recreation.[189] Furthermore, these perspectives, like those of the eighteenth-century encyclopedist Denis Diderot, seemed to see nothing in civilization worth teaching to the African. The Tutsi and their perceived athleticism could easily have been the subjects of the European question: "[W]hat would the savages have to learn from us, since they are already better than we are?"[190]

Tutsi corporeality can also be seen as a reflection of the power of *gusimbuka* to create in the European a sense of wonder. For the Europeans, the measured jumps were, indeed, wondrous enough to stop them in their tracks and to become the subject of their gaze and their written and visual records. But this model of display coexisted with another, that of *gusimbuka*'s ability to "reach out beyond its formal boundaries to a larger world." This resonated with the European's own high-jumping forms and, as I have shown above, echoed a (perceived) age that existed prior to the present state of Western degeneration. Stephen Greenblatt argues that the impact of most exhibitions (and here I have no reservations about including *gusimbuka* as an exhibition) is enhanced if an initial appeal to wonder then leads to a desire for resonance.[191]

The view of Tutsi—or any other group of people, for that matter—as natural athletes ran counter to the views of the 1930s anthropologist Marcel Mauss, who termed activities such as running and jumping "techniques of the body," which he saw as a human being's first "technical object."[192] He pointed out that we have to learn the technique involved even in spitting.[193] What often appear to be the most basic and natural of bodily movements are cultural and social activities, the result of techniques that possess geographical and historical variability. The suggestion, for example, that jumping is as natural as birth or death is a negation of its historicity and of its different configurations and objectives. Where the idea of the natural athlete was a recurrent theme, it is especially salutary to note that such appeals "to the natural tend to dissolve the traces of training and cultural work done on the body and its movements."[194] In addition, it can be argued that by representing the Rwandan athlete as natural and associating him with nature, the African is excluded from civilized society.[195] Writing the natural athlete could also be seen, therefore, as a mode of negation.

The notion of natural athletes cannot be divorced from the widespread racial rhetoric of 1930s track-and-field sports. I have already alluded to Webster's physiological comments, and now want to briefly situate the readings of Tutsi athleticism within the broader discourse of the naturalness of the black athlete per se. The Americans Dean Cromwell and Al Wesson saw Tutsi as typical of the black race, but their explanation for this seemed to be based more on environmental determinism than on qualities of physiology, training, or tradition. Cromwell was the track coach at the University of Southern California and, with Wesson, he believed that the black athlete excelled in the sprints, long jump, and high jump

> because he is closer to the primitive than the white man. It was not so long ago that his ability to sprint and jump was a life-and-death matter to him in the jungle. His muscles are pliable, and his easy going disposition is a valuable aid to the mental and physical relaxation that a runner and jumper must have.[196]

Focusing specifically on the high jump, the two insisted that the black U.S. sports champions of the 1930s—"colored boys" such as Mel Walker, Ed Burke, Dave Albritton, and Cornelius Johnson—owed their success to their "excellent relaxation." While it was patently obvious that white men *could* jump, it was the Negro who would dominate because "the lithe, pantherlike spring of the colored stars combined with their complete freedom from tenseness will always make them outstanding."[197] A similarly essentialist view was communicated from Europe. In the 1940s and 1950s the colonial powers of France and Britain witnessed an African high-jumping presence as part of a broader black impact on European sports. In 1947, the Nigerian Prince Adegboyega Adedoyin won the British high jump championship, and in France in 1950 the Senegalese Papa Gallo Thiam broke the national high-jump record. In 1954 another Nigerian, Emmanual Ifeajuna, won the British Empire Games title, and other Nigerian and Ugandan athletes reached world-class standards.[198] "The true negro," wrote the author of an early geographical essay into sports studies, "has longer arms and legs than the Nordic type and this, in the case of athletics, is all too obviously a great advantage." Johnson's high-jump success at Berlin was cited as evidence.[199]

Webster, writing a few years earlier than Cromwell, was not quite so forthright. As noted earlier in this chapter, Webster believed that all black Africans had natural "spring." But he also argued that they had a particular aptitude for "momentum events"—that is, the sprint and the long jump. Webster felt that what remained of the Negro's "former state of savagery" included "the ability to gather himself quickly for a brief effort and a certain explosive force," something that he must have had in order "to preserve his life in his uncivilized state."[200] However, it was acknowledged that while explosive events such as the sprint and the long jump required innate momentum and were thus naturally suited to the black athlete, success in the high jump, with its specialized requirements, was beyond him until he could fully master the required stratagems. In the late 1940s, an anonymous British writer explained that even Tutsi needed training. Having witnessed a performance of *gusimbuka-urukiramenede,* he agreed that they had "spring" but needed to be trained in a way that did not infringe the international rules.[201] For such writers, in contrast to others noted earlier, a seamless merging of the primitive native with the modern athlete would be impossible.

Some observers took a quite different line and emphasised the considerable training that was believed to have been undertaken by Tutsi athletes. In the 1920s a sports physiologist Professor Schmidt from Bonn, while accepting that Tutsi were undoubtedly gifted at sport, was also careful (and untypical) in adding that details of their training were needed before a full understanding of their performances could be obtained.[202] Kna rejected any notion of innate physical characteristics (or "auto-didactic short cuts") as the determinants of athletic performance and stressed the rigorous daily training undertaken by the jumpers. Indeed, he emphasized the importance of training in order to counter—or at least complement—the environmentally deterministic notions that, as noted earlier, often accounted for Tutsi jumping capabilities.[203] More recently, Ndejuru has used Western criteria and definitions of training to show that the *intore* were, indeed, undertaking a practice that he felt characterized a sport.[204] On occasion, the emphasis placed on training seems to be as idealized as the notion of the natural athlete (and it must be admitted, the notion of natural ability could easily become one of natural *advantage*—that is, could be presented as a form of negation). The emphasis on the great amount of training needed for such corporeal skills was typified by Attilio Gatti, who claimed that Tutsi athletes trained for eight hours each day.[205] Weidenfeld alluded to "peculiar high jump performances" involving the younger men jumping from a knees-bent position, with both feet stamping on the ground, from which they would jump straight up and land back on the same spot.[206] Diem specified one of the techniques of training in a drawing showing an athlete attempting to kick a suspended object placed above his head; the origins of the drawing were not cited.[207] Schumacher was left to conclude that in the production of an athletic body, the *intore* was in no way inferior to the European.[208] Drawing further analogies with ancient European traditions, it was also noted that the Tutsi jumpers "trained in a Spartanlike regime practically from birth."[209] Natural athletes and highly trained Hellenized high jumpers could both be readily accommodated by colonial rhetoric.

The idealized view of the Tutsi high jumper as the noble savage bears some final readings. First, the emphasis on natural athletes is not simply a "reassertion of nature in a machine culture"; it can also be read as providing compensation on the symbolic level for the political and economic processes that had destroyed the traditional fabric of non-Western societies.[210] By representing individual instances of courage, beauty, and athleticism, Western representations of Africa offered a kind of "substitute gratification for what would otherwise be an overwhelming sense of loss."[211] This is not to deny that the emphasis placed on the athleticism of the African may have reflected a kind of fascist aesthetic that celebrated—or fantasized—the physical over the mental and combined a "celebration of the primitive" with "situations of control."[212] A second point to bear in mind is that racialization is not simply the result of a contemptuous attitude toward the indigene. The image of the noble savage, like that of the savage, was still a product of the taxonomic imagination.[213] It could become a positive stereotype, but it was still a Western stereotype.

Nor can it be discounted that the seminaked displays of power and grace may have provided an arena for the homoerotic imaginings of the European male. After all, Jean Genet argued, male adventure had become a vehicle for homoerotic fantasy and an inspiration for homoerotic writing.[214] But it is impossible to say to what extent the representations shown in this and the following chapter were fields of homoeroticism "wherein the Other becomes a terrain for the forces and energies of suppressed desire."[215] Finally, it should also be pointed out that the vivid and striking descriptions of *gusimbuka* are, as I have noted, generally nonthreatening. These athletes seem to be ostensibly elevated as natural, but paradoxically this renders them harmless. The writings do this by "making them exotic, other, and generally disconnected from our lives."[216] The athletes are idealized, but distance is retained.

Negation: Champions Denied

The rhetorical mode of negation is widely regarded as being the most common form of representing Africa and the African from the eighteenth century onward. It sees the Other as absence, emptiness, or nothingness. Africa is read as an empty space waiting to be appropriated and then filled or developed. It is a negative space, a spatial void. Pieterse notes that "the icon of the nineteenth-century savage is determined by *absences*: the absence or scarcity of clothing, possessions, attributes of civilization."[217] Negation also implies the possession of a negative history, the inability to leave a permanent mark on the landscape. It is often allied to the rhetorical mode of debasement (and denial). It is possible to negate African corporeality by defining it out of existence or rewriting its history. Negation is the negative stereotype at the polar opposite of the positive that is found in rhetorical modes such as idealization and naturalization. African corporealites, like other aspects of their non-Western Otherness, were paradoxically "ridiculed for their attempt to imitate the forms of the West"[218]—witness, for example, the reaction to the performances of "native" peoples during the "anthropology days" of the 1904 Olympics (cited earlier in this chapter). As late as the 1940s, some still argued that it was impossible to make sports stars out of Africans.[219] Viewing Africa through a lens focused entirely on Europe, Jokl observed that "it is a peculiar fact that primitive people, e.g. the numerous aboriginal people of the African continent, do not indulge in athletic exercises such as hurdling, high jumping, long jump, pole vault, shot put and javelin throwing." Having appropriated *gusimbuka* (which he translated as "high jumping"), Jokl was forced to make it his single exception to an African absence from athletics.[220]

In the context of this book, negation is somewhat muted in comparison with the other rhetorical modes, but can, nevertheless, be seen lurking in the discourse of *gusimbuka-urukiramende*. That the African was a natural sportsman (the gendered noun is deliberate), as noted earlier, often ran parallel to the view that there was no sport at all in precolonial Africa. This was one of the contradictions of colonial discourse, but it can be explained by Spurr's observation that "the concept of *nature* must be available as a term that shifts in meaning, for example, by idealizing or degrading the savage, according as the need arises at different moments in the colonial situation."[221] The contradiction also arose because the fluidity of the word *sport* encouraged both alterity and mimesis. On the one hand, it could be applied to events of the modern global sports system which, when seemingly absent from the African context (via the rhetorical mode of negation), could be used to maximize the cultural distance between the African and the European. On the other hand, when physical form was divorced from social function, the visible similarities of indigenous body cultures with those of Europe could be used to exemplify the noble savage (or natural athlete) and his appropriation for the sportized European realm. Yet the natural could also be read negatively. Combined with the imagery of the giant (the titles of two papers by Attilio Gatti were "The Jumping Giants of Rwanda" and "The Kingdom of the Giants"[222]) a freakish quality could be attributed to the Tutsi. Such freakishness moderated the idealized view that was also painted of him and rendered less significant his apparently outstanding athletic performances. As noted earlier, his supposed natural ability could also be read as giving him an unfair advantage over the European. The notion of the natural athlete also ran parallel with a discourse that essentialized the Tutsi as lazy. This situated the Tutsi within the equally essentialized category of the African, who had been negated in this way from the mid–nineteenth century. Mecklenburg noted that the Tutsi had "indolence in their gait"; Geoffrey Holmes thought that they were "above anything that savours of manual labour ... living in a state one might almost say of luxurious vice and refined sin"; and Sharpe recognized degeneration among the once warlike Tutsi who, he reckoned, had by 1920 become "invariably lazy."[223]

The most negative form of recording *gusimbuka* has been to deny it. The rejection of Rwandan athletic performance is illustrated by Peter Rummelt's rejection of the *intore*'s leap of 2.50 meters, as asserted by Mecklenburg in 1907.[224] Nowhere in Mecklenburg's published accounts did he claim to have actually measured the jump, but Rummelt is not satisfied with this tacit admission of an estimate.[225] Instead, he refers to a very detailed inventory of the equipment taken by Mecklenburg (which included seven cigars) and observes that there is no mention in it of a measuring tape. It is difficult to believe that a "scientific" expedition would not have included some kind of measuring equipment, but this is not the point. Rummelt denies Rwandan corporeality. He also denies athletic competence on the grounds that no Tutsi was ever chosen to represent Belgium in international sporting competition, despite the fact that he earlier accepts that *gusimbuka* was not a sport in the modern sense of the term. He reads physicality, athleticism, and corporeality through a lens constructed solely by modern sport. Having adopted this lens, he then proceeds to deny *gusimbuka-urukiramende* by citing heights quoted by Attilio Gatti and Jokl that are well below those mentioned elsewhere by the same writers.[226] In addition, he argues that because pre-Mecklenburg and contemporary visitors to Rwanda appear to know nothing of Rwandan high jumping, it did not exist. Here he also draws on the writing of the French journalist Achôt Melik-Chaknazarov, who claimed that his respondents from a number of central African nations (including Burundi where, as noted earlier, there is no evidence of any indigenous form of high jumping ever having been practiced) and other, widely scattered African countries, could not confirm or verify Tutsi— or Rwandan—high-jump achievements.[227]

Negation appears writ large in a doctoral dissertation presented to the University of Rostock in 1940 by the German anthropologist, Karl Reutler. In it he claimed that the Duke of Mecklenburg denied that *gusimbuka* was an indigenous body culture, despite Mecklenburg's claims in his letter to Kna in 1928 (and implicitly in his initial report) that it originated in Rwanda (see chapter 2). Reutler described an interview with the Duke as follows:

On August 9, 1939 at the Institute of Physical Education at the University of Rostock I held an interview with the leader of the expedition, the

Duke of Mecklenburg. He said, "We came with our expedition to see the Tutsi. At the sight of their stature a thought came to me. I suggested to my adjutant that these men should know how to perform the high jump. Under the adjutant's supervision, high jump stands were made out of thin tree trunks in which notches were cut and a rope laid across the top. My suspicions were confirmed when the lads cleared astounding heights— some up to 2.50 meters. The height of a termite mound, serving as a springboard, was small (5–7 centimeters) and of no significance." No particular jumping technique was observed. The Duke clearly stated that the Tutsi have only done this high jumping once—to be precise, on the day of the Duke's visit—and as a result of his proposal. The Duke emphasized that the Tutsi had never before, and probably never since, done the high jump ("Die Watussi haben niemals vorher und wohl auch niemals mehr später den Hochsprung gemacht"). Regarding the idea that a boy's high jumping was a ritual form of entry to manhood, as averred by Professor Weidenfeld from Leipzig, the Duke could not comment. From what Mecklenburg researched and saw, he did not take the same line. In summary, the Watussi high jump was a *unique European experiment* ("ein einmaliger Versuch von Europäern"). The assertion of Professor Weule, that the high jump is the main sport of the Tutsi, is a mistake and basically false. The high jump had nothing to do with their economic and racial characteristics, it has not developed, it did not remain with them, nor has it been adapted to their way of life nor been adopted.... To talk about sport for primitives is nonsense.[228]

Mecklenburg had claimed *gusimbuka* as a Tutsi tradition in 1928 (see chapter 2) and, given his interest in both Africa and body culture, it seems difficult to believe that he would have been unaware of the many reported and photographed performances of it during the 1920s and 1930s. How, in 1939 at the age of sixty-six, he could have denied it is open to speculation. Ndejuru implies that Reutler simply misquoted Mecklenburg and rewrote history. He attributes these views to the zeitgeist of late 1930s Germany, as typified by Reutler's opposition to the word *sport* being applied to "primitives."[229] Such a view refused to accept the athletic ability claimed for the black African and is the only instance, to my knowledge, where it is contended that *gusimbuka* was introduced by Europeans.

Such an interpretation appears to be fully consistent with the prevailing Nazi body cultural ideology. By the 1930s books were already being rewritten by their authors "to conform to the dogma of the [Nazi] regime."[230] In addition, the academic conventions of a racist state in which the selection of scholars had become Aryanized (Jews having become ineligible for university posts from 1933) seriously influenced aspects of representation. It has long been customary in Germany for students submitting a doctoral thesis to include personal details in a curriculum vitae at the end of their dissertations. Among the details required by 1940 was a statement that the student was of Aryan descent, part of a move to "systematically check and catalogue the racial provenance of persons involved in German cultural life."[231] Given that it was a requirement that dissertations should be widely circulated, any public declaration of Aryan ancestry would necessarily have had to be supported by the kinds of observations made by Reutler, who was, in any case, a member of the Nazi party.[232] However, in cases where it was undeniable that African Americans had defeated Aryan athletes, as in Berlin in 1936, they were simply read as being nearer to animals than to athletes. They were said to have "a natural and almost animal-like way of running and jumping."[233] Here naturalization amounted to negation, the athletes' very effortlessness signifying a lower value.[234] Adolf Hitler himself conceded some kinds of athletic superiority to black athletes, but viewed Negroes as representing unfair competition and, following their victories at Berlin in 1936, argued that they should be excluded from future games.[235] This was part of a total theory within which a wide range of attributes formed the basis for the categorization of people in macro-groups (e.g., Negroes).[236]

The juxtaposing of the modes of negation and appropriation is exemplified in a more recent example of the denigration of Rwandan jumping achievements. Rummelt obtained "scientific evidence" which, he claimed, showed that if factors such as the uneven surface of the ground and the takeoff mound were taken into account, the laws of mathematics and physics would predict that Tutsi performances would have been modest by Western standards, a tactic used by earlier quantifiers. By employing expert advice from scientists in Berlin and Bochum and using various simple mathematical calculations, Rummelt was able to conclude that the 2.50-meter jump claimed by Mecklenburg could be converted from one culture to another and become the equivalent of a modern high jump performance of between 1.87 and 1.89 meters. My interest here is not the accuracy of his claims, but with the fact that he had first to appropriate *gusimbuka* in order to compare it with the Western model before being able to negate it as a high jumping legend.[237]

Absence, denial, and legends—these rhetorics exemplify the mode of negation, a mode that privileged European athletic prowess over that of the African. Rwandan high jumpers were projected as fantastical, freakish, or, having been scrutinized by Western objectivity, simply not as good as first impressions may have suggested or never having existed at all. They could also be read as animals. In an odd way, negation and naturalization combined together to prepare the way for the excesses of the European sports model. On the one hand, sport did not exist and an empty Africa awaited colonization by Western athleticism; but on the other, the natural athletes were available to be processed for the anticipated world of achievement sports.

Finally, it has to be noted that academic books and articles which allege to cover what are often called the "traditional sports" of Africa have frequently excluded *gusimbuka* from their pages. It is not cited in Kendall Blanchard's standard text on the anthropology of sports, even though other indigenous sport-like activities are. Nor is it mentioned in works on games and sports in precolonial African societies, notably that by anthropologist John Blacking (though he does refer to the high jumping of the neighboring Banyankole of Uganda).[238] These writers seem to fail to connect with the possibility that *gusimbuka* might have existed. Of course, their omissions may not be conscious; one can only cite what one has already sighted. But the implied certainty that *gusimbuka* did not exist reveals that these authors and others occupy a particular social space, an authorial space where they seem to think that they are the only people doing academic (or journalistic) work on African body culture.[239] Applying Barnes's words, they did not make explicit that their task—to know all about African body culture—while necessary, is impossible.[240]

Conclusion

As an inspired metaphor for postcolonial analysis, Henning Eichberg has suggested that when pointing in one direction, three fingers will always point back to oneself. In this chapter I have tried to avoid following the index finger ("look at those others"), but instead have followed the three other fingers ("look at what we have been writing").[241] And what might each of these three fingers reflect? By a convenient coincidence, the fingers pointing back can serve as metaphors for the three body cultural configurations of high jumping—the sportized, the welfare, and the folk models. While tending to point *gusimbuka* back to the sportized model, the European did not do so in an unambiguous way, but trialectically. My application of Eichberg's notion of body culture does, I believe, overcome the danger of the word *sport* connoting a different kind of body culture from what actually existed. But none of these strategies, nor a wide variety of other experiments in writing culture, are above criticism. They simply reflect the initial problem of how to represent research.[242]

This chapter has considered the various modes of colonial rhetoric that were applied to an African body culture and communicated to a European public. Such imagined sports, like the empires in which they were found, were verbal acts.[243] Yet the rhetorical modes selected to structure this chapter show that the European projection of African corporeality in the early twentieth century was far from one of negation, a set of verbal acts frequently associated with much colonial writing. The continent was not always seen as empty or an embodiment of nothingness. Here were found natural athletes and superhumans whose physicality exposed the white man as feeble by comparison. However, colonial rhetorics conflicted with one another. The juxtaposition of the quantified record of *gusimbuka* with the naturalized Tutsi athletes demonstrated vividly that in travel writing "science and sentiment code[d] the imperial frontier in the two externally clashing and complementary languages of bourgeois subjectivity."[244] At the same time, it was possible to see in the modes of appropriation and idealization a lurking sense of negation.

This chapter also shows how colonial discourse about Africa was not only a "European discourse about non-European worlds,"[245] but also a sportized discourse about nonsportized worlds. Those who placed the Tutsi as future Olympians failed to see the significance of almost everything except sports. Such a view ignored history, anthropology, linguistics, and politics. And, I should again stress, it was almost always the Tutsi who were rhetorically privileged as athletes. How could the writers of the aforementioned texts have been so sure that there were no Hutu—no Banyarwanda—among them?

Drawing on Mariana Torgovnick's comments on "primitive" art, the fact that context controls the message sport or nonsport indicates is one of the many continuing problems in the representation of precolonial body cultures.[246] In other words, *sport* is a highly ambiguous term and carries, as I have stressed in this chapter, quite specific cultural connotations, the result of its specific logic and specific practice.[247] As Torgovnick additionally points out, in asking Eurocentric questions about "primitive" cultures, we miss important opportunities—"the opportunity to preserve alternative value systems, and the opportunity to re-evaluate basic Western conceptions from the viewpoint of systems of thought outside ... those of the West."[248]

In deconstructing conventional accounts of *gusimbuka* from the total colonial archive, I have not shunned "scientific" texts and journals, but have also made extensive use of relatively popular books and magazines. Indeed, in representing the image of the Rwandan athlete—and, it might be added, the corporeality of colonized people per se—such nonliterary sources as travel writing and sports magazines should not be underestimated. After all, they contribute to the production and circulation of commonsense reasoning that impacts upon public opinion.[249]

So I must fully agree with Hoberman, who observes that our knowledge of racial biology and the evolving scenarios for a prospective black athleticism may originate "less in the knowledge of human biology than in an imaginary realm that has been shaped by the *National Geographic*" and other such noncanonical sources of popular imperial myth.[250] After all, colonial inscription and the resulting popular imagination about black athletic potential were surely more likely to be achieved and fueled by travel writing for the masses than by the scholarly versions of Africa's "imaginative sports geography" targeted at academic elites. The colonial labeling of African athleticism, therefore, seems to be as much the result of the literary and textual shortcomings of Africanist authors of popular travel (and other) writing as of the scientific misreading of human biology and genetics.

In the case of the Rwandan spring-artists, the realities never corresponded to the imaginary pictures that the Europeans had of them. Professor Jokl's certainty, from a 1950s perspective, that the Tutsi were "bound to play an increasingly important role in the Olympic Games in the future" was never reflected in actuality, though by the 1960s he had accepted that nobody could predict how the "new political situation" would affect Tutsi "development."[251] In fact, the high jumpers of Rwanda never competed in the Olympic Games, nor did they break the official world record of the Western sports system. Instead, their records have remained as inscriptions in colonialist writing and photography—testaments to a European presence that was able to capture *gusimbuka-urukiramende* only as a way of seeing.

CHAPTER 4

Visual Images and
Foreign Bodies

A depiction is never just an illustration.

—Gordon Fyfe and John Law, "On the Invisibility of the Visual"

The late nineteenth century saw photography emerging as a popular means of recording the worlds of both sport and travel. The use of negative film from 1884, and of the user-friendly Kodak camera from 1888, blurred the distinction between the professional and amateur photographer. By the end of the century, photography was part of mass leisure. Travelers to Africa could now take a camera as well as a notebook. With the help of a reduction in exposure time, they could record spectacle as well as scenery. The result was a genre of popular travel photography that included "photographing the natives."[1] At a more technical level, Étienne-Jules Marey and Eadweard Muybridge had become, in the 1880s, the first photographers to establish the camera as a scientific means of recording and analyzing human movement, including what would today be called "sports techniques."[2] They were concerned with improving human athletic performance and worked closely with athletes in a variety of sports. By the turn of the nineteenth century, the camera had become, in a variety of ways, much more suited to the overlapping spheres of scientific sport and popular travel.

Although Said all but ignored the visual arts in his exploration of imaginative geographies, there seems little doubt that photographs played a major part in the construction of those geographies, in which distant facts were often transformed into Western fictions. As Linda

Nochlin has stressed, the photograph "is hardly immune to the bland-ishments of Orientalism."[3] The late nineteenth and early twentieth centuries saw the increasingly popular recording of Africa and the African by means of the camera and cinematography,[4] and the final decade of the nineteenth century witnessed the production of the first photographic records of Rwanda. Between the late 1890s and the early 1950s, travel photography, which recorded this small kingdom, placed considerable emphasis on the corporeality of the politically dominant Tutsi. Unlike written texts, (photo)graphic modes of representation try to establish an *iconic* relationship to that which it attempts to represent.[5] This may make such representations more powerful and realistic, "offer-ing a sensual immediacy that cannot be rivalled by print media."[6] It is the sight of the body, more than of mere words, that arouses the voyeur and the athletic coach. Even so, photographs can be as misleading as the written word. Invariably, captions are needed to explicate a meaning of the image (see below).

Photographs of *gusimbuka* reveal it as something that could be readily domesticated and turned into Western forms of athletic sport via such rhetorical modes as appropriation and surveillance. Alongside these can be seen the tropes of idealization and naturalization. Indeed, these photographs contain many of the characteristics of the modern sports photograph, the main object being the human body, the triumphant body, but one that is gendered and racialized.[7] Only rarely did the pho-tographic record emphasize negation; "savage" and "primitive" are hardly words that are encouraged by the visual records of *gusimbuka*.[8]

Photography resonates strongly with geography. It has been observed that "cameras are boxes for transporting appearances."[9] The photograph, like the metaphor, is a means of communication that car-ries an image from one place to another—and, I might add, from one time period to another. Roland Barthes used geographical and spatial metaphors to describe the photographic message—"a *source* of emission, a *channel* of transmission and a *point* of reception."[10] However, Deborah Poole's notion of an "image world," through which representations flow from nation to nation and from culture to culture, helps us think more critically about images and invites a political geography of representa-tion.[11] Photography has the power to enable an event to be visualized without it having been witnessed directly by a geographically distant audience. It is usually able to convince those who were not at the scene of the photograph of its immutability. Hence, photography can be seen as geographically important because of the relation between visual-ization and space.[12]

In the academic disciplines of anthropology and geography, pho-tography has long been central to the ways in which people and places are represented to those faced with learning about the world and its peo-ples. The early twentieth-century British political geographer, Halford Mackinder, regarded geographical education as a form of "visual disci-pline" and a means of capturing the sites and sights of empire for a mass audience.[13] Indeed, such was the camera's scientific symbolism in inves-tigating colonial lands that Michael Taussig suggests that "photography seems to be emblematic, to verify the existence of the scientific attitude as much as the existence of that which was photographed" (as shown in Figure 2.4).[14] The growing academic awareness of photography has meant that in recent years a more specialized interest in the photographic record has been demonstrated in geographical and anthropological scholarship.[15] Indeed, Felix Driver sees critical reflection on the photo-graphic representation of people and places as a theme that presents a current challenge to cultural and historical geographers.[16] In this chap-ter, I attempt to provide a visual analysis of the substantial (though hith-erto largely unknown) photographic archive of *gusimbuka-urukiramende* and, in doing so, reflect the view that photographs help tackle the visual strategies that underlie geography's intellectual traditions.[17]

Photography fitted perfectly into the ethos of the late nineteenth- and early twentieth-century travelers who journeyed to the world's remaining terrae incognitae. The instant record provided by the "truth-telling eye of the camera" seemed to be the ideal medium for recording the lifestyles of peoples who would shortly disappear forever.[18] Paintings and prints—as well, of course, as writing—had long served to provide European armchair travelers with images of Africa and the African.

Indeed, some paintings of distant lands were held to be "dauntingly objective and scientific," as in the case of the work of the French orientalist painter Jean-Leon Gérôme.[19] Yet then, as now, paintings were obviously handcrafted images. Photographs, on the other hand, belied the status of paintings as statements about the world "and seemed instead to be truthful, uninflected restatements of that world."[20] The photograph, along with a number of other panoptical Victorian innovations, involved collection, display, and discipline, from which "objectively sound 'factual' knowledge" could be obtained.[21] Photographs could also be used as a summary of a culture and as a source for categorization and classification. In addition, they recorded more information than was possible by pencil and notebook, and as a result could be repeatedly scrutinized for more and more information upon returning from the field. This could be of particular interest for those doing research in physical education and body culture, for whom careful analysis of technique and body management was important. But the apparent authority of the photograph, brought back from Africa and published in the commercial world of travel writing (and elsewhere), was not without contradiction and ambiguity. It was about more than the simple collection of facts. After all, the camera, like the gun and the phallus, involves *aiming* and *shooting*. In the English language, anyway, we *take* a photograph or make a snap "*shot.*"[22] However, as Donna Haraway has noted, the camera was "ultimately so superior to the gun for the possession, production, preservation, consumption, surveillance, appreciation, and control of nature."[23] The camera turns people into objects that are symbolically possessed and often "mounted" like the hunter's trophies; here, the camera is described graphically in the language of power. Today photographs exemplify various ways of seeing the world and its peoples. Often, they are interpreted according to a Western way of seeing, with little or no reference to the significance of their content in their indigenous context. In this way, the images become, in reality, the image of the Occident.[24]

Many of the European and North American travelers—adventurers and scientific explorers—who witnessed *gusimbuka-urukiramende* in

Rwanda between the early and mid-1900s obtained a photographic record of it. The fact that they felt it was worth photographing suggests shared aesthetic values, resulting, it could be argued, from their shared social background.[25] I will examine many of these photographs later in this chapter, but at this stage I would like to note that many of them were probably taken with the intention of subsequent commercial publication, supplementing the kinds of written works referred to in the previous chapter. Few, if any, were primarily intended for the emerging market in books, magazines, and manuals connected with track-and-field athletics or with sports in general. An unknown number of amateur photographers took many snapshots that were never intended for commercial or academic use, and the majority remain unpublished. It is simply not known how many dusty photograph albums including snapshot images of *gusimbuka* might be found in the German or Belgian homes of former colonial residents of, or visitors to, Rwanda.

In the context of travel photography, however, the distinction between amateur and professional seems difficult to sustain. So pervasive were the forms of imagery of the Other that it is arguable that, by the early twentieth century, nonprofessionals were adept at modeling their photographs on those whose work was widely published. Faris has suggested that "order and control," "*their* power confined," and their domestication "was evident even in the photograph of an amateur."[26] Nevertheless, photographs from diverse sources, many of them "unscientific" in character, were absorbed by anthropology and geography and became academic through their use rather than any scientific intent.[27] Any photograph is "open to appropriation by a range of 'texts,' each new discourse situation generating its own set of messages."[28] The famous Mecklenburg photograph (shown in Figure 4.1) reveals such intertextuality. Used first in the discourse of travel writing, it later appeared regularly in the discourse of European sports science, including a book on sport and race from the Nazi period, a British book on athletic training from the 1930s, and a coaching manual from the former German Democratic Republic.[29]

Realist Traditions

It is implied in the writings of many travelers that the aim of their visits, armed with a camera, was to record the "real" Africa. An event could be seen in Europe and America as the explorer had seen it in Rwanda, the photographic image adding greatly to the satisfaction of armchair travelers from Los Angeles to London. After all, given the shortcomings of linguistic representation, what better way to achieve mimesis than by capturing it visually? In claiming impressive performances for the Rwandan high jumpers, Kna felt that the Duke of Mecklenburg could be accused of being mistaken, but that it was the camera that provided the "undeniable photographic proof" (Figure 4.1), a sentiment echoed thirty years later by Martin Birnbaum.[30] If T. Alexander Barns was in any way representative, the objective of the travel writer and photographer who explored the Africa of the 1920s was "to place before his public the beauties of this African Wonderland which still lie hidden from so many."[31] The Italian millionaire-explorer, Attilio Gatti, sought "the routing of disbelief, for the conquest of new bits of information, for triumph over age-long mysteries."[32] William Roome's objective was to demystify the Dark Continent. "All progress from savagedom to civilization," he wrote, "is measured in the mastery of these mysteries."[33] Photography was the medium that could master, record, and reveal "some of the secrets that wild and savage Nature hides so securely from all save those who seek her treasures in remote corners of the world."[34] In seeking to reproduce an accurate image of the more mysterious and "remote" parts of the world, the anthropological and geographical photographer would, through the traditions of realism, seek "to preserve the purity of the cultural other that he represents."[35] Mecklenburg described his expedition as a "*systematic* investigation"; Gatti undertook what he perceived as a "*scientific* expedition."[36] In their representations, there would be no room for connotations.[37] Today, however, the photograph is regarded, at best, as a "naive representation of the object that it depicts—the object is transformed from its original lumpy and awkward state into a two-dimensional docile form."[38] Photographs are also recognized as having the ability to connote as well as to denote. They additionally constitute an intersection of several gazes, among them those of the photographer, the subject, the editor, and the reader.

In Gérôme's "scientific" representations of the oriental Other, the European was never included in any of the scenes. Indeed, "one of the defining features of Orientalist painting is its dependence for its very essence on a presence that is always an absence."[39] The same might have been said of an Africanist photography that longed for the invisibility of its producer—a dream of purity of image "in the quest for an unblemished primitivism."[40] The photograph would provide "total visibility and knowledge of 'the other.'"[41] To include a European traveler as an unfortunate trace in an otherwise "accurate" representation of African places or people could, according to this view, be a means of disturbing the effectiveness of the photograph as an anthropological record or "an image of uncontaminated difference."[42] The presence of a westerner would be "a sort of scratch on the negative, a blemish which betrays the presence of the photographer and his culture." It was re-production, not production, that should be stressed.[43] Yet in the first half of the twentieth century, Europeans *were* central to many photographs of foreign people and places. This apparent contradiction raises a number of questions of representation and is the focus of this part of this chapter.

In passing, I note that another paradox of photography's realism: Most travel photography that covered the corporeality of the Banyarwanda was printed in black and white, a suitable symbolic dualism for African and European shown together, but representing a world drained of color. This was in spite of the fact that color and tinting processes had been available from the nineteenth century. As far as I am aware, no color photograph of *gusimbuka-urukiramende* has ever been published.[44] According to Graham Clark, the veracity of the traditional "documentary" image is increased with the absence of color, but he notes the paradox that "we equate black-and-white photographs with 'realism' and the authentic."[45] If that were the case, the representations shown in the following pages would have been viewed as "authentic."

In what follows, I will illustrate the variety of visual representations of *gusimbuka* made by Western photographers. I will first refer to examples of colonial photographs in which the European presence was far from accidental and, through visual analysis, explore the composition and possible meanings of such photographs. I will secondly review the equally wide variety of photographic arrangements that typified the visual representations of *gusimbuka* in which Europeans were left outside the frame. Finally, I will allude to the significance of other kinds of visualizations and to written texts that accompanied such representations, drawing particular attention to the importance of captions.

Tramp(l)ing through Africa

In Germany the reproduction of the photographs taken by the Duke of Mecklenburg's expedition was said to have "roused great interest" among ethnologists, travelers, and sports historians.[46] Among the five thousand photographs taken on the Mecklenburg expedition, (at least) three were of one display of *gusimbuka* at Nyanza. Two of them were included in the duke's book, *In the Heart of Africa*, published in English in 1910. His chapter on Rwanda and Burundi—including these two photographs—was reprinted in *National Geographic* magazine two years later.[47] A third picture (Figure 4.2) is clearly recognizable as having been taken at the same event and was first published in Jan Czekanowski's report in 1911.[48]

Undoubtedly the most well-known of the Mecklenburg photographs, and by far the most frequently reproduced among those that represent *gusimbuka-urukiramende*, (Figure 4.1) has already been noted. Indeed, it is arguably the most frequently reproduced photograph of any single Rwandan event and of the Duke of Mecklenburg. It shows the duke and his uniformed adjutant, von Weise, standing between the two high-jump uprights with a high jumper passing over their heads to clear, according to Mecklenburg, a height of 2.50 meters. *National Geographic* magazine carried this photograph, full-page, twice in seven years.[49] As noted earlier, it continued to be widely reproduced in subsequent decades in a variety of popular and academic publications. In the 1990s alone these ranged from (yet again) *National Geographic* to the cover of a book on German foreign policy in Rwanda in the early

Figure 4.1

twentieth century, and from Allen Guttmann's *Games and Empires* to a copy of the *Times* (London) newspaper and the International Amateur Athletics Federation magazine.[50] It can be read as the quintessential iconographic representation of African athleticism. It can also be seen as a work that has shaped subsequent representations. It is, in the words of Greenblatt, one of those "images that matter"—that is, "those that achieve reproductive power, maintaining and multiplying themselves by transforming cultural contacts into novel and unprecedented forms."[51] It appears to have set a precedent for subsequent representations of high jumping, in which the European was included with the Rwandan jumper as part of the overall image. According to Hintjens, it was "one of the most common images of the colonial era" in Rwanda.[52]

In addition, this photograph connects with the question of representation. The athlete is performing or "re-presenting" with his body the characteristics of one form of Rwandan body culture and his own athleticism. But these characteristics are also being represented to the

Figure 4.2

Western world in the very different language of sport—a language that, as I noted in the last chapter, appropriates Banyarwanda body culture in Western terms. Mecklenburg's two other photographs of the high jump event did not contain any Europeans. This may be one of the reasons why they have not been reproduced so frequently, despite being somewhat more pure (though, as I shall show, far from accurate) anthropological records.

Some people, when viewing the photograph in Figure 4.1, believe it to be a forgery—an "unproven" photo.[53] Many photographs of the period were indeed reconstructed as montages, modified to provide readers with what the photographer wanted them to see.[54] However, two photographs from the Mecklenburg expedition (Figures 4.1 and 4.2, the latter including Mwami Musinga to the left of the left-hand upright)—seem to me to be more the result of retouching than of montage. This was a common practice, "an absolutely routine procedure in publishing at this time,"[55] especially when film that had to be transported from Africa to Europe was damaged. However, the speculation of forgery (i.e., montage) is not central to my present discussion. What is important is that these photographs follow the trope of colonialism— they have been set up for the camera (a metaphorical montage, if not a literal one).

The representation of the Tutsi high jumper, as captured in this classic image (and in several others that follow), may be read on several levels. This is typical of representations that "[are], by themselves, often too ambiguous to convey a simple, single message. Indeed, the very abundance of information in photographs, invariably well in excess of that intended by the photographer, opens them to a multitude of uses and meanings."[56] It certainly denotes an African clearing a rope above the heads of two Europeans. But what does it connote? Is it a sign of an African or a European triumph—or both? There is no one meaning, and many acceptable meanings could be taken from it.

Certainly, the objects of the camera's gaze have the potential to become objects of supervision, if not of discipline.[57] Simon Ryan notes that a "dissociation of the see/being seen dyad ... represents the visual desire of the explorer to reduce the threatening complexity of interactive observation by distancing the observer from the observed, and to construct observing moments as a 'small theatre' and the indigene as an 'object of information,' never a subject of communication."[58] The "super vision" of the camera can assume the role of supervision. However, this super vision recorded a body, not an identifiable person. Figure 4.1 illustrates the Europeans not only (through the accompanying text) as named people, but through the clarity of their faces, identifiable as such. In contrast, the face of the athletic object (especially in Figure 4.2) is reduced to an almost blank surface, to little more than a silhouette. Although this may have resulted from an inadequacy in the photographic technology, it classically symbolizes the athlete's objectification. His face is unimportant; it is his body that is valorized and which provides the necessary message.[59]

Figure 4.1 also seems to illustrate a landscape of discipline. The clear demarcation of the Africans and the Europeans suggests an emphasis on difference; the photograph stresses the binary opposites of white and black, European and African, dressed and seminaked. The juxtaposition of nakedness and clothed bodies reinforces the view that, while nakedness signifies "uncivilized," clothing, an obvious appendage of civilization signifies "civilized."[60] The attraction (for the viewer and subject) of the European photographed with the Rwandan may have lain in these contrasts or in the simple "co-presence of two discontinuous elements, heterogeneous in that they did not belong to the same world."[61] At the same time, it can be suggested that while the image was, to be sure, one which showed the indigene as different, he was also shown as similar. After all, he was undertaking an activity with which the Europeans felt they could identify. Regardless of the way in which they were read, representations of Europe meeting Africa in this kind of duality, and in this particular version of the "contact zone," became common from the 1910s to the 1940s.

The presence of two kinds of image (i.e., African and European), side by side, may create meanings not produced by either image on its own.[62] Bringing the Tutsi and the European together, the photograph connotes feelings of power (or, possibly, of reciprocity) that would be absent in two individual representations. The African objects of the gaze are captured, but the overdressed Duke of Mecklenburg and his militarily uniformed adjutant are also shown, standing somewhat stiffly and self-importantly, under the seminaked athlete as he clears the rope between the two uprights. As the Germans distance themselves from local life by their attitude and posture (these are most definitely not men about to "go native"[63]), they also demonstrate the European power contained centrally within the image. The positioning of the camera enables the jumper to be outlined against the sky, hence (literally) heightening the dramatic effects of his performance (and a technique replicated in other photographs of Tutsi high jumping, shown later in this chapter). Yet it cannot be said unequivocally that he is given visual primacy over the German visitors. Although the *gusimbuka* performance is regarded as the object of the photograph in most of its captions, the Europeans' centrality, upright posture, and military uniform carry messages of power and control as the condition of European dominance over Africa. However, it is not known whether the pose of the Europeans reflected an awareness of the symbolism of the photograph's spatial organization. Hence, it is unclear whom the photographer wished to privilege.

The scene was perfect for reproduction in *National Geographic*, which was fond of showing not only the juxtaposition of the binary opposites of black and white, and civilized and primitive, but also the control that white domination bestowed on the tropics.[64] The Europeans command the center, even if they are not the objects of the photograph. The man next to the upright (seemingly questioning the entire episode) is present in each of the three photographs of the event. In none of them is his gaze directed at the athlete. He appears to be some kind of assistant (whether to the Germans or the jumper is not clear). He is certainly not in charge; he knows his place. But this assistant could be read as part of a cultural—even a racial—hierarchy. Whatever his role, for me he produces a kind of "sensitive point"[65] that disturbs the symmetry of the rectangular *urukiramende* and the vertical Europeans topped by the more horizontal Tutsi athlete. He appears to me as a rather poignant figure, all the more poignant if the jumper is read as representing a stereotypical, dominant, powerful Tutsi and he—the passive attendant, an imperfect body compared with the perfection of the Tutsi, and located at the margins of the action—a stereotypical Hutu or Twa.

Other important questions are raised by Figure 4.1. Was the high-jump event a Tutsi-initiated performance, or was it set up by the European visitors? Was it, in other words, a vision of authentic primitiveness, or one of hybrid reality?[66] The photograph itself makes the event a European production. Mecklenburg, in a 1928 letter to H. Kna, wrote: "[S]ince we perceived with them the pleasure they [i.e., the Tutsi] take from this sport we [i.e., von Weise and Mecklenburg] organized the high jump event."[67] The photograph illustrates the power of the European to orchestrate or negotiate the reenactment of indigenous performance genres.[68] It thus illustrates less an act of discovery than it does a sign of German beneficence—organizing (more effectively?) for the African what he was already practicing. It also reveals the presence of colonial culture within the reenactment—what Michael Taussig terms "copy *and* contact"—a case of an "image *and* bodily involvement of the receiver of the image, a complexity we too easily elide as nonmysterious."[69]

Though the most famous and most widely reproduced of photographs of *gusimbuka*, this photograph contains so much evidence of the photographer's culture that it is arguably the *least* typical photograph of *gusimbuka* ever taken, and as such can hardly be regarded as a valid photograph of Rwandan body culture. The bags of sand at each end of the rope are reminiscent of the apparatus used for jumping in German school gymnastics. The rough-hewn branches comprising the uprights with their crude calibrations, or notches, in which to rest the rope are also untypical of the conventional apparatus shown in other early photographs of *gusimbuka*, in which long, angled, rigid reeds form both the upright and the crossbar.[70] How much of the photograph's content is, in fact, Rwandan? On the one hand, with its calibrated upright and a European presence, this photograph can be read as a discourse of progress, from which it gains its meaning. On the other hand, the more typical images that include the plain reeds, drawn from nature, gain their meaning because they can be read as showing tradition and stasis.

Mecklenburg and his adjutant were not unfortunate traces in the photograph that spoiled an otherwise anthropological record, but central elements in its construction. However, it also reminds us of the inadequacy of the word *representation* in the sense that usually it simultaneously depends upon and erases "the networks of associations conjoined by the notion of the mimetic."[71] In this case, the photograph not only recorded—or reconstructed—an indigenous custom and live objects of display; it also revealed all too clearly a European power that, at the same time, it reinforced. Yet, as noted earlier, this is widely thought to be the first photograph of *gusimbuka*. If this is the case, no first instance of anything approaching authenticity seems to exist. Mecklenburg's photograph looks second-hand, impure and artificial. There appears to be no "referent lodged in an allegedly pristine real."[72] But could there ever have been? Once the Europeans had encountered *gusimbuka*, whatever their involvement, it could never remain pure. The photograph itself made sure that this body cultural activity was to become part of a postcolonial world of visual images and international publishing. It was also to become part of the worlds of politics, anthropology, and sport, as testified by the variety of its published destinations.

The microgeography, as shown in the photograph, also reveals *gusimbuka* as a site of power orchestration. It is an image of order; African corporeality is confined to a cleared space. There is ample room for the event, and it takes place in an atmosphere of structure and, possibly, rehearsal. The audience (Czekanowski stated that they were mainly Tutsi plus a few "Askari"[73]) are orderly and well-controlled. Seminudity and exotic activity identify the Africans, but the photographic frame and the European-imposed order domesticate them.[74] Power and oppression are not the sole properties of this image, however, and I cannot deny that the photograph also idealizes—even promotes—the Tutsi. It projects corporeal achievement. Not for this athlete (nor for the others shown in this chapter) does the camera's gaze record "blunt frontals" of the head-and-shoulders variety used for the anthropomorphic sur-veillance of native "types."[75]

For Nicholas Thomas, an emphasis on European power would be much too obvious a way of reading this and other such images. To read such a photograph solely like this could be interpreted as being

> complicit in the result of the photographic process and to pass over the fact that this enactment [of *gusimbuka*] must have been the outcome of some sort of deal or negotiation. Even if the capacities of the European photographer and the [Rwandan] actors to shape the terms of the arrange-ment are unequal, the [Rwandans] were possessed of a kind of agency and willed involvement which the photograph effaces, and [in the years to come] they may well have been familiar with the kind of image that [the Europeans] sought to produce. In other words, what is true of the repre-sentation that reached a public in ... Europe is not true of the colonial encounter from which it derived.[76]

This quotation, used by Thomas to describe a posed photograph of Fijian stereotypes, is an important reminder of the possibility of Rwandan complicity in, or subtle resistance to, the European photo-graphic venture. The authenticity of all the photographs in this chapter is fundamentally unsettled by the conditions of their production. Did the Mecklenburg party and later photographers offer gifts or payment to those who were photographed, hence further destroying any notion of authenticity? Stephen Greenblatt stresses that representational modes may give themselves over to whom ever embraces them, to be assimi-lated for their own ends.[77] This is a subject I will touch on later in this chapter, and I deal with it in rather more detail in the final chapter. These thoughts apply to all the photographs included in the pages that follow, though ultimately it was the European who was "taking" the African, in visual and written form, for the European and American mar-kets in images.

The third of the photographs taken by the Mecklenburg party shows a jumper failing to clear the height at which the rope was set, thereby dislodging it from the uprights.[78] That this picture has rarely been reproduced is understandable, as it reveals the Tutsi as being normal and capable of failure. "Travel scripting," as Gregory calls it,[79] often required specific "objects"—in this case, *gusimbuka*—to be seen in specific ways—that is, the athlete making a successful clearance—and in the overwhelming majority of representations of Rwandan jumping, the athlete is shown clearing the bar. To be seen knocking the bar off or falling onto a person standing underneath would be antithetical to the mode of idealization and to the perceived Tutsi ideal. Therefore, the photographic representations of *gusimbuka* cannot in any way be said to "conform to preconceived ideas of the racial inferiority of Africans and then presented as evidence of such ideas."[80] Far from it. Instead, they typify much more the problematical reconstruction of the African as an athlete in the Olympian mold.

More Than a Scratch on the Negative

Following the publication of Mecklenburg's book in Germany, Britain, and the United States, and the relatively widespread publicity afforded the Tutsi high jump image by *National Geographic*, the notion of the Tutsi as superathletes seems to have spread among the traveling classes. By the 1930s, Euro-American visitors to Rwanda were said "infallibly" to stand under the crossbar at a high jump exhibition.[81] This may have been hyperbole, but it was not uncommon for them to return with photographs of the event similar in arrangement to that of the Duke of Mecklenburg. It seems that a sort of "structure of expectation" had been created in which "the pictures circulating around sights were more important than the sites themselves."[82] It could be argued that the prior expectations of Europeans, which were set up by Mecklenburg's famous and powerful image, framed what would be subsequently seen.

Soon after the First World War, Alexander Barns, another fellow of the Royal Geographical Society, accompanied by his wife, ventured into Rwanda. The records of their visit produced what was probably the first published British photograph of *gusimbuka-urukiramende*.[83] Standing between the uprights in Figure 4.3 is the apparently relaxed figure of Mrs. Barns, who assumes the role of Mecklenburg. Mwami Musinga is the tall figure in white on the left of the photograph. In 1925, Prince Eugène de Ligne of Belgium and his wife adopted a similar, if rather more nervous-looking, pose as the blurred figure of a "Watutsi" soared over their heads.[84] Fast shutter speeds and short exposure times were not ubiquitous by the mid-1920s. Queen Astrid of Belgium, while taking part in a royal visit to the Belgian Congo, Rwanda, and Burundi in 1934, was featured in a similar picture (Figure 4.4). However, she appears to have adopted a more formal posture than that of Mrs. Barns. Do these pictures show European power displayed in female form? Alternatively, do they depict two centrally placed ladies, with the native high jumper and the accompanying crowds merely decorating the overall representation?[85] Perhaps they are both.

Figure 4.3

Figure 4.4

Musinga also appears in Figure 4.5 (the tall figure dressed in white to the right of the high jump), a photograph that seems to be full of ambivalence. It was taken around 1920. At its center is an unknown military man who appears much more part of the event than many other Europeans photographed in this position. He not only holds the crossbar in place, but his less serious demeanor matches that of some of the crowd. This jovial European is not shown as someone who is distant, detached, unapproachable, "scientific," and dominant, as are Europeans in some other photographs (especially Mecklenburg). It is almost as if there is dialog between European and African here, perhaps he is even a friend of the Banyarwanda, and, while not "going native," he is shown as someone who seems to be enjoying a local body cultural display. A second photograph of the event (Figure 4.5) also includes the apparently benign soldier and Musinga and was published as a Belgian postcard during the 1930s and 1940s.[86] Visual analysts regard the postcard as a sign of reality that confers a spurious truth and authenticity when modernization starts to corrupt the world of the primitive. The postcard is a

Figure 4.5

commercial product, part of the tourist industry, and as such consists of images that best fit consumers' expectations. *Gusimbuka*, a fragment of Rwandan culture, comes to represent the unchanging world of the noble savage, providing a relic or an icon of the tourist experience.[87] Purchased by nontourists, it is a collectable artifact that confirms the exotic stereotype of "the African"—a kind of enshrinement and consumption through mechanical reproduction.

Figure 4.6

Attilio Gatti's portfolio included, among a number of pictures of Rwandan high jumping, a photograph of three members of his expedition under the high-jump bar as a jumper clears it with apparent ease (Figure 4.6).[88] Here, again, the Europeans appear relaxed and seem at home, with folded arms and smiling faces. The English explorer Patrick Balfour was similarly photographed in a relaxed pose, with hands in pockets (Figure 4.7), as was the smiling American traveler Martin Birnbaum.[89] These more informal representations suggest a reading in which much less emphasis is placed on power relations. Instead, they invite consideration of dialog, festivity, the meeting of two cultures. In some of these photographs, the European could be said to be the one who is "playing the clown." There is even the possibility of reciprocity—"If

Figure 4.7

you will stand under the bar, we will jump over your head."[90] If that was the case, they may have posed as they did to avoid looking (more) foolish (than they already were).

The arrangement of Figures 4.2 through 4.7 (and, to an extent, others shown in this chapter) recalls the sense of order I referred to in relation to Mecklenburg's memorable photograph (Figure 4.1). These images recall V. Y. Mudimbe's reading of a photograph of the Belgian artist Pierre Romain-Desfossés surrounded by his African students. In the composition and space of the photograph, says Mudimbe, there is an "overly well-organized balance" with "subtle arrangement," "geometric positioning" and the "exploitation of nature." There is a "regression of sensibilities" from the "master" through the young artist toward the "symbolic unconquered forest." The only white figure is in the center. Mudimbe reads this as "a gradual progression from nature to culture.... Following Freud one might refer to a will to master a psychic topography."[91] The centrality of the European in photographs of Tutsiness was clearly a common form of spatial arrangement. But the relaxed and jovial demeanor of several of the Europeans in these images does not necessarily conflict with their being (intentionally or not) representations of power.

Figure 4.8 is a photograph taken in 1930. Once again Musinga is shown, this time standing close to the high-jump upright facing the oncoming jumper. The presence of the *mwami* in several of these photographs further suggests a degree of Tutsi participation in their arrangement. However, this photograph also reveals how visual images could be modified to suit the design of an author or publisher. The version shown here (held in the archives of the Koninklijk Museum voor Midden-Afrika, Tervuren, Belgium) suggests that the photographer was careful to include a pith-helmeted European prominently placed in the foreground. The *mwami*'s position in the (relative) background reduces his significance. Though the European's role in the proceedings is unclear, his presence is given a high degree of visual prominence. However, on the left-hand side of the original print (held in the Church Missionary Society Archives in London) two other Europeans dressed in tropical suits and pith helmets are included.[92] Located, as they are, near the frame, the three Europeans could have been conveniently erased had the need arose; all of the Europeans were cropped from a third version of the photograph that was published in a British missionary publication about a Tutsi chief.[93] Presumably, the sponsors of that publication required a purer image of African physicality; it was not to be spoiled by the white man's presence.[94]

In other cases, a Western visibility was not excised, but made to appear less obvious. For example, in a 1940s photograph of the high jump, a Belgian mission station, clearly shown in the background, symbolizes the European realm.[95] In other photos the similar positioning of a European automobile serves the same purpose. In this case, rather than erase evidence of a European presence, such images could be used to symbolize the machine age in opposition to the physicality of the African athlete.[96] In the early 1950s another high-jump photograph (Figure 4.9) was included in *National Geographic*.[97] Probably taken in the late 1940s, its highly professional-looking composition portrays a less

Figure 4.8

blatant—though, nevertheless, very evident—occidental presence. Two European influences are shown: Tourists are in the center, and one of the White Fathers is on the right. But with the whiff of independence in the air, he is symbolically positioned in the background. An amateur photographer, Joseph Ghesquiere, also included a missionary, as illustrated in one of his snapshots from 1950 (Figure 4.10). Here a White Father, though at the edge of the frame, is nevertheless an essential part of the representation.

As the pressures for the decolonization of Africa became greater from the late 1930s onwards, the visibility of the European in travel photographs in Africa seemed to decline.[98] Eventually, in photographic representations of *gusimbuka* the European seems to have been replaced by the *mwami*, as in a highly professional photo taken in 1939 and published

Figure 4.9

in a Belgian government–produced travel guide.[99] Shown as Figure 4.11, it includes the *mwami*, Rudahigwa, rather than a European next to a high-jump performance—and next to *his* athlete. This image hints at a more fascistic aesthetic, at least as defined by Susan Sontag.[100] People are shown grouped around an all-powerful leader who, in this case, is manifested athletically by his athlete.

I now want to return to the European presence in photographs of *gusimbuka* and to tease out some further ways of reading such depictions. There are some obvious reasons why Europeans should have included themselves in the photographic record of the African. One would have been to provide a scale by which to gauge the height of the jumps.

Figure 4.10

Another was to demonstrate to the reader that the traveler involved in writing the text really was there—a means of authenticating the expedition. These images may have provided personal mementos of the African visit. It was also possible that these travelers, though not "scientific" anthropologists, may have followed something akin to "anthropological methodology and orientations ... showing the ethnographer in-there-with-them, as [became] characteristic of ethnographic anthropology."[101] However, a number of other interpretations can be adduced, based on an exploration of more symbolic meanings of the European presence. These may be apparent from my review of the social and political background to Rwanda in chapter 1, and to which I will return in the concluding chapter.

As noted earlier, it is virtually certain that the event photographed by the Duke of Mecklenburg's expedition was actually organized by the duke himself. But the setting up and the taking of the photograph—

Figure 4.11

itself a demonstration of surveillance and appropriation—was not always enough, and I would argue that the physical presence of the European was thought necessary to reveal and make explicit the colonial power. Central to the popular European imagination in the early twentieth century was the notion of occidental superiority. To be included in a photograph of native lands and/or people suggested asymmetric power relations. Whether it was the African's athletic power or the European's political and cultural power that was being shown to the European audience, the African was still being frequently photographed for purposes he did not define.[102] In several of the photographs considered here, the Europeans tended to be placed in a posed, central position. They were framed not only by the edge of the picture, but also by the rectangle of the high jump equipment (seemingly emerging from the portals of Africa) with clear evidence of the African Other (spectators) in the background. There is again a visual hierarchy (Mudimbe's "psychic topography") in which Europeans are at the center and Africans occupy various degrees of peripherality, symbolizing a map of the colonial world system.

In most of these cases, I would suggest that the presence of the European served to deflect the attention of the (European or North American) viewer from the ostensible African object of the photographs—who also happened to be performing what were perceived as stupendous feats of athleticism. In photographs of the high jump, the European could not stand over (literally) or look down upon (figuratively) the African—a popular positioning in the relation between African and European in many of the photos carried in (for example) *National Geographic*.[103] Power over the African by means of the central positioning of the Europeans was the next best thing, and it symbolically portrayed them as reaching out into African space and appropriating it as their own.[104] Indeed, if the African was viewed as part of the natural world the authority of the photographs could be exploited within a conventional iconography of human dominance over nature. This was not so different from the poses adopted by triumphant Europeans when photographed with dead animals (their "trophy") after a successful "sporting tour."[105] At the same time, however, the European presence served to normalize the African subject and remove him from his wider cultural environment—performing, to an extent, the same iconic function as the standardized measuring screen against which subjects were placed during the practice of anthropometric photography.[106]

Many photographs of African "types"—whether as individuals or groups—were obviously posed; the Africans were clearly "put there."[107] In the photographs showing Tutsis and Europeans, the pattern seems to be inverted. The African high jumper usually appears more natural than the self-objectified European, and thus it may be less easy to see in these pictures the African as a European "trophy." The presence of explicitly threatening postures in the more posed photographs might have defeated their objective of showing Tutsi-European compatibility. Paternalism—or maternalism, in the cases of Mrs. Barns and Queen Astrid— seems a better description. Chrétien applies the term *apostles* to the Tutsi relationship to Europeans in other photographic contexts (though through the appropriative characteristics of photography, the Tutsi obviously were, ultimately, trophies).[108] The Western presence cemented the contact between the European and the African,[109] but with the possible exception of Figure 4.5, the photographs under consideration here seem to reflect a "look, but don't touch" relationship with the "objects of vision," which are well removed from the body of the observer.[110] Yet in photographs of Europeans at displays of jumping, it is also possible to see representations of a peaceful yet uneasy relationship, one possessing a tension which had yet to explode.[111]

A paternal presence was certainly found only rarely in photographs of African dancing. As noted in the previous chapter, the African tradition of dancing was "obviously" savage, by European standards, and so different from the European equivalent that there was little need for any Western presence in its representation to demonstrate occidental superiority. In a rare example of a depiction of a European accompanying African dancers, James Augustus Grant (traveling companion of John Hanning Speke) is shown incongruously assuming the formal movements of the (superior, more controlled) Western dance style in contrast to the uninhibited movements of the African.[112] But *gusimbuka-urukiramende* was not savage; its exotic character was tempered not only by its perceived gracefulness, but also by the similarity of its form (though not its function) to that of the Western high jump. Its superficial similarity to the Western form of jumping made for its easy rhetorical and visual appropriation and provided a means of domesticating and reconstructing distant places as images of home. At the same time, however, *gusimbuka* was too close to the Western model for comfort, and Europeans themselves felt threatened. Marc Augé has observed that what the European finds difficult is the mirror in which he sees the spectacle of his own image. *Gusimbuka* appeared as familiar as it was foreign; the superathletes "seemed less like an exotic invention than like what we might see in a magnifying mirror."[113]

Under such circumstances, difference had to be sustained by a visible and recognizably European presence. The apparent superiority of the Tutsi over the athletes who had established Western and Olympic records needed countering by the maintenance of cultural distance. The Europeans could not be recorded as matching the astonishing heights of the "natural" Tutsi jumpers. Nor, given their lack of training and their traditional reluctance to learn how to perform the body cultures of indigenous people, could they even use the Western high-jump technique to make their presence felt by taking part.[114] What is more, they could not mimic the Tutsi by posing in their clothing and replicating their customs in the way that some orientalists did, by taking on the image of the East.[115] But through the photograph they could, by their very presence, posture, and dress style, communicate to a European audience their cultural superiority over the African, and, at the same time, preserve the essential difference (culture/nature) between European and African in the multicultural content of the photographs. Despite the interlocking practice of high jumping, a display of power asymmetry could be retained.[116]

Lutz and Collins suggest that photographs which show a Western traveler in a non-Western setting have complex effects on viewers. They represent quite explicitly the contact zone—the point at which intercultural relations took place between—European and African. Such pictures "may allow identification with the westerner in the photo and, through that, more interactions with, or imaginary participation in, the photo."[117] Hence, the presence of westerners in the photographs allows us to be more aware of ourselves (or, at least, of the West) as actors on the world stage. Of course, whether Europeans physically appeared in such pictures or not, they were still present. As Lutz and Collins have noted, "[I]n pictures that include a Westerner, we may see ourselves being viewed by the other, and we become conscious of our relationships and ourselves. The act of seeing the self being seen is antithetical to the voyeurism which many art critics have identified as intrinsic to most photography."[118] The traveler, photographed with the primitive, was made as much a star of the story as was the Rwandan.

Play and Power

Not all photographs of *gusimbuka-urukiramende* include obvious evidence of a European presence. In these cases (probably the majority) the European was kept behind the camera. A diversity of styles typified such photographs. Some stressed the orderliness of the high-jump occasion, despite the closeness of the spectators to the athlete, as in the scene of a gathering at Nyanza in 1922 (Figure 4.12). In other cases, as in the photograph taken by an English missionary, probably in the 1930s (Figure 4.13), Rwandan boys seem to display a more playful, innocent image of *joie de vivre*, free of a large audience in a more playlike setting. Figures 4.13 and 4.14 are among a relatively small number of images that show a Rwandan standing underneath the bar. The extent of this practice— whether it was central to the pre-European presence in Rwanda, or whether the man between the uprights is mimicking Europeans by adopting this pose—is unknown. Most likely taken in the late 1920s, Figure 4.14 again illustrates high jumping as part of a rural idyll. The "natural" athlete in a quasi-natural setting invokes a homology between figure and background.[119] These naturalistic views may be worthy of comment, because *gusimbuka* was popularly associated with the courtly exhibitions and training of the *intore*. By appearing somewhat distant from an aristocratic spectacle, such images of a natural body in a natural landscape may imply (intentionally or not) a more widespread practice of *gusimbuka* than was, in fact, the case. More importantly, however, in these images man and nature can be seen as one—an aesthetic that creates a sense of innocence. To some extent, it is reminiscent of some of Leni Reifenstahl's Aryan images in her classic film *Olympia* and of her later photographs of the Nuba.[120] It is also possible to read these images as the perfection of a fantasy. The bucolic milieu and the physicality of the athletes can be read as "a lyrical affirmation of the human, especially the male, body."[121] Sontag argues that "Fascist aesthetics is based on the containment of vital forces; movements are confined, held tight, held in."[122] However, images such as those in Figures 4.13 and 4.14 are ambivalent if it is not physical strength that is being lauded in them. It is debatable, therefore, that they exemplify a fascist—or even a fully masculine—aesthetic. They do not reveal extravagant effort or the endurance of pain, considered by Sontag to be preoccupations of a fascist aesthetic.[123]

Indeed, it is possible to suggest that some of these representations exemplify what has been seen as a feminization of African men. The

Figure 4.12

Italian Africanist Pompilio Schiarini described Tutsi as having a "quasi-feminine" character, and Alexander Barns described the Tutsi chief, Rakwataraka, as having facial characteristics that were "refined to a point of womanhood."[124] While Tutsi men were often seen in gentlemanly terms in comparison with other black races, they could, at the same time, be read as representing the typically feminine features of the white race. Their athleticism was represented as graceful, aesthetic, almost feline—features typically represented as feminine—and many of the earlier (and some later) photographs display them in long, flowing robes. This might illustrate the way in which the rhetoric of gender was used to make increasingly refined distinctions between the different races. This reflected a long-standing view, popularized by Gobineau, who argued that different races had different sexual characteristics. Masculine races were Aryan and Germanic; the black races were negated as being feminized.[125] Yet, in this context, athleticism and effeminacy appeared compatible, unlike their discordance in orientalist discourse.[126]

Figure 4.13

In the case of Figure 4.15, a low-angle shot has enabled the photographer to place greater emphasis on power, height, and achievement. Placing the Tutsi athlete against the sky (and, in other examples, the Hutu against the ground) served to perpetuate class stereotypes.[127] Yet the dress of the "page boy" on the left, and of the audience, suggest aristocratic, regal, or feminized bodies. This was a style typically adopted by Attilio Gatti, and could be read as a way of presenting a Tutsi athleticism that reflected power, but not the more threatening brute force of other groups. Such contrasting views again demonstrate the flexibility of colonial representation. It could show the high jump as both an idealized form of innocent, feminized, child-like playfulness and as corporeal power, a contrast which itself is far from absent in fascist aesthetics.[128]

Returning the Gaze

In considering the variety of gazes involved in the creation and consumption of the photographs of *gusimbuka*, I have largely been dealing with those of the photographer and the reader, with only passing

Figure 4.14

reference to the gaze of some of the Europeans within the photographs. These were generally directed at the athletes and dignitaries, but would be, in the words of Lutz and Collins, "distinctly colonial," since they do not seek a relationship but see others as ethnic (or, in the present

Figure 4.15

context, athletic) objects.[129] Among the various gazes, Lutz and Collins suggest that none is more significant than that of the subject.[130] In almost all the photographs considered thus far, the subject is the athlete. However, when Europeans are also involved, the question of who is the primary focus of the photograph seems more problematic. Moreover, in many of the photographs there is a large number of native spectators who are also subjects of the camera's gaze. What, then, was the Rwandan gaze? For my present purpose, there are two main types of gaze of the Other. The first is to look at something or somebody within or beyond the frame of the photograph; the second is to confront the camera. Three photographic representations illustrate these gazes.

The first of these (Figure 4.16) was taken in the mid-1920s by an unknown photographer (possibly by Roome or Smith) and shows the "champion high jumper of Ruanda," Kanyamuhungu.[131] Because the Rwandan high jumpers were usually collapsed and essentialized as anonymous Tutsi athletes—ideal types or iconic symbols of African athleticism—photographs of them as individual human beings in anything other than action shots are rare. In this case, however, Kanyamuhungu poses somewhat stiffly, obviously placed for the camera, the polar opposite of the fluidity of his body as he leaps to great heights. While posed for the photograph, his gaze refuses to acknowledge the eye of the camera and runs off into the distance beyond the frame. Lutz and Collins observe that this behavior can suggest radically different things about the subject's character. In the Rwandan context, it seems to be consistent with a person (a member of the *intore*?) showing pride and determination, focusing on heroic tasks ahead of him.[132] For the admiring westerner, having a subject face away from the camera may have reflected the Western view that this pose was to be reserved for the more sophisticated classes, who in doing so made themselves less available.[133] This would certainly have fitted the early twentieth-century European view of Tutsi court behavior and their general style. The text accompanying the photograph tells the reader that it "will give some idea of his phisique [*sic*]." So despite the athlete being named, in the caption he is still regarded as a body to be seen.

While leaping the bar, the high jumper is concentrating on his performance and cannot return the camera's gaze. For the spectators at an event featuring *gusimbuka*, it is often impossible to see any gaze, as they are part of the distant crowd. According to Lutz and Collins, this kind of picture (for example, the one in Figure 4.8) can be read as being about the activity or the communication of "a sense of nameless others."[134] In other cases, however, it is clear that some spectators are either looking at the athlete, at other spectators, or at the camera. Generally, the African spectators in the photographs included here seem to be concentrating on the jumping rather than looking at their compatriots or the

Figure 4.16

Western visitor(s) with (or without) the camera. This suggests a degree of authenticity in the performance. Looking at the photographer might be expected to occur if something were reenacted only for the camera.

Figure 4.17, taken in 1933, is rather different from any of the others included thus far. Here, the relative mixing of European and African bodies is somewhat unusual. In this anonymously photographed image, the roles of the respective actors are highly ambivalent. The African jumper is not so obviously objectified. The Europeans appear to occupy the center, but they are not rigidly separated or demarcated from the Africans in some kind of territorialized space on the basis of ethnicity. The conventional neatness of the spatial distribution of participants is less evident, and the relative crowding of spectators, interwoven with Europeans, is unusual and, to some extent, perhaps even unsettling. Nor does the photograph appear have been posed, as have some of the others illustrated thus far. Every spectator has his gaze fixed on the athlete.

The second type of gaze, which is returned by the local to the camera, is seldom found in photographs of *gusimbuka*. It is exemplified,

Figure 4.17

however, in Figure 4.18. This is a rare example of a photograph of four high jumpers pictured posing for the camera, taken in 1950 by the Belgian physical anthropologist Joseph Ghesquiere. It is not an intimate portrait, and the young men have not been caught unawares. Unlike Kanyamuhungu, they return the camera's gaze. Photographs that show the gaze being returned are regarded as the least candid and potentially the most influenced by the photographer. However, "the return gaze does not contest the right of the viewer to look and may in fact be read as the subject's assent to be watched."[135] The look into the camera obviously acknowledges the European photographer, though some theorists

Figure 4.18

suggest that this gaze may short-circuit "the voyeurism identified as an important component of most photography: there can be no peeping if the other meets our gaze."[136] This may also be interpreted as a site of resistance.[137] Because looking into the camera could indicate both accessibility and confrontation, it is the facial expression that is important, not the return gaze per se. Posed frontally, therefore, the representation allows scrutiny of the face and eyes (and perhaps the "soul"). The young athletes shown in Figure 4.18 are certainly not smiling, which may be taken as a sign of oppression or at least subservience.[138] Yet they appear somewhat arrogant, defiant, almost haughty, perhaps military, and with a hint of aggression and confrontation. Indeed, there may be a double meaning in their gaze. The athletes' names do not appear on the handwritten comments on the back of the original print. To do so might have been thought unimportant, tedious, or irrelevant.[139] Their anonymity is compounded by the identical (Western?) uniforms they wear and their possible adoption of Western postures. As in some of the other photographs under consideration in this chapter, the nature of the Western clothing has "framed" the body, normalizing it to Western athletic standards.[140] But the athletes could be read as conforming to a Tutsi stereotype—slim, tall, and proud—and such visual evidence could be read as confirming an athletic type.

Picturing Power / Living Diagrams

The technical dimensions of *gusimbuka-urukiramende* were a concern of at least some of those who represented it photographically. Here was a form of body culture that could be envied, eulogized, and measured, but also where technique could be subjected to kinesiological and physiological analysis. Two examples are found in other photographs taken by Ghesquiere. Having already alluded to some of his pictures, it is appropriate to note that he took a large number of photographs of Rwandan high jumping which he has retained in his private collection and which were never intended for publication. Professionally his data were quantitative rather than photographic, his specialty being physical anthropology and anthropometry. Though being of good quality, Ghesquiere's photographs are, by his own admission, those of a relative amateur—a European track-and-field fan who happened to be in Rwanda in the 1950s advising on the development of physical education in the region.[141] Some of his photographs, however, seem to betray his scientific training. Most of them show athletes clearing the bar during a demonstration of their skills in Kigali in 1950. However, on another visit in 1958 the *mwami* invited an athlete to perform for him, and the photographs of this performance reveal a more clinical concern with technique. Two of them are shown as Figure 4.19. Together, they depict (a) a high jumper with his foot placed at the angle at which (the reader is led to believe) he would take off from the termite stone, and (b) the position of both legs at the point of an actual takeoff. It also provides clear details of the takeoff stone. It is not my concern here to debate the accuracy of the posed images in Figure 4.19. I am more interested in how Ghesquiere is unable to resist technical representations, with the intrusion of the close-up further exemplifying Africanism as a history and discipline of detail in which every minute aspect of Tutsi body culture could be recorded.[142] A concern with technique is also evident in two of Ghesquiere's other photographs, which were taken from different positions to show the layout of the body at different stages of clearing the bar. One is taken from behind and the other from the side. In these examples the photographs precisely, and with geometric clarity, provide technical proof of its object of knowledge. In these images, in contrast to many of the others shown in this chapter, the African is isolated as a scientific specimen to be ordered by the Belgian scientists. The arena had become a laboratory.

Bodily movement was, of course, central to the execution of *gusimbuka*, but in its representation in the photographs (and written texts) I have considered thus far I have hardly mentioned the actual movement of the athletes themselves. Although the athletes were obviously moving when photographed and written about, there is little sense of movement within these representations. The photograph of the moving athlete is a permanent record of a temporary phenomenon—in this case, a unique movement. The freezing of an image for contemplation is something quite different from what is experienced in the "real" world.[143] This change of context results in the respective meanings of the photograph being different. A concern to capture the stages of movement of the Rwandan athletes is implicit in Figure 4.19, but Jokl demonstrated this in a much more ambitious examination of technique. He applied to *gusimbuka* the nineteenth-century experiments of photographers who sought to identify the movement characteristics of the human body. These experiments were most popularly associated with the work of Eadweard Muybridge (1830–1904) and Étienne-Jules Marey (also 1830–1904), each of whom included examples of high jumping in his experiments.[144] Whereas Muybridge's approach presented separately framed images, Marey's technique had enabled him to depict all the

Figure 4.19 a

recorded successive positions of a single athlete within the same frame (see appendix). From such photographs, measurements could be produced that would enable a more efficient training regimen for the bodies involved. Jokl's representation, based seemingly on the ideas of both Muybridge and Marey, classically illustrated the modes of surveillance, idealization, and appropriation noted previously. Marey's—and, I would add, Jokl's—objective was to capture and measure moving bodies that had seemingly eluded representation.[145]

During the late 1930s, Jokl, with the financial support of Sir Ernest Oppenheimer, allegedly visited Rwanda to study traditional

Figure 4.19 b

high-jumping ceremonies.[146] In 1941 he published a short paper on the technique of *gusimbuka-urukiramende* and, as part of his search for "the mechanical elements of technique efficiency," he selected cinematographic films of it for pictorial analysis. He claimed that his analysis of an explicitly Tutsi body culture was "the first scientifically analyzed observation in primitive men of a movement pattern which, because of its degree of differentiation, has hitherto been thought to belong to the category of technically involved muscular actions."[147] He added that

> the jumper attains perfect kinetic utilisation of his take-off effort by rotating his longitudinal body axis from the vertical position, during the take-off, into a horizontal position while crossing the bar [and achieves] an extraordinary exactness of what is called in athletics "timing"; the highest point of the curve of a jumper's centre of gravity is reached precisely at the moment when the jumper crosses the bar.[148]

The language here is idealized, to be sure, but it is also one of power and of bio-technicalities, standing in contrast to that used to idealize the gracefulness of Rwandan jumping, which I noted in the previous chapter.

Jokl's analyses produced a set of diagrams, shown in Figure 4.20. Such figures have been said to stand "at the point where the heterogeneity of ... the field study gives way to the relative homogeneity and tractability of the two-dimensional sheet of paper. And they represent a convenient medium for economical juxtaposition and display of what might never otherwise have been put together at all."[149] Here we witness the modeling of the Tutsi where science replaced the sentiment of some of the photographic representations. The diagrams can be read as a form of spatial analysis, collapsing *gusimbuka-urukiramende* into a set of depersonalized lines (of approach), points (of takeoff), and trajectories (of jumping). Superimposed on the body of the athlete is a trace—a path—that is charted to show a general pattern of efficient and effective movement. The diagrams also serve to generalize the Tutsi as athletes and the awkward presence of any European (indeed, any extraneous

noise) is erased. Once seen, everybody will know that this is not a particular Tutsi high jumper, but rather that the Tutsi per se are good high
jumpers. At the same time, however, it can be read as scientifically legit-
imating the Tutsi as a docile technoathletic object, perhaps part of "an
alienated world of bodies in autonomous motion."[150] Such abstractions
can further be read as a juxtaposition of bodies and machines—"the
translation of the natural into abstract and disembodied laws of force."[151]
Jokl's diagrams (and the kinds of photography on which they were based)
made it possible "to pierce the apparent opacity of the body bringing
to the surface new visibilities: visibilities that help propose a machine
analogue" for the athletic body—a body that would thence be rede-
signed to synchronize with the technical rhythms of sport.[152] According
to Mark Seltzer, these kinds of representations are "the calibration
of body movements, the conversion of bodies into living diagrams, the

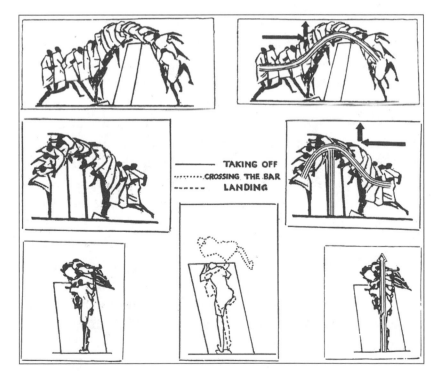

Figure 4.20

practices of corporeal discipline that appear at once as a violation of the natural body and its transcendence."[153] Of course, technique, which the representations sought to identify and perfect, was central to the modern sports movement to which, through the diagrams, *gusimbuka* was symbolically appropriated.

Moving Pictures

There is a long tradition of filmmaking in Rwanda, often associated with broader projects involving films about the Congo (which, in many movies, included Rwanda and Burundi). Cinematographers were sometimes included among the early twentieth-century visitors from Europe to Rwanda. Mecklenburg himself claimed to have obtained pictures with an "excellent cinematograph apparatus" though any resulting films seem to have been consigned to obscurity.[154] The Belgian Colonial Ministry had its own chief cinematographer who was able to record the entire celebrations of a fete—including high jumpers—organized by Mwami Musinga in 1919.[155] Indeed, by the early 1920s it was claimed that an explorer's equipment was not complete without a "cinematograph outfit as well as one for still photography."[156] The missionary William Roome exemplified this with his still photographs (e.g., Figure 2.1) and his mid-1920s film of Church Missionary Society work in Rwanda, which included scenes of Kanyamuhungu clearing 7 feet 6 inches.[157]

Realist ethnographers felt that film had advantages over writing, making the experiences of the films' objects more natural. It is now recognized, however, that documentary realism is "as much a constructed text as are written books" and can therefore be read in much the same way as writing. Furthermore, ethnographic films need to be distinguished from the broader category of documentary.[158] The movies I will discuss below do not posses the characteristics of what anthropologists would regard as ethnographic film. The only voice is that of the European commentator, distanced and detached. Even Western music, such as *Finlandia*, was used as incongruous background sound. In several cases, notably of films produced by or for the White Fathers or White Sisters, or as a record of, say, a royal visit, the documentary depictions of

Rwanda appear to be blatantly propagandistic.[159] They tend to show an idealized world lacking in social and political tension and with evidence of considerable benefits resulting from Catholic missions and Belgian influence. Native life is often depicted in a folkloric style and, in the tradition of binarism, is compared with the benefits of Belgian influence. Invariably, there is a happy ending. Tutsi featured prominently in virtually all films of Rwanda up to the mid-1950s. Indeed, a feature of many of them is that Tutsi, Hutu, and Twa were categorized and presented in quite separate segments. The notion of presenting the population as Banyarwandan would presumably be less exotic than showing what emerged as the clearly defined traits of the three "classes."

It can be argued that physical exploits are central to the cinematic experience. When dealing with Tutsi, it was their relatively wild dancing that tended to dominate, viewed by the camera as a spectacle. *Gusimbuka* was shown less frequently, but that is not to say that it was ignored. In addition to the savageness of the dance, grace and athleticism have been recognized as the major elements of Tutsi cinematography. In films where *gusimbuka* was included, its representations can be seen as what Ramirez and Rolot termed an "aesthetic valorization of performance."[160]

Terres brûlées (Scorched Earth) was made as a popular documentary for mass circulation in 1934 by Charles Dekeukeleire, a well-known avant-garde filmmaker in Belgium. It proved to be very successful and, though mainly about the Congo, was marketed by including references to Tutsi athleticism that was shown in the film. Promotional blurbs for the film included allusions to the Tutsi as accomplished high jumpers. It was claimed that they were "truly world champions," jumping 2 meters 30 centimeters "without a springboard—it's extraordinary!"[161] A poster for the film featured a light-skinned high jumper among an assortment of African images, showing that during the mid-1930s *gusimbuka* retained considerable iconographic status (Figure 4.21). But an icon of what? From the advertisement alone it was not evident that the high jumper was from Rwanda, and he appeared as one of a number of representations of various exotica from the broader realm of Belgian colonization. *Congo, terre d'eaux vives* (Congo, Land of Living Waters) was

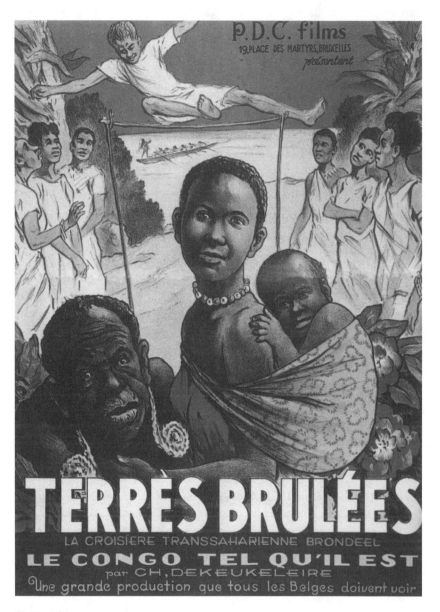

Figure 4.21

made in 1939 by the doyen of Belgian documentary filmmakers, André Cauvin. It includes coverage of a fete at the court of the *mwami*, and although, as was typical, more time was devoted to the *intore* dance, a few minutes were given to *gusimbuka*. Some spectacular leaps were recorded, and the French-language commentary explains that these are the "best high jumpers in the world." *Gusimbuka* was also included in one of Cauvin's later films, *L'equateur aux cent visages* (The Hundred Faces of the Equator), made in 1948. Produced in collaboration with the Colonial Ministry and organizations such as the Belgian airline Sabena, it includes Rwanda as part of a voyage made by two European tourists, a tactic that served to emphasize difference and the possible gains to be obtained from Europeanization. Images of Western sports were included in order to reflect Belgian munificence. But "traditional" Rwanda was also displayed in an arena with a large crowd watching "folk events" such as the *intore* dancers, archery, sacred longhorn cattle, and *gusimbuka-urukiramende*. As in written texts, the commentary explicitly states that the Tutsi are excellent jumpers, and notes that they are clearing 2.40 meters. About ten athletes are shown clearing the bar, which is raised at regular intervals. No athlete appears to dislodge the bar. Some of the jumpers are wearing white sports shoes. Having cleared the bar, they somewhat self-consciously jog back to the start of their run-up, where again all execute successful leaps. Overall, this sequence in the film appears as a choreographed promotion of Tutsiness. It is followed by an equally stereotypical view of the Twa.

Feu de Brousse/Doorbraak in Afrika (Brushfire in Africa) is a film made for the White Fathers in 1947, but includes material made earlier. Part of it is structured around the filming of the baptism of Mwami Rudahigwa in 1943 and is, I think, worthy of more extended comment. Before the depiction of the ceremony, the film focuses on the body cultural gains to Rwanda resulting from missionary education. A caption reads "A Young Church Grows," and the film shows, as part of the church's work, Rwandan children engaged in simple but regimented physical exercise. Young girls clothed in white dresses take part in a carefully choreographed Western dance. These are followed by scenes of

youths involved in Western gymnastics and sports. Swedish-style regi-
mentation, with exercises in straight lines, vaults over wooden boxes,
displays on parallel bars, and other physical exercises typify these activities. Some pole-vaulting (Figure 4.22 shows a vaulter starting his run-up)
and a game of soccer—welfare and sportized forms of body culture—are
also depicted.[162] Time and space limits are imposed on these activities,
and they are carefully subjected to surveillance and regulation by the
White Fathers and European physical education instructors. The ceremony surrounding the *mwami*'s baptism then occupies a few minutes.

Following this is a great celebration that is devoted to folk activities, a reminder of their continuance, (albeit in selective and somewhat
folklorized form) under colonialism and Catholicism. Performing before
a large crowd, the inevitable display of *intore* dancing features in these
post-baptism events. It also includes exhibitions of indigenous musical
instruments, the sacred longhorn cattle, and *gusimbuka*. Filmed from a
variety of angles, four athletes (not identified as Tutsi) are shown jumping in rapid succession, returning to the position from which they started
their run-up, and jumping again, with the bar being progressively raised.
Again, none appear to dislodge the bar. Figures immediately surrounding the event are African; the only Europeans are in the more distant
crowd of spectators. The sequencing of *gusimbuka* in this film clearly

Figure 4.22

reveals it as something different from, say, gymnastics, pole-vaulting, or soccer, and this is surely intentional. It is clearly distanced from sport both culturally and symbolically through the structure of the narrative. This is quite different from its treatment in almost all literary sources, where, as I have shown in this chapter, the term *sport* is widely identified with it.

L'Afrique vous appelle (Africa is Calling You) made for the White Sisters in the early 1950s, also includes fleeting scenes of *gusimbuka*. They are relatively close-up shots of athletes making, according to the commentator, "prodigious jumps" of 2 meters 35 centimeters. He goes on to note that these athletes would not be out of place in the Olympics, a common allusion to what was perceived as a seamless attachment to modern sport, as noted in chapter 3. Of greater interest, however, is his reference to the athletes as de-ethnicized "natives of Rwanda" rather than as Tutsi high jumpers. This could reflect either a 1950s political sensitivity, as ethnic labels became much less popular and were actively discouraged, or a general shift in Belgian discourse that began to de-emphasize Tutsi superiority.

From the mid-1950s the number of movies that showed *gusimbuka* declined, and by 1960 allusions to the Tutsi-Hutu differences appeared muted or absent. The benefits of being a colony of Belgium continued to be stressed, as in the documentary *Ruanda-Urundi 1949*. This was also illustrated in the movie *Tokèndé*. Made in 1958 by Gerard de Bos on the occasion of the World Exposition in Brussels, it stresses the benefits of Belgian colonization. Rather than showing Africans engaged in tradi-tional physical activities, emphasis is placed instead on the playing of Western sports and participation in regimented physical jerks. Likewise, in a documentary movie on universities in the Congo and Ruanda-Urundi made in 1960, students are shown taking part in pool, table ten-nis, handball, track racing, and soccer. These represent the modern world. What are perceived as folk activities are premodern and in the past; they are excluded and unworthy of a place in the modern univer-sity. And in these depictions of Western sports, no distinction is made between Tutsi and Hutu.

Captured by Captions

Photographic images are invariably surrounded by written text. Among the most potent forms of such texts are photographs' captions, which serve to guide the reader or suggest one of several possible meanings of the photograph.[163] In the case of film, the spoken or titled commentary (intertitles) could be said to serve the same purpose. They are, therefore, what Gren calls "semantic significations" because a particular part or arrangement of the photograph is distinguished from another in defining or describing the representation.[164] Consequently, the caption can sometimes assume supremacy over the image and can divert the audience's attention away from what might, at first sight, appear to be the central object of the photograph. In such cases, "the image no longer *illustrates* the words; it is now the words which, structurally, are parasitic on the image."[165]

The main way in which words assumed supremacy over the image was when it informed the reader that the athlete was a Tutsi. This was something that the reader could not possibly have established with any certainty by simply looking at the photograph. And in the great majority of cases there was no doubt in the mind of those who wrote captions that the jumper was a Tutsi. More subtle relations can also be exposed. The captions to the photographs of the Rwandan jumpers that featured Europeans often referred to both the African and the westerner. The caption accompanying the picture in Figure 4.6 indicated the following: "This fellow easily leaps a good foot over the heads of the members of the Gatti expedition."[166] The caption to another photograph stated, "While the author [Martin Birnbaum] stood his ground, one after another of these tall natives demonstrated that they could top the official world's record."[167] By making reference to both African and European, these captions detract from a Rwandan presence and performance by noting the European "standing his ground." In addition, it establishes African and European as two types. From these examples, we know the author is Birnbaum; we are told the expeditioners are with Gatti. Whereas the Europeans are named as individual human beings, the African high jumpers are essentialized. They are generalities—"a Tutsi," "a tribesman," "tall natives," or "a fellow." This was part of a discourse that represented the African as an object "to be looked at rather than [regarded as] a self-constituting subject," a body transformed from an individual person into a specimen, "a mere statistical anonymity."[168] Their names were irrelevant to ostensibly scientific expeditions.[169] It was a rhetorical form of negation that was almost ubiquitous in the visual and written representation of the Rwandan high jump, despite the fact that high jumpers' names were known and recorded orally by the indigenous culture.[170] The only photograph I have encountered whose caption names a Rwandan athlete is that of Kanyamuhungu, shown in Figure 4.16. A less serious misreading of the image could show how the caption could change one thing into another. For example, the *gusimbuka* performance in Figure 2.2 was described on the caption accompanying it as a *Stabhochsprung* (pole vault).

Over time, a photograph could be accompanied by different captions in a variety of publications. Such recaptioning provides insight into changes in the interpretation of other societies and into the caption's general role.[171] In its German source, the most famous of the Mecklenburg photographs (Figure 4.1) was simply captioned "Hochsprung eines Mtussi (2.50 m.). Niansa." When reproduced three years later in *National Geographic*, its caption was amplified as "The champion high jumper of Africa." In Guttmann's *Games and Empires*, however, it is captioned as a "Wattussi tribesman leaping over the head of Herzong [*sic*] Adolf Friedrich von Mecklenburg, leader of an ethnographic expedition to German East Africa."[172] In the first case, as in many others, the caption appropriates the Tutsi and *gusimbuka* by substituting a European term—here, the German *Hochsprung*—and by applying metric measurements; in the second caption, the contemporary occidental idea of a champion is applied as a further form of appropriation; and in the third, the caption engages in Othering the African by naming only the European and mistakenly naming the Tutsi as a "tribe."

Among its numerous reproductions, the Mecklenburg photograph also appeared in one of the many coaching manuals written in the 1920s and 1930s by F. A. M. Webster.[173] While it was not uncommon for

Rwandan athletes to be photographed with Americans (for example, the explorers Martin Birnbaum and the Americanized Italian, Attilio Gatti, and his colleagues), Webster's compilation is different because each of the Americans who are included is an African American sportized jumper. This provided representational space for an essentialist view of the black athlete. The compilation fills a single page and starts, at the top, with two long jumpers—the "Canadian Negro" Sam Richardson, champion of the British Empire, and Jesse Owens. Below these are photographs of Cornelius Johnson, the world high-jump record holder and Olympic champion, and next to it the much-reproduced Mecklenburg photograph of "a Watufessi [sic]" high jumper. Each of the four photographs has a brief caption (e.g., "Jesse Owens, USA, world's long jump record holder 26′ 8¼″, Olympic champion 1936"). The general caption for the four images is simply "Negro jumpers." The juxtaposition of the four photographs, plus their collective caption, seems to establish two significant messages. One is that sportized jumping is a cultural universal. By dissolving cultural context, *gusimbuka* and Western high jumping are fantasized as being essentially equivalent. As illustrated and annotated, the Rwandan is performing (literally and metaphorically) *alongside* the Olympic champion from the United States. Secondly, this compilation of black jumpers essentializes "the Negro." Irrespective of their cultural background (Canada, the United States, Rwanda), it suggests that black athletes per se are in some way privileged as long *and* high jumpers. Here, explicated by the caption, a Tutsi body becomes part of a crudely defined racial representation.

I have stressed that, during the first half of the twentieth century, it was invariably made explicit that it was a Tutsi who was being represented in visual depictions of *gusimbuka*. But there were exceptions. The Belgian postcard I alluded to earlier in this chapter was simply titled "Jumping exhibition" with no reference to Tutsi, sport, or competition; likewise, the caption to the photograph in the book by Pagès termed the peformance "Le saut en hauteur" ("The high jump").[174] And in later years, the ethnic dimension in photographic captions of *gusimbuka* seems to have changed. In some French-language academic works there is a much greater sensitivity to identifying anyone as a Tutsi or a Hutu. Hence, the caption to a photograph taken in 1939 (at the event shown in Figure 4.12), but appearing in a Rwandan-authored book published in 1995, is "Saut en hauteur à Nyanza, en présence du Mwami Rudahigwa" ("High jump at Nyanza, in the presence of Mwami Rudahigwa").[175] In a post-genocide context it was thought to be inappropriate to make any allusion to the ethnicity of the athlete.

Conclusion

The complexities (the variety of representational modes, the ambivalence, and contradiction of written and visual works) revealed in this and the previous chapter are hardly likely to lead to a comfortable or easy set of concluding images. Michael Curry alludes to the easy image as "the essence, the one thing that will turn what was rough and confusing into something tamed."[176] Here, I have tried to avoid searching out a series of easy images. Had I found them I would have ended up with a single occidental gaze (negation *or* idealization, for example). The easy image of what Mecklenburg's expedition witnessed in 1907 would have been presented as a "native event." Professor Jokl, the scientist with his biomechanical diagrams, saw simplicity in complexity. My readings of *gusimbuka* see complexity in simplicity.[177] An easy image would have been to write a conclusion that attempts to bring everything together. Much of the representation of *gusimbuka* was out of place. It consisted of sets of normalizing practices that provided a particular view of the body culture of a very small proportion of Rwanda's precolonial and colonized population.

I recognize the danger of overgeneralizing the condition of postcoloniality and of ignoring the specificities of a particular place. As I noted earlier, Rwanda is a unique place. It is not a reduced mirror image of the rest of Africa. The universalizing views of many of the travel writers, while bringing Rwanda rhetorically into the world of modern sport, confused place with space. They assumed that a particularity was a generalization. In their writing of Rwandan body culture, they confused Rwanda with the world—hence the ease with which they seamlessly merged those who practiced *gusimbuka* with "sportsmen." What I have tried to show is that in writing about the imaginative sports geography of Rwanda, the topography is, to use appropriate metaphors, uncon-formable and riven with fault lines. But this is not to say that no lessons can be learned from traversing it.

The illustrations that I explored in this chapter produce a variety of ways of seeing Africa and the African: as exotic, mysterious, power-ful—and as athletic. Having said that, the photographs also seem to connote the power and control of the European over the African. The presence of the European in the high-jumping photographs served to emphasize difference and power, but this is not to ignore the fact that, at the same time, they could present the African as vastly superior to the European. A further reading is that the European presence made Tutsi more like the European (a traditional interpretation in travel writing) than Hutu. As noted in chapter 1, the Tutsi ruling elite were anything but passive in transforming the relations between Tutsi and Hutu. From a Tutsi perspective, a European presence in the photographs could have been encouraged to display Tutsi superiority over Hutu, but at the same time to have it recognized symbolically by a European presence and through the Europeans's eulogistic interpretations of Tutsi athleticism. It implies that the photographs of the European presence at a Rwandan high-jump event—or, perhaps more accurately, a Rwandan performance at a European-orchestrated event—was a form of mimicry.

In this chapter I have alluded to the theme of black athleticism, a subject that together with "racial science" has attracted renewed inter-est in recent years.[178] Although I have focused on the 'racialization' of the Banyarwanda, I have made limited reference to Western readings of *gusimbuka* in relation to the debate about black corporeality per se. Fre-quently, such work (like this one) takes Gobineau as a seminal figure, but works through the essentialist proposition that the black athlete pos-sesses unique genetic structures that are expressed in qualities such as rhythm and relaxation. However, it should have become clear that, in Rwanda, the presence of the three ethnicized groups plus the Europeans made the binary dualism of black and white inappropriate as the sole organizing framework. Within the space of a tiny political unit, a variety of racial types could be culturally constructed, each possessing different degrees of physical prowess, but with the textually homogenized Tutsi at the top of the hierarchy. In the instance of Rwanda, it was far from being a case of the West representing the black athlete per se as a natural athlete.

I also have tried to suggest ways of seeing a particular kind of visual representation that was common during the first half of the twentieth century. It should not be difficult to detect the modes of idealization and appropriation in these visual strategies; photography was not solely a mode of surveillance. Taken in conjunction with the written representations noted in this chapter, the representation of *gusimbuka* can be read as presenting a Tutsi stereotype. There is an implicit but consistent emphasis on difference between Tutsi and Hutu, the nature of which I outlined in chapter 2, and will return to in the concluding chapter. This stress on difference can be interpreted within the political history of twentieth-century Rwanda as being part of a broader process of Tutsification, racialization, and traditionalization, and, indeed, is a form of political propaganda.

In addition, in both this and the previous chapter I have shown how bodily performances such as *gusimbuka*, while obviously occurring in a particular space, need not be seen as being set in the rational space of the taken-for-granted—that of spectators (sometimes including Europeans) simply watching a spectacular form of corporeal entertainment. The space of *gusimbuka* is not completely knowable and transparent. A space that constitutes the rationality of the European and invariably male observer may also be a space permeated with a variety of fears, fantasies, and festivities.

Through the publicity afforded by popular travel writing and photography, the space of *gusimbuka* became almost canonized in a "geography of attractions"[179] and as such satisfied the various fantasies of the European gaze. But fears that the African could not only entertain but also assume athletic dominance in future Olympic Games were also played out in these spaces. In some ways, it may have been like the "non-white actor [who] performed on western stages, his/her body [carrying] a kind of mystique that both heightened and detracted from its significance."[180] The rhetorical and visual modes of representation were not only preparing—indeed, constructing—a future African athleticism for the potential European consumer, but also constructing a specific form of Tutsi imagery based on physical prowess and corporeal power. The political ramifications of these images, and the way in which they could be read as related to the aspirations of Tutsi and their eventual downfall, are subjects I take up in the concluding chapter.

Finally, let me return to the presence of Europeans in the photographs of Tutsi athleticism. Among the questions that might be raised about photography's mimetic claims is that, even without the European in the photographs discussed here, claims of mimesis are exaggerated. Yet these photographs did serve to establish the European presence in Africa. Of course, the Europeans were there even if absent from the photographs, but the fact that they were sometimes included arguably presents a more accurate, scientific picture of the "new" Africa than if the Europeans had simply stood behind the camera in search of what they perceived to be authentic images. As with other photographs, those I have discussed above may not have been perceived as scientific but they may tell us more in a modern documentary sense than do many photographs intended as scientific records.[181] While we may denounce the colonial presence and the authority relations illustrated in several of the photographs shown here, these themes are not hidden in them; "even the authorities are captive."[182] It is to what the representations say about Tutsi-Hutu—and Tutsi-European—relationships that I finally want to turn.

Epilogue

Complicity is not sudden, though it occurs in an instant.

—Anne Michaels, *Fugitive Pieces*

Rhetorics and Relativism

The main theme of this book has been the variety, ambiguity, and inconsistency of European representations of a Rwandan corporeality, which in fact tell us more about Europeans and their ways of seeing than they do about Rwandans. In particular, I have shown how the language of European achievement sport was used to write an indigenous body culture, though not without equivocation. But are all of the rhetorical modes that were used to project representations of *gusimbuka* to their distant markets of equal significance? In this chapter I try to justify the privileging of one of the several modes used in the previous chapters. In revisiting these representations, I relate them to Hutu-Tutsi-European relations during the period covered by this study. I try to read the written and photographic texts as cultural products of the interactions between colonizers and colonized.[1] In addition, I allude briefly to the extent to which these representations may have been circulated among Rwandan people. Finally, I suggest that the representations of *gusimbuka* could be associated tangentially with the Tutsi genocide. None of this means that the book ends with an easy image or a neat and tidy conclusion. I do not suggest any causal relationships, but simply offer tentative associations.

The kind of study that does little more than recognize the inconsistency of Western voices and gazes has been described as a "postmodern 'certainty' ... that everything is *just* representation and that no judgements can be made about adequacy, accuracy or inaccuracy, truth or falsity."[2] Such an approach fails to prioritize or privilege a particular mode as being of greater significance or importance than others, and seems dangerously close to a relativism that revels in its unwillingness to recognize any underlying ethical or moral position. This can be countered by arguing that "representations of people and places, or races and regions, can be re-examined and repudiated precisely because they are *in*authentic depictions or characterisations of the known subject and its habitus."[3] Underneath academic methods reside politics, power, and morals.[4] One could go slightly further and argue that a moral reading of a corporeal performance overshadows athletic or aesthetic readings of it.[5] Each of the rhetorical modes used to structure chapter 3 are clearly political. But in the context of this book, and given the importance of the positive stereotyping of Tutsi (and, concurrently and interrelatedly, the negative stereotyping of Hutu), the rhetorical mode of idealization can be read as the most significant and the most dangerous. This leads me to a more political reading of *gusimbuka* and its representations.

Through a Political Lens

Should any worthwhile account of the representation of *gusimbuka-urukiramende* include some discussion of Hutu? Was the textual presence of Tutsi corporeality an example of textual violence towards Hutu? And can the textual images of *gusimbuka* from the first half of the twentieth century be said to "bleed" into the physical violence of the terrible events that have taken place in Rwanda in recent decades?[6] I think the answer to each of these questions has to be in the affirmative. Indeed, I believe it would be irresponsible to exclude them from consideration, for an appreciation of the representations of *gusimbuka* would be incomplete without reference to both Hutu and the genocide. I will return to these questions later. For the moment, it is sufficient to note that the limitations of looking solely at representations without looking also at how they are used are revealed by the fact that meanings are transformed as they are encoded and decoded by producers and consumers over time and in different contexts. It has been suggested that, as texts are produced, they are incorporated into larger (symbolic) systems. As another, different audience encounters a representation, its meaning may be transformed and fed into everyday life. Eventually, these representations may be introduced to new and different textual forms (representations) that lead to new ways of seeing, resulting in what has been termed a "circuit of culture."[7]

It is also arguable that there are political ramifications to any production of knowledge. Gren observes that "any representation feeds upon various hidden assumptions that also structure its form and content in various ways. In that respect, a representation is not politically, morally, or ethically neutral. On the contrary, it is an intervention in the world."[8] Mitchell implies that politics is so central to the construction of representations that it is "hardly something that can be adequately undermined by subversive readings and mere meaning-construction (no matter how important these practices may in fact be)." Power, he argues, should not be reduced to the status of a text.[9] Texts, therefore, are not autonomous entities created in a vacuum.

The kinds of texts I have been examining in the preceding chapters were produced by power resulting from several sources. The first was the status of the speaker. People such as the Duke of Mecklenburg or Professor Ernst Jokl had the power through photography, writing, and access to publications to create the Tutsi athlete. The second was the site from which the statement was made—the commanding sites of the German and Belgian empires or of the Royal Geographical Society in England, from which an Africanist photographer and writer could orchestrate and capture the Rwandan performance. And the third was the position of the subject of the discourse—the output and œuvres of travel writers and photographers in relation to the entire discourse of Africanism, both political and cultural.[10] In these ways, the representations of a reified Tutsi athleticism illustrate Western power in the production of African images. However, as suggested in previous chapters, the involvement of a Rwandan (principally Tutsi elite) influence cannot be ignored. It is also worth noting, I think, that there seem to be parallels between visual and political representation that are clearly exemplified in the context of *gusimbuka*. Indeed, it is possible to argue that the technologies of textual and visual representation are political in character.[11] For example, the representations of *gusimbuka*, an activity performed by a small proportion of the Rwandan population, served to typify Tutsi males per se, not simply the *intore* or the aristocracy. Likewise, the broader racialization of Tutsi can be viewed as the solidification (i.e., a re-presentation) of what was a heterogeneous group. In each case—the Tutsi as athletes and the Tutsi as a race—heterogeneity is reduced to homogeneity. Narrowly defined, therefore, the written text and the photograph are politically relevant documents.

The representations discussed above and in the preceding chapters are, I suggest, part of the broader stereotyping of Tutsi—and (by implication) of Hutu. Alain Destexhe notes that in the Rwandan context,

> the caricature of physical stereotypes ... was manipulated to provide proof of the racial superiority of one group over the other. The present generation has internalized this ethnological colonial model, with some groups deliberately choosing to play the tribal card. The regimes that have ruled Rwanda ... since independence have shown that they actually need ethnic divisions in order both to reinforce and justify their positions.[12]

If the new reality of mid–twentieth century Rwanda was made up of three groups—heroes, tillers of the earth, and clowns,[13]—it should be obvious into which category the representations of supreme athleticism placed the idealized and naturalized Tutsi. The extent to which a traditional body culture was incorporated into a broader Tutsi ideology (crystallized in the publications of Kagame and others) is difficult to estimate, but it is easy to see representations of *gusimbuka* as a symbol of Tutsi superiority. The black stereotype is usually trapped by its binary structure, usually split between the two extremes of "barbarian" and "noble savage." In the case of Tutsi, I have tried to show that while the mode of negation was applied, it was rather muted when compared with other rhetorical modes. It was the more common rhetorics of idealization, naturalization, and appropriation that together reflected the construction of a broadly positive stereotype. The other end of the scale was reserved for Hutu and Twa. But the Tutsi stereotype was still a stereotype, based on massive generalizations and oversimplifications. As is often the case, it was not recognized that the differences within groups are greater than those between groups.

Twentieth-century representations of *gusimbuka-urukiramende*, even if created innocently enough, were fully consistent with the broader Tutsification of the nation during the 1920s and 1930s. In the re-presentation of Tutsi as superman, the significance of intentional European complicity is not known, but Europeans would have had everything to gain from painting flattering pictures of the Tutsi. Tutsi court administrators drew on European powers of representation for their own ends. The bodies of those athletes represented in writing and photographs of *gusimbuka* could be read, therefore, as being not simply athletic and aesthetic, but also critical and insurgent. Power is usually seen as belonging to the colonizers who use it to dominate the colonized. But power can move between multiple sites.[14] While Europeans were representing themselves in one way, Tutsi can be seen as establishing themselves in another. While the European discourses assisted the colonial project, they also implied the continued assertion of Tutsi superiority over the Hutu and Twa. Hence, a Saidian binary of colonizer and colonized is inappropriate in a Rwanda that experienced dual colonization. At one level, the dominant powers could be seen to be first Germany and then Belgium, but for much of the first half of the twentieth century this had to be reconciled with the internal dominance of the Rwandan monarchy and its authority over most Rwandan people.[15]

The ways in which *gusimbuka* and the Tutsi athlete were shaped and represented evokes the notion of invented traditions, that is traditions "invented, constructed and formally instituted or those emerging in a less easily traceable manner within a brief and dateable period."[16] It is the latter category that may apply most readily to *gusimbuka* and its representations between about 1920 and 1950. This is not to say that *gusimbuka-urukiramende* was a colonial invention, though the colonial invention of African traditions for Africans was far from unknown.[17] Rather, it may be better defined as an amplified tradition. *Gusimbuka*'s precolonial origins were confirmed and refined, and its Tutsiness promoted, by German-, Belgian-, British-, American- *and* Tutsi-orchestrated representations. "The rewriting of history is easier when there is no writing" observes Fisiy, and *gusimbuka*, like other elements of culture, can be read as having been "socially constructed to validate the position of the dominant power."[18] The apparent ability of the Tutsi at high jumping—a Western sport—was totally consistent with his status as an honorary European. He appeared to take part in Western pursuits such as the high jump, he could improve on Western institutions such as the world's record, and he was a potential Olympian. Through this lens, the Tutsi appeared European in taste without having been educated in European ways. He appeared as a mimic (sports)man who was able to translate—even to anticipate—European body cultures without training. All this was part of Rwanda's (or, more accurately, in this case, Tutsi) mythico-history—a subversive "recasting and reinterpretation of the past in fundamentally moral [and corporeal] terms."[19] Hardly any of the photographs of *gusimbuka* reflect the anthropometrists' physiological view of docile bodies drained of life, but they can, nevertheless, be read as constructions of an ethnic athletic stereotype. They were almost always *Tutsi* high jumpers, seemingly never East African or Hutu and only very rarely Rwandan high jumpers. As racial exclusion was implied in these images, Hutu did not need to be explicitly excluded.[20] American, British, and numerous other European writers, travelers, tourists, and photographers can be seen as having been unwittingly complicit in the positive stereotyping of the Tutsi. It was a stereotyping which was to clash with the revolutionary political trajectories that contributed to the massacres of 1959 and, later, the genocide.[21]

The photographs shown in the previous chapter are far from being pure scientific documents (of course, they never were). As noted earlier, the Tutsi elite were (slyly, or comically?) giving the European photographers what they wanted. The Tutsi high jump with the accompanying European visitor, can, therefore, be seen as an ironic or "satirical narrative of colonial life."[22] That Tutsi and Europeans should be represented together in a sporting event was natural. It was also in the interests of Tutsi elites to have Europeans idealize the *intore* as natural athletes and to have their athletic abilities made visible and communicated to a European public. Racism, the zeitgeist, and administrative expediency had created a superior race image of the Tutsi. Hence, however different their priorities, Belgians and Tutsi were united in their need to manipulate the situation protectively. The Tutsi elite needed to maintain its place in the national political arena; the Belgian colonialists needed to retain (until the 1950s) the support of Tutsi.[23]

All this illustrates the assertion that stereotypes are most commonly based on a combination of real-life experience and the world of myth. The two become entangled to form fabulous images, neither wholly of this world nor of the province of myth.[24] The representations of the "stupendous" feats of "natural athletes" in one of their "traditional" forms of body culture can be read as one (often unwitting) element in the conversion of Rwanda's history into a "tool for political propaganda."[25] An internalization of invented traditions would certainly have encouraged uncritical observers to use terms such as "long before the emergence of modern sports movements" to describe the distant origins of *gusimbuka-urukiramende*.[26] And tradition could have also been reflected in the way in which the presence of Europeans in the photographs of the high jump was matched by the presence of the *mwami*.

Throughout the period of colonialism, I see *gusimbuka* and its representations serving a quite different function from that often attributed to modern sport. One of the accepted functions of Western achievement sports is that they are *representational*, in the sense that they represent collectivities such as schools, universities, cities, or nations. For a time, at least, heterogeneous groups ally themselves in support of "their" team or "their" athletes. Allen Guttmann notes that sports are "one of the frail institutions that leaders of ... ethnically divided societies call upon to resist the factionalism that threatens to devolve into fratricidal conflict."[27] They represent what are often socially and culturally divided nation states as unities. *Gusimbuka-urukiramende*, and the interpretations placed upon it by Europeans, served the opposite of this bonding function. Instead, it represented Tutsi, through their (imagined) corporeality and athleticism, as different from—and superior to—the numerically dominant Hutu; it can be read as contributing to Tutsi bonding while marking "ethnic" boundaries within the Banyarwanda.

One question remains. Did the images also speak to the people of Rwanda? The jointly produced Tutsi-European history of Rwanda was, as Alison Des Forges observes,

> shaped in Rwanda and packaged in Europe, and then delivered back to the school-rooms of Rwanda by European or European-educated teachers. In addition, the results of the collaborative enterprise were accepted by intellectuals in the circles around the court, even those without European-style schooling—and integrated into their oral histories. It was not surprising that Tutsi were pleased with this version of history. But even the majority of Hutu swallowed this distorted account of the past, so great was their respect for European-style education. Thus people of both groups learned to think of the Tutsi as winners and the Hutu as losers in every great contest of the Rwandan past.[28]

It seems plausible that some educated Tutsi, like almost all Europeans, internalized an association between *gusimbuka* and Tutsiness. Kagame himself had identified *gusimbuka* with "sons of the Hamitic nobility"— i.e., Tutsi.[29] And it seems possible that, by the 1930s, educated Hutu would have also been aware of the symbolism of the superathlete, if (as it is claimed) refined Rwandan traditions were made available to "schoolchildren, readers of newspapers in African languages ... and all those who attended missionary and administrative centres."[30] For Europeans, this was part of a reassuring, normalized, and even westernized view of Rwanda. This was especially the case when *gusimbuka* was presented in folklorized form, in the kinds of movies described in the previous chapter. Even if they had only been consumed by a small number of Banyarwanda, the representations of *gusimbuka* did nothing to temper the pro-Tutsi attitudes of those Europeans who had read the travel literature and sports books that extolled Tutsi athletic virtues.[31] But the question of whether the broader, uneducated Rwandan population ever identified *gusimbuka* with Tutsi is simply unknown, despite the European hyperbole, discussed in earlier chapters, that claimed it was the "national sport."

A Conclusion

The primary theme of this book has been an examination of sporting imaginations. The colonial images of *gusimbuka-urukiramende* raise many questions about the abilities of Europeans to provide representations of native body cultures. Many of the colonial texts explored here did not extol the anthropological (and geographical) fantasy of unhindered, pure observation of native life, but more likely resulted from the interactions between colonizers and colonized. They may have supplemented Tutsi traditions, and were often peddled by Rwandan and Belgian racial theorists. Intentionally or unintentionally, many of them elevated (literally) the Tutsi to the top of the social and corporeal hierarchies, reinforcing their imagined superhuman status. Devoid of any military overtones, and replacing power with grace, what better symbol of racial authority could there be than that of the high jumper? But I have also shown that other rhetorics sought to devalue the very athleticism that those of surveillance, idealization, and appropriation encouraged.

Some researchers see the genocide as partly the result of economic and global factors relating to such things as the fall in world coffee prices.[32] At the same time, it has been argued that "representations of the body can be seen to underlie much of the politics and the violence that has occurred in Rwanda."[33] I am anxious to avoid any hint of a suggestion that European images of Tutsi corporeality were of any serious significance to the causes of the post-1959 tragedies and the Rwandan genocide. But what if these images *were* read as being symbolic of Tutsi power by Tutsi and Hutu elites? Some observers aver that "racist prejudice was a structural feature of Rwandan society."[34] Likewise, others argue that "the genocide that broke out on April 6, 1994—far from being an abrupt irrational explosion or an unavoidable predetermined event—followed decades of political myth-making and ethnic polarization, conscious manipulation of extremist ideologies, and incitement to political violence."[35] During the twentieth century, the political elites of the two major groups in Rwanda had embraced colonialist rhetoric, each for their own ends. The representations of *gusimbuka-urukiramende* were, I suggest, nothing more and nothing less than a small part of that mythmaking and expressed an ideology of racial division. They were consistent with the forging of a Tutsi identity, leaving national identity to be usurped in the 1960s by the Hutu elite.

The period covered by most of this study ends with the demise of Tutsi supremacy. However, with the taking of power in the early 1960s by the Hutu, the racial theories of the former decades were kept alive. In the early 1990s appalling visual stereotypes of the Tutsi were published as cartoons in the extremist Hutu press.[36] The Hamitic hypothesis was used to justify the killing of the Hutu's former "Aryan" masters, a perverse form of "strategic essentialism,"[37]—that is, the use of essentialist forms of identity in a conflict that pitted one group of Rwandans against another. It can be argued, therefore, that anything that contributed to the hardening of—even the very recognition of—difference between Hutu and Tutsi from the mid–nineteenth century onward was complicit in the genocide.

The messy discourse of *gusimbuka-urukiramende* was constructed by several groups. Among these were individuals from the academic disciplines of anthropology, physical education, and geography. Also represented were the industries of photography and publishing. In addition, there were historians, gentlemen's clubs such as the Royal Geographical Society, the tourist industry, the International Amateur Athletics Federation, German and Belgian individuals with political ambitions, and others who had their own personal motivations. Perhaps this discourse is analogous to that which constructed the elitist physicality of the Aryan body in Hitler's Germany, where the fascist body was championed in the context of modern sports via a variety of texts.[38] These included stone statues, paper posters, comic caricatures, calendars, and parts of

Leni Riefenstahl's classic movie, *Olympia*, or, more dramatically in her more explicitly propagandistic *Triumph of the Will*.[39] As Hitler's photographer, she was, of course, a willing propagandist. It would be absurd to suggest that (m)any of the Europeans who represented the performances of *gusimbuka* in writing, photography, and film were consciously or deliberately engaged in acts of indoctrination or pro-Tutsi propaganda; there was no Rwandan Riefenstahl. But surely the contribution to ethnic stereotyping "is no less real if unintended."[40] At what point does complicity stop?

Three Configurations
of High Jumping

Citius, Fortius, . . . and Altius: The Achievement Model

In 1887 it was observed that in sports "perhaps nothing is so pretty and interesting as a High Jump."[1] A decade later, however, aesthetics were dismissed when it was pronounced that "popular opinion has always held the view that the high jumper is a freak of nature possessed of wonderful 'spring,' the seat of which is supposed to be in the instep or toes."[2] This may or may not have been the case. My point here is that although an aesthetic dimension is clearly present in achievement-oriented high jumping, its importance is not elevated above that of technique. It was technical improvement, not aesthetics or the freakish, innate ability of individuals, that had produced the "extraordinary improvement" in high-jumping performances in the British Isles during the nineteenth century. Well before the end of the nineteenth century, the style of running at ninety degrees to the bar, with both legs tucked up against the chest, was in decline and the "scissors" technique, using an approach from the side, was favored.[3] Progress in high jumping was attributed to careful training and assiduous practice, two characteristics strongly associated with modern sport, but not its distant relative, disport. As early as the 1880s the idea was advanced that daily training lay at the heart of the "higher" element of the Olympian triad of "faster, higher, stronger."[4]

   The first recorded—or quantified—high-jump performance is said to have been a leap of 5 feet 2 inches (1.575 meters) by the Scotsman

Adam Wilson in 1827.[5] Claims of higher jumps were common, evidence of an early concern with quantified records. Donald Walker, in his *British Manly Exercises*, published in 1834, stated that "a good high leaper will clear 5 ft., a first rate one 5½ ft. and an extraordinary one 6 ft."[6] This may have been hyperbole, but by the mid-1860s professional jumpers had cleared over 5 feet 11 inches (1.80 meters), and amateurs, led by the Oxford University student Marshall Brooks, reached similar heights by the 1870s. The careful training and attention to technique shown by high jumpers at this time (and subsequently) undoubtedly helped the progress of high jumping in the twentieth century. The years after 1900 have witnessed the constant refinement and modification of technique and the closely associated influence of changing technology.

In the 1890s performance-orientated high jumping assumed a variety of forms. There was the running high jump, the standing high jump, and the running high jump "taking off from a wooden block."[7] There was also the "hitch-and-kick," which involved competitions to see who could achieve the highest kick. Robert Templeton's standard textbook from the 1920s on high jumping records how Michael Sweeney had achieved a world's record for this variant of high jumping, reaching 9 feet 4 inches.[8] Performances in these kinds of events were recorded and ranked. Gradually, however, they became marginalized, and high-jumping space was purified with the running high jump as the dominant form. During the twentieth century it was characterized by a variety of jumping styles and techniques. The scissors style was compared with the "eastern cut-off," and as the sport became increasingly international, the cut-off was largely replaced, from 1912 (when *gusimbuka* was first being publicized in Western media) by the "western roll." The "straddle" (Figure A.1) appeared during the 1930s, and became the dominant style until the late 1960s when the "Fosbury flop," named after the 1968 Olympic champion, became widely adopted. Such changes in technique correlated with improved performance.

At the time of Mecklenburg's visit to Rwanda, the best recorded high-jump performance in the world of sportized athletics was 1.97 meters. The first "official world record" following the establishment, in

1912, of the governing bureaucracy for athletics throughout the world, the International Amateur Athletics Federation (IAAF), was held by the American Harold Osborn, who cleared 6 feet 7 inches (2.007 meters). By 1940, the record had reached 6 feet 10⅜ inches (2.09 meters) set by Melvin Walker, and by 1960 John Thomas had reached 7 feet 3¾ inches (2.22 meters). All three of these athletes each came from the United States, but by 1980 Europeans were dominating the event, and at the end of that decade, it was Gerd Wessig of Germany who held the record at 2.36 meters. The seemingly inexorable colonization and globalization of achievement-related high jumping is exemplified by the Cuban holder of the current world record, Javier Sotomayor, whose best performance is 8 feet 0½ inches (2.45 meters).[9]

During its existence the IAAF has been censorious in its attitude toward technique. Until 1936, for example, athletes had to clear the bar leg first. Diving over, head first, was not permitted. In 1924 the afore-mentioned Osborn broke the world record with a leap of 6 feet 8¹⁵/₁₆ inches (2.0559 meters), but it was in an exhibition event and was there-fore unrecognized by the IAAF, which drew a clearly defined line between competition and exhibition. In 1954 an American acrobatic champion, Dick Browning, cleared seven feet from a two-foot takeoff with a back-ward somersault.[10] This would have broken the existing world record, but the IAAF requires that the jumper take off from only one foot. Con-sequently, the performance was not accepted as a new record. In the 1970s, several Soviet high jumpers experimented with jumping with a built-up sole on their takeoff shoes. This enabled them to obtain greater leverage in the conversion of their bodies' horizontal speed to vertical thrust. The IAAF responded to these experiments with disapproval and stipulated that the thickness of the sole of a high jumper's shoe should be no more than 13 millimeters, later, a heel thickness of 19 mm was accepted. An equally specific measurement, typical of this genre of jumping, requires that the length of the crossbar must be between 3.98 and 4.02 meters in length, and its weight must not exceed 2 kilograms.[11]

Women high jumpers have followed the same direction as men. Having started competitive jumping later, their records have improved at a faster rate. The earliest measured high jump on record by a woman was by Emma Baker, who cleared 1.17 meters in 1895 at Poughkeepsie, New York. Superior results were achieved by clearing a rope or bamboo cane. The leap of 5 feet 4 inches (1.6256 meters) by the English athlete Joan Balasco in 1920 was not bettered in "standard" competition with a rigid wooden bar until 1932, when Jean Shirley cleared 1.65 meters. Until the late 1980s, progress toward better and better performances had been inexorable. Rosie Ackermann was the first to clear 2 meters in 1977, and the world record at the time of this writing is 2.09 meters, established by the Bulgarian Stefka Kostadinova in 1987.[12] It has been suggested that the gap between the best women's performance and the best of the men is gradually closing. If the improvement were to continue at the existing rate, it has been estimated (or speculated) that sometime during the twenty-first century, the men's and women's world records will become equal.[13]

The kinds of precise and detailed measurements noted in the previous paragraphs reflect the characteristics of standardized global sport. Its measured space and time enable it to function as a form of international cultural currency. The ability to measure performances that are (thought to be) meaningfully comparative requires a standardization of rules and, ideally, a standardization of the micro-environment of competition. The athlete in Figure A.1, Gene Johnson, was from the United States, but the photograph was taken at a track meet in Växjö, Sweden. Yet neither he nor the spectators in a country distant from his own had any problems identifying with the event in which he was performing. In modern sports—unlike the "folk" analogs—there is always a globally intelligible script and it is its organization at the international, or non-local, scale that some scholars recognize as the main difference between modern sport and its traditional analogs.[14] At the same time, the statistical character of achievement sport forms the basis from which results are valued over performance.[15]

The standardized conditions that are necessary for such international comparisons are an outcome of changing technology. Until the 1970s, high jumping had been performed on a variety of surfaces. These included grass and a number of cinder-type surfaces of differing hardness and drainage capacities. Today, all arenas for major competitions need precise standardization, as does the character of the equipment used. In much of the Western world surfaces are made of synthetic substances that drain easily, do not deteriorate with use during a competition, and provide a consistent environment from place to place. It is what might be called an environment of "placelessness."[16] With its associated accuracy of measurement and geometrically perfect equipment, it is hardly surprising that a neo-Marxist observer of modern sport noted that "the reduction of space to geometry, the abstraction of what is concrete, real, and tangible in nature, is carried to the ultimate extreme in sport."[17] In

Figure A.1

1900, high jumpers were landing on grass. In the 1950s, athletes landed in pits of sand. Today, their descent onto inflatable airbeds cushions their falls and does not inhibit them in the execution of their performances. The people who inhabit the world of achievement sports are "experts" such as trainers, medical scientists, pharmacists, technologists, and engineers.

Another dimension to the technologizing of high jumping was the introduction of photography, which contributed to the improvement of high jumping performances as early as the 1890s. The French pioneer of photographic applications to sport, Étienne-Jules Marey, utilized his "chronophotography" at the Paris Olympics of 1900. His results revealed that the Americans had a "real advantage over the others, thanks to ingenious tricks that the rules did not prohibit, that they did not even foresee, but that make comparisons among different competitors of the form they use in the same sport impossible."[18] In achievement sport, form had to give way to "tricks," which would improve results. Tricks continue to impact on the event in other ways, namely through the application of pharmacology. Arguably, it is modern athletes who best exemplify the cyborg (the ultimate hybrid). After all, "they are experimented upon in much the same way as rats in kinesiology laboratories; they are exploited for their animal aggression by the producers of sports spectacles; they are fine-tuned and chemically manipulated by techno-science; they are circuits in the network machine of the high-performance sport system."[19] The modern sport body is here presented as the rational body; it explifies the machine-nature of our bodies. During the 1980s, the world high-jump record went from 2.35 meters to 2.44 meters. In the 1990s, the men's record increased to only 2.45 meters, and the women's record has not been improved on since 1987. This suggests that new tricks may need to be introduced for records to continue to improve at the previous rate.

The achievement model of high jumping has deadly seriousness as its focus. Traditionally, people watched the high jump performance in absolute silence so that the athlete could obtain maximum concentration. However, in the 1970s and 1980s a more carnivalistic, folk, or dialogical style occurred as the crowd began to rhythmically clap their hands as the jumper approached the bar. This has now become the norm.[20] What is more, achievement-oriented high jumping has been accompanied by more than clapping, with occasional attempts to spectacularize it by the playing of amplified rock music of the athlete's choice. In addition, this dramatic form of sport has, from time to time, left the confines of the concrete stadium and moved into the multifunctional spaces of the city square, town center, or shopping mall. The guardians of the sport's records would not accept a world record set in such unstandardized surroundings, but such developments (or regressions) show that modern achievement sport can assume a form closer to that of a circus. This is not to deny that such developments may be driven by the world of commerce. From the above discussion, it can be seen that three key words characterize this mode of jumping in its pure form or ideal type. They are *progress*, *quantification*, and *record*, and each is central to achievement sport.

Posture and Hygiene: The Gymnastic Model

In 1599, Arcangelo Tuccaro published his manual of jumping and gymnastic skills, which seems to have been deemed still worthy of consultation into the twentieth century.[21] The intricate diagrams contained in this remarkable work reveal a fascination with technique in the production of the athletic—and in this case, also the aesthetic—body. For Tuccaro, jumping was an art. In early modern Europe, it appears, jumping was considered as one of several courtly exercises appropriate for the promotion of manly vigor. It also assisted in fitness for warfare and was regarded as a means of obtaining a good name "among the multitude."[22] The good name came from good posture, but manly vigor had to be compatible with moderation in exercise. Strenuous movement overstepped what was proper and was "more appropriate for tumblers," wrote J. du Chesré in 1606.[23]

High jumping as a component of gymnastics arguably reached its greatest popularity during the late nineteenth century. The turner movement (*Turner* is the German for "gymnast") was inspired by the thoughts of the German physical educators Friedrich GutsMuths (1759–1839) and Friedrich Ludwig Jahn (1778–1852), and spread rapidly through Germany, parts of central Europe, and Scandinavia, where it was modified by the Swedish physical educator Pehr Henrik Ling (1776–1839). In Jahn's *Turnplatz*, constructed in the second decade of the nineteenth century, high-jumping equipment was erected as a permanent structure, along with a variety of other gymnastic apparatus. It consisted of two vertical standards fixed rigidly into the ground with moveable pegs placed in holes in each stand. Across the pegs was a rope with small, weighted bags of sand at each end.[24] In France, gymnastics, as part of physical education, was seen as a means of national regeneration. It also diffused, with some success, to the United States. In some ways, it was similar to the sportized model of achievement sport (i.e., through the keeping of records) but the turner movement opposed the more serious competition favored in the English sports. Instead, it concentrated on the development of good posture.

A comparison of jumping as a component of gymnastics with that practiced as a sport was graphically illustrated by the comments of the Danish *gymnastikinspectør*, Knud Anton Knudsen. On a visit to England in 1895, he witnessed a competition between Finnish and English jumpers. His evaluation was that

> the English had only one thing in mind: to get over the rope, no matter how. They did nothing to conceal the exertion caused by their efforts to perform the jump and they gave the spectators the impression that the clearance of greater heights depended on certain tricks. They placed themselves at angular positions to the rope and landed on all fours. The Finns ran frontally to the rope, straightened their bodies as soon as they had cleared it, came down with knees slightly bent, and immediately went into an upright position as if it had been no effort at all.[25]

The clear difference between the body management of the Nordic jumpers from that of the English lay in the difference between their respective approaches to the high jump. The former stressed an aesthetic dimension, whereas the latter emphasized effectiveness. The former exemplified the symmetrical body; the latter the asymmetrical. It was a case of form versus the record. The English approach betrayed the strenuousness that had been so deplored in the medieval pedagogical treatises. Knudsen did not appear to realize what was at stake. He assumed that the English had simply not discovered the "correct" way to perform bodily exercises and that, in time, they might learn to do so. His Nordic-conditioned gaze focused emphatically on exercise, but what were important in sports were quantifiable results. In sportized high jumping, no prizes were given to stylish jumpers. And by the 1930s, it was prizes, press coverage, and the mania of the record that were seen by a Danish supporter of gymnastics to be an "odious system [that] must, of course, be entirely banished from the physical exercises in schools."[26]

The fitness model of high jumping exemplifies the values of health and well-being in both a physiological and a sociophysiological sense. Eichberg sees physicians and pedagogues as the experts involved in the overall configuration of such jumping. They exhort us to perform the correct ways of moving our bodies and encourage good posture.[27] A series of diagrams shown in Figure A.2 (taken from Knudsen's textbook of gymnastics) illustrates the technical dimensions of the Swedish gymnastic high jump. Apart from the ideological differences, there were some differences in the equipment used in gymnastics from that used in sportized

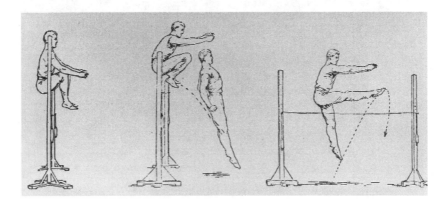

Figure A.2

high jumping. The former had, for example, the weighted rope instead of the rigid bar. More significantly, perhaps, it often had a springboard for purposes of takeoff. In other ways, however, gymnastics and sport were similar. Each required technical development—for improved posture, in the former, and improved results, in the latter. To this end, just as science impacted on the sportized version, scientific methods of analysis, such as the technical photography of Marey and Muybridge, were also applied to the gymnastic form of jumping.[28] An example of Marey's work is shown in Figure A.3. Taken in 1886, it shows the performance of Schenkel, one of the top members of the Parisian gymnastic societies. Another similarity between both modes of jumping was the presence of surveillance, exemplified by the monitoring of posture and fitness. There was order in the gymnasium, in much the same way as order and instruction existed in the athletic arena. But whereas the objective of sportized high jumping was the production of results and records, that of the gymnastic model was the reproduction of a healthy community and workforce.[29] This association between the labor force and gymnastics was taken furthest, perhaps, in the Soviet Union, where, during the 1920s, competitive sports were denounced as unhealthy and bourgeois. "Socialist competition" did not gain acceptance until the 1930s.[30]

Figure A.3

The welfare model has as its central concerns the learning of fitness, hygiene, and posture, but although a competitive and quantified format was initially rejected, gymnastic high jumping was, by the 1890s, assuming some elements of sportization. For example, gymastic jumping was being measured and recorded. The notions of national records and champions were applied.[31] And, just as some elements of serious, sportized jumping have become less serious and more dialogical with crowd involvement and musical accompaniment, some elements of achievement sport had entered the world of gymnastic jumping. Elements of cross-configurational hybridity were present.

To some extent, the gymnastic model of body culture posed a threat to the hegemony of the achievement or sportized model.[32] During the late nineteenth century the sportized and gymnastic models of high jumping were contesting the social space of sports, and in Germany and Scandinavia fierce debates often raged about which one should be prioritized among the population. During the twentieth century gymnastics became sportized and much more individualized, and the gymnastic form of high jumping fell into abeyance.

"Folk" Traditions

For many centuries, a variety of folk forms of high jumping have been found in many parts of the world. They comprise a diffuse range of activities. It has been asserted that as long ago as 1829 B.C.E jumping took place at the Tailtin Games in Ireland. Apparently, Cuchalain (the "Irish Hercules") learned the "salmon leap," by which he was able to clear castle ramparts in order to win Emer, daughter of Forgall the Wily.[33] The factual accuracy of this legend is not important. It shows not only that jumping was practiced, but also that from an early date it carried rather precise social and personal signification. Legend or not, it is reasonably certain that jumping—sometimes with the aid of a pole—was practiced in many countries of Europe. In Britain, a regional form of nineteenth-century high jumping was exemplified by the "high leap" at the Scottish Highland Games. In this case, it appears that although the height of the jump determined the winner, the participants also had to land on their feet.[34] It was a mixture of performance and style. At Winchester, in the south of England, frequent archive references allude to "Cat's Gallows"—the high-jump stand and bar used for recreational (and, later, competitive) purposes from the early nineteenth century.[35] In the early 1900s at Vassar College in Poughkeepsie, New York, young women took part in "fence vaulting"—like a high jump, but with one hand used to assist the clearance of a rigid structure such as a fence.[36] It was neither high jumping nor pole-vaulting, and although records were kept it was not an activity that was widely practiced.

There were also widespread turn-of-the-century traditions of different forms of high jumping that were associated with the circus, the music hall, vaudeville, and sideshows. Typical of this genre were performances in the late 1890s at the Pavilion Theatre, in London's Piccadilly Circus. Among a range of routines which lay somewhere between acrobatics and high jumping were several trick jumps such as the extinguishing of a candle on a man's hat with the jumper's foot while jumping over him. There was also the example of jumping over a "human wall."[37] From the world of high culture, ballet has provided other examples of leaping and jumping. From the milieu of the street, on the other hand, children have long taken part in widespread but informal high-jumping events. In the alleys of 1950s industrial England, for example, the improvised vertical supports for the crossbar were made of materials such as broken house bricks piled one on top of the other. Variations on these unstandardized forms of jumping probably took place throughout Europe and North America.

Different kinds of high jumping also existed among the indigenous peoples of North America, Asia, and Africa.[38] These, like some of the Western forms described above, are sometimes known as "folk" traditions of jumping, though such is the range and variety of such activities that to accommodate them under a single label may be a gross oversimplification of the extent of their common characteristics. Some examples illustrate the variety. In the 1870s it was recorded that a chief of the Canadian Iroquois, White Eagle, was "able to jump over a man's head without the slightest effort."[39] In northern Canada, men and women of the Dene and Inuit peoples continue to take part in *aratsiaq*—a one-legged jump to kick a suspended target. *Akratcheak* involves kicking the target with both feet.[40] In Asia in the early twentieth century, a German ethnologist, Kauffman, recorded a strong preference for high and long jumping over the competitive races that were held among the Thadou Kuki of Assam.[41] High jumping has also been recorded on the Indonesian island of Nias, where villagers jump for pleasure over a specially constructed setting of stones (over 2 meters in height) using an inclined stone takeoff.[42]

The contrast between folk body cultures and those of the achievement and welfare models has been clearly made by both Allen Guttmann and Henning Eichberg, though their interpretations differ in one important respect. Guttmann implies that achievement sports are characteristically modern whereas folk games are typically premodern.[43] Eichberg, by contrast, does not necessarily see folk games as antecedents of modernity or as "primitive" forms of high jumping, but as a different form of folk body culture in modernity.[44] Additionally, Eichberg points to examples of the apparent continuation (or revival) of folk activities that may be read as alternative forms of modernity rather than as residuals of a bygone age or as folkloric exhumations. Such regressions reflect a move away from the serious sportized model, but at the same time, they may be driven by capital and may reflect certain characteristics of achievement sport.

Notes

Introduction

1. For reasons of preference and consistency, I use the postcolonial spelling Rwanda rather than the colonial spelling Ruanda throughout this book; likewise, I have used Burundi rather than Urundi. The only exceptions are where cited quotations have used the colonialized spellings. I have also adopted the terms Hutu, Tutsi, and Twa, except when in quotations where other words (usually prefixed) are used (e.g., Watutsi, Mtussi). In postgenocide Rwanda, attempts have been made to build a nation in which these terms will become obsolete, but the threefold division is, nevertheless, still widely used. See Taylor, *Sacrifice as Terror*.

2. Bryant, "Major's Mission Seeks Leap of Faith." The idea of using athletes from the colonies to represent European nations in sports is not new. Having witnessed the success of African Americans at the 1936 Olympics, French journalists, anticipating the French team for the (aborted) 1940 Games at Tokyo, remarked that research should be undertaken "in the bush" so that the "French race" could be represented by the "outstanding contribution" of Africans from the colonies. Quoted in Deville-Danthu, *Le sport en noir et blanc*, 68.

3. Livingstone, *The Geographical Tradition*, 221–41. According to the geographer Ellsworth Huntington, central Africa was an area of low "climatic energy," ibid., 231.

4. Ryan, *Picturing Empire*, 30. On the term *explorer* see Ryan, *The Cartographic Eye*. It is beyond the scope of this book to provide detailed background information on the writers and photographers who contributed to the

knowledge of westerners about *gusimbuka*, or Rwandan high jumping. I have tried to provide the context of some of those who were of importance in this respect and, in the notes to chapter 2, I supply brief biographies of two of the major publicists for *gusimbuka*, the Duke of Mecklenburg and Professor Ernst Jokl.

5. Barnett, in "The Cultural Turn," wryly notes that "clinging to 'the geographical,' 'the spatial,' or even 'the environmental' is one way of managing the anxiety that comes when faced with an essentially un-'masterable' field of cultural theory," (390).

6. Said, *Orientalism* and *Culture and Imperialism*.

7. Barnett, "The Cultural Turn," 380 (emphasis added).

8. James et al., "Introduction: The Road from Santa Fe," 2.

9. Curry, *The Work in the World*, 17–42.

10. Gren, *Earth Writing*, 18.

11. Curry, *The Work in the World*, 201–6.

12. Livingstone, "Reproduction, Representation, and Authenticity," 15.

13. Olsson, *Lines of Power/Limits of Language*, 174. See also Olsson, *Birds in Egg/Eggs in Bird*. In the mid-1970s, one of Olsson's ardent supporters observed that only he "among contemporary geographers has made a serious attempt to address the broad and important issues of how language ... makes us prisoners in our own house, and how it leads us to make status quo and normative statements which are not necessarily intended." See Symanski, "The Manipulation of Ordinary Language," 605. There are inevitably antecedents. For example, see Tuan, "Use of Simile and Metaphor in Geography"; and Darby, "The Problem of Geographical Description." For an overview of geography and literature, see Brosseau, "Geography's Literature." Olsson's legacy is a concern with representation in human geography. For example, see Barnes and Duncan (eds.), *Writing Worlds*; Duncan and Gregory (eds.), *Writes of Passage*; Duncan and Ley (eds.), *Place/Culture/Representation*; Gren, *Earth Writing*; and Curry, *The Work in the World*.

14. Gregory, *Geographical Imaginations*, 73. Examples of some works in sports studies that have transgressed the boundaries of conventional writing genres are reviewed in Bruce, "Postmodernism and the Possibilities for Writing."

15. Rose, "Teaching Visualised Geographies."

16. A postcolonial focus for geography was stimulated in large part by the richness of the geographical allusions and metaphors found in Said's work. See

Said, *Orientalism*. Note also the geographical metaphors in the titles of Baucom, *Out of Place*; Gikandi, *Maps of Englishness*; and Ryan, *The Cartographic Eye*. While geographers (and researchers in sports studies) may, in their embrace of postcolonial studies, have been said to be "busy grabbing their share of colonial guilt," they can hardly avoid doing so if they are "not to lose out on their share of the spoils of the most exciting and innovative realms of contemporary theory" (Barnett, "Awakening the Dead," 418). On the interconnections between postcolonialism, postmodernism, literary studies, and anthropology, see Gregory, *Geographical Imaginations*, 134–5. In that both postmodernism and postcolonialism "refuse to turn the Other into the same" they can be seen to be clearly allied. See During, "Postmodernism, or Post-Colonialism Today," 125; and, in more detail, Quayson, *Postcolonialism*, 132–55. For a critique of a postmodern approach in a postcolonial sports context, see Morgan, "Hassiba Boulmerka and Islamic Green."

17. Childs and Williams, *An Introduction to Postcolonial Theory*, 7; and Quayson, *Postcolonialism: Theory, Practice, or Process?*, 9.

18. Ashcroft, "Constructing the Post-Colonial Male Body," 207.

19. Ashcroft et al., *The Empire Strikes Back*, 64. Ashcroft and his colleagues point out strategies serving to distance the Western author from the worst excesses of Eurocentrism. These include "editorial intrusions" such as the footnote, the endnote, and the explanatory introduction where these are made by the author as well as the explication of the author's own position within the text. Yet these and other strategies are continually in danger of appearing merely cosmetic. Note the following example from Australia.

In a class with a large Aboriginal enrollment, an instructor making a presentation on the construction of Aboriginality was careful to stress that it was not his views that he was presenting. He threw out a safety net of quotation marks to signify that at least some of the words that came out of his mouth ... were not his words or even approximations of the truth. In doing this, the lecturer used his pedagogical authority to de-authorise—to render "untruthful"—colonial discourse. Despite these efforts, some of the Aboriginal students staged a walkout. This was not a misrecognition of the use of quotation marks, but a response to their inadequacy in transporting racist discourses from their place in the history as colonial "truths" to their present place as postcolonial "fallacies." There is, then, no predictable relationship between the political intentions of those who employ the interpretive strategies of social constructionism and their effects. See Jackson and Jacobs, "Introduction," 2. Of particular importance in the present context is the uncritical use of the word *sport*, which, in the past, has led to quite erroneous impressions and expectations of African body cultural practice. For example, colonial writers in Kenya predicted that the Masai would be fantastic athletes, whereas it turned out that it was the Kalenjin who, in fact, excelled at track running. See Bale, "The Rhetoric of Running."

20. Ryan, *The Cartographic Eye*, 15. Among good introductions to post-colonialism are Childs and Williams, *An Introduction to Postcolonial Theory*; Boehmer, *Colonial and Postcolonial Literature*; Ashcroft et al., *The Empire Writes Back*; Loomba, *Colonialism/Postcolonialism*; and Gandhi, *Postcolonialism*.

21. Boehmer, *Colonial and Postcolonial Literature*, 50.

22. Barnes and Gregory (eds.), *Reading Human Geography*, 138. Existing work in sports studies that shows how written texts can "create" body cultural practices is best exemplified, perhaps, in Oriard, *Reading Football*.

23. Slater, "Geopolitics and the Postmodern," 324.

24. Duncan, "After the Civil War: Reconstructing Cultural Geography as Heterotopia," 406. This kind of work is exemplified in Phillips, *Men and Empire*; Driver, "Visualizing Geography" and "Geography, Empire, and Visualisation"; and Ryan, *Picturing Empire*. Note also, and from a different perspective, Gregory, "Imaginative Geographies" and "Between the Book and the Lamp."

25. Massonnet, "Rôle et place du sport et du jeu au Rwanda," 59-63.

26. See several of the essays in Godlewska and Smith (eds.), *Geography and Empire*; and Driver, *Geography Militant*.

27. Driver, "Submerged Identities: Familiar and Unfamiliar Histories."

28. This is based on Crush, "Postcolonialism, De-Colonisation, and Geography." On postcolonial geography, see also Blunt and Willis, *Dissident Geograpies*, 162–207.

29. Eichberg, *Body Cultures*. See also Korsgaard, *Kampen om Kroppen*.

30. Brownell, *Training the Body for China*.

31. Spurr, *The Rhetoric of Empire*, 22.

32. Mirzoeff, *Bodyscape*, 3 (italics added).

33. Pratt, "Scratches on the Face of the Country," 139. On the "postcolonial body," see also Ashcroft et al., *Key Concepts in Post-Colonial Studies*, 183–86.

34. See Rothenberg, "Voyeurs of Imperialism," 170–71.

35. Hoberman, *Darwin's Athletes*, 103. Hoberman is principally referring here to the prominence of East African middle- and long-distance runners and of African American and West African sprinters.

36. Ashcroft, "Constructing the Post-Colonial Male Body," 209.

37. Gregory, "Imaginative Geographies," 453.

38. In Said's major works the only sport-related citation is Mangan, *The Games Ethic and Imperialism*; see Said, *Culture and Imperialism*, 417, n. 128. Said barely mentions sport in writing about culture and imperialism, and he barely mentions imperialism when (on a rare occasion) he writes about sport. See Said, "John McEnroe Plus Anyone." I leave readers to make their own interpretations of this apparent paradox. Some writers on postcolonialism from a background in literature do pay some attention to sport. For example, Ashcroft, "Constructing the Post-Colonial Body," 215–17; Baucom, *Out of Place*, 135–64; Gikandi, *Maps of Englishness*, 9–14; Montefiore, "Latin, Arithmetic, and Mastery"; and, notably, Farred, "The Maple Man."

39. Although the work of such varied scholars as, for example, James, *Beyond a Boundary*; Klein, *Sugarball*; Mangan, *The Games Ethic and Imperialism*; and Beckles and Stoddart (eds.), *Liberation Cricket*, is clearly postcolonial writing, none of it utilizes textual and visual analysis of colonialist texts on precolonial body cultures.

40. On body building, and its early twentieth-century representation, see Garb, *Bodies of Modernity*, 55–79.

41. Such writers included Richard Burton, Rudyard Kipling, Benjamin Disraeli, and Lewis Carroll. See Bivona, *Desire and Contradiction*, in which it is noted that for much of the Victorian period a "game" was read as a "lark" or a "trivial pursuit." Nevertheless, it was the Victorian era that witnessed the growing seriousness of games and the application of the word *sport* to many of them. Lewis Carroll, among others, opposed the earnestness with that sports were taken. See Blake, *Play, Games, and Sport*. See also Montefiore, "Latin, Arithmetic, and Mastery."

42. Quoted in Hoberman, *Darwin's Athletes*, 100.

43. On colonialism and mountaineering, see Kearns, "The Imperial Subject," 457–58.

44. Guttmann, *From Ritual to Record*. For a critique, see Blake, *Body Language*, 69–82.

45. Mentore, "Society, Body, and Style," 66.

46. Kirby, "The Construction of Geographical Images," 55.

47. Malkki, *Purity and Exile*. Malkki applies the notion of "mythico-history" to Burundi, but it is equally applicable to Rwanda.

48. Eagleton, "Postcolonialism and 'Postcolonialism,'" 26.

49. Jackson and Jacobs, "Editorial," 1.

50. James, *Beyond a Boundary*, viii.

1. Writing Rwanda

1. Mitchell, *Cultural Geography*, 232.

2. Newbury, "Ethnicity and the Politics of History in Rwanda," 9; Vansina, "The Politics of History and the Crisis in the Great Lakes," 41; Jefremovas, "Treacherous Waters" and "Contested Identities."

3. Gregory, "Social Theory and Human Geography," 104.

4. Quayson, *Postcolonialism: Theory, Practice, or Process?*, 67.

5. Owusu, "Ethnography of Africa." The records of meetings and exchanges in this contact zone are mainly attributed to Europeans, but native interpreters, whose role in the subsequent European record is rarely hinted at, would have filtered language through the various qualities of translation. As a result, Western geographies and body cultural studies may bear traces of African knowledges. See Sidaway, "The (Re)Making of the Western Geographical Tradition and "Postcolonial Geographies."

6. Clifford, *The Predicament of Culture*, 259. Indeed, Walter Benjamin warned against attempting to recognize the past as it "really was". Quoted in Gidley, *Edward S. Curtis*, 283.

7. Fyfe and Law, "Introduction: On the Invisibility of the Visible," 1; Sekula, "On the Invention of Photographic Meaning," 92.

8. Barthes, *Image, Music, Text*, 28. See also Foucault, *The Archaeology of Knowledge*.

9. Berger and Mohr, *Another Way of Telling*, 120–1 (parentheses added).

10. Walder, *Post-Colonial Literatures in English*, 58.

11. Curry, *The Work in the World*, 5.

12. This draws on thoughts in Tyler, "Post-Modern Ethnography." See also Gidley, *Edward S. Curtis*, 8. It has been noted that "to be ironic is to recognize self-consciously the near impossibility of what you are trying to do but then do it anyway." Quoted in Barnes, *Logics of Dislocation*, 211.

13. Newbury, *The Cohesion of Oppression*, 2.

14. Jefremovas, "Contested Identities."

15. Here I draw extensively on the geographically informed review by Franche, *Rwanda: Généalogie d'un génocide*. I am extremely grateful to Clare Slater-Mamlouk, of Keele University, for her translation from the French. Other important sources are Des Forges, *Defeat Is the Only Bad News*; Newbury, *The Cohesion of Oppression*; and Newbury, "Ethnicity and the Politics of History in Rwanda."

16. Gilroy, *Between Camps*, 46.

17. Mitchell, *Cultural Geography*, 234–35.

18. See, for example, Maquet, *The Premise of Inequality in Ruanda*.

19. Newbury, "Ethnicity and the Politics of History in Rwanda," 10.

20. Newbury, "Understanding Genocide," 84.

21. Franche, *Rwanda: Généalogie d'un génocide*, 18.

22. Des Forges, *Defeat Is the Only Bad News*, i.

23. Newbury, "The Clans of Rwanda: An Historical Hypothesis."

24. Jefremovas, "Contested Identities," 96.

25. See Pottier, "Representations of Ethnicity in Post-Genocide Writings on Rwanda."

26. Franche, *Rwanda: Généalogie d'un génocide*.

27. Des Forges, "The Ideology of Genocide," 44.

28. Des Forges, *Defeat Is the Only Bad News*, 10.

29. d'Hertefeld, "Mythes et idéologies dans le Rwanda ancien et contemporain," 235.

30. Franche, *Rwanda: Généalogie d'un génocide*.

31. Ibid.

32. Des Forges, *Defeat Is the Only Bad News*, 2.

33. Newbury, *The Cohesion of Oppression*, 186.

34. Linden, *Church and Revolution in Rwanda*, 18.

35. von Götzen, *Durch Afrika von Ost nach West*; Kandt, *Caput Nili*; Parish, "Zwei Reisen durch Ruanda"; and Mecklenburg, *In the Heart of Africa*.

36. Note the appropriateness of the title of the paper by Tamplin: "Noble Men and Noble Savages."

37. Pratt, *Imperial Eyes*.

38. Louis, *Ruanda-Urundi*, xvii.

39. Des Forges, *Defeat Is the Only Bad News*, 96.

40. Admiralty Naval Staff, *The Belgian Congo*, 161.

41. Codere, *The Biography of an African Society*, 39. For an overview of the period of German colonization, see Kabagewa, *Ruanda unter deutscher Kolonialherrschaft*.

42. Mamdami, "From Conquest to Consent as a Basis of State Formation," 11; Prunier, *The Rwanda Crisis*, 25.

43. Camus, "Le Ruanda et l'Urundi"; Mamdami, "From Conquest to Consent As a Basis of State Formation," 11.

44. Linden, *Church and Revolution in Rwanda*, 193.

45. Prunier, *The Rwanda Crisis*, 29. Jean-Baptiste de Lamarck's scheme (1) embraced the doctrine of the inheritance of acquired characteristics, and (2) attributed the directive force of organic variation to will, habits, or environment. See Livingstone, *The Geographical Tradition*, 188.

46. Prunier, *The Rwanda Crisis*, 36.

47. On the varied histories of the Hamitic thesis, see Sanders, "The Hamitic Hypothesis." See also Taylor, *Sacrifice as Terror*, 55–97.

48. On Gobineau, see Young, *Colonial Desire*, 99–109; Todorov, *On Human Diversity*, 125–40; and Franche, *Rwanda*, 29–31.

49. Parish, "Zwei Reisen durch Ruanda," 7. This antisemitism is repeated in Sander, *Die deutschen Kolonien in Wort und Bild*, 446. These comments, which distance the Tutsi from the Jew, were opposed by other examples of antisemitism that equated the Tutsi with the Jew (as a form of negation). For example, the Roman Catholic Missionary Father Paul Barthélémy observed in 1900, "Les Batutsi sont des vrais Juifs: ils sont rapaces, flatteurs et surtout hypocrites." Quoted in Kabagewa, *Ruanda unter deutscher Kolonialherschaft*, 72. This exemplifies, again, the inconsistency of colonial discourse.

50. Gatti and Gatti, *Here is Africa*, 138–39.

51. Rigby, *African Images*, 67.

52. Kesby, *The Cultural Regions of East Africa*, 141–42.

53. Genetic research in the 1980s, if it can be upheld, suggests that Tutsi and Hutu *may* have ancestors who came from northeast Africa. But such findings neither address nor support the claim that the Tutsi are a superior race. Quoted in Taylor, *Sacrifice as Terror*, 63. See also Mamdami, *When Victims Become Killers*, 45–46.

54. Gilman, *Difference and Pathology*, 18. It has been suggested that "racial ideologies have survived independence in Rwanda and Burundi. Indeed, they have thrived in post-independence Rwanda and even in Belgium itself." Quoted

in Hintjens, "Through the Looking Glass." Tutsi stereotypes—often recycled from colonial times—were widely depicted in cartoons and writing in Rwandan newspapers and magazines during the early 1990s. See Chrétien, *Rwanda: Les médias du génocide.* I am grateful to Helen Hintjens of the University of Wales, Swansea, for this reference.

55. Sibley, "Creating Geographies of Difference," 125–26.

56. Gilman, *Difference and Pathology,* 19 (emphasis added).

57. Ibid., 20–21.

58. Jamoule, "Notre mandat sur Ruanda-Urundi"; J. Gahame, "Le Burundi sous administration belge." Quoted in Sellström and Wohlgemuth, "Historical Perspectives." These statements contradict the oft-quoted view that the Tutsi are lighter-skinned than the Hutu. Recent observers in Rwanda also refute such a statement. See Keane, *Rivers of Blood,* 15.

59. It has been suggested that the first of the White Fathers had been educated through works that highlighted the merits of the Franks who, under Clovis, had converted France to Christianity. A schema of invasions and racial divisions thus permeated their consciousness, and the Hutu and Tutsi were seen as the Gauls and Franks of Africa. See Franche, *Rwanda,* 34. Franche quotes an extreme example of Father Martial de Salviac, who saw the descendents of the Gauls as Hamites because of the coincidental similarity of the words Gaul and Galla, the name of one of the "Hamitic" groups of east Africa.

60. Quoted in Linden, *Church and Revolution in Rwanda,* 261. It would be wrong, however, to assume that all Europeans eulogized the Tutsi. For Father Alphonse Brard, a contemporary of Barthélémy (see note 49 above), "the Tutsi mystique soon wore off." Ibid., 38.

61. Grogan and Sharp, *From Congo to the Cape,* 119.

62. Barns, *The Wonderland of the Eastern Congo,* 40. The Bantu referred to were the Hutu. This is not to say that there were no alternative or contradictory voices. While Captain Geoffrey Holmes, for example, felt "how anyone with a changed heart could help falling in love with the Batusi would be beyond" him, he also saw them as "proud, arrogant and cruel." Quoted in Holmes, [untitled article].

63. Boehmer, *Colonial and Postcolonial Literature,* 82.

64. This view was associated with the German anthropologists von Eichsted and Spannaus. Quoted in Chrétien, "Tutsi et Hutu au Rwanda et Burundi," 138.

65. Rykmans, *Dominer pour servir*. Quoted in Prunier, *The Rwanda Crisis*, 11.

66. *Rapport Annuel de territoire Nyanza* (1925). Quoted in Prunier, *The Rwanda Crisis*, 6. But contradiction was certainly present in the representation of Hutu, who could also be described as athletic. See, for example, Schantz, "Urundi, Territory and People," 342.

67. Decle, "The Watussi"; McDonal et al., *Area Handbook for Burundi*; Gatti, *South of the Sahara*, 164. See also Gatti, "Jumping Giants of Africa," 25. Italics added.

68. Mecklenburg, *In the Heart of Africa*, 370.

69. Hintjens, "Through the Looking Glass"; Des Forges, *Leave None to Tell the Story*.

70. Franche, *Rwanda*, 12.

71. Lemarchand, *Burundi*, 7. Lemarchand also notes that a description of the differences between Hutu and Tutsi, carried in the prestigious journal the *Economist*, is almost a "travesty of reality."

72. Franche, *Rwanda*, 12. It is also noted that the French nobility and bourgeoisie had lighter skin and more delicate hands and features than those of the peasants.

73. de Waal, "Genocide in Rwanda," 1. The tallest of the Tutsi, it has been argued, were a "selectively bred caste." See Kesby, *The Cultural Regions of East Africa*, 144.

74. Malkki, *Purity and Exile*, 79. Malkki shows how such stereotypes live on today among Hutu refugees in Tanzania.

75. Mamdani, "From Conquest to Consent As the Basis of State Formation," 10.

76. For example, Pagès, *Un royaume hamite au centre de l'Afrique*. On the role of missionaries in Rwanda's history, see Linden, *Church and Revolution in Rwanda*.

77. Mecklenburg, *In the Heart of Africa*.

78. Fabian, *Out of Our Minds*.

79. Mecklenburg, *In the Heart of Africa*. The most detailed account of the Mecklenburg expedition is the work of the Polish anthropologist Czekanowski, *Forschungen im Nil-Congo-Zwischengebiet*.

80. See, for example, Mecklenburg, "A Land of Giants and Pygmies"; Hildebrand, "The Geography of Games"; and Shantz, "Urundi, Territory and

People." Shantz was probably taking poetic license in assuming that *gusimbuka* was practiced in Burundi.

81. d'Hertefelt and de Lame (eds.), *Societé, culture, et histoire du Rwanda*. Oddly, the one reference to a paper dealing with *gusimbuka* is included in a section on dance. Being located in academe and in Belgium, d'Hertefelt and de Lame failed to include much English-language or popular writing that referred to Rwandan folk culture.

82. Jokl, "High jump Technique of the Central African Watussis"; "African Man-power"; *Physiology of Exercise*, 124–28; and *Medical Sociology and Cultural Anthropology of Sport and Physical Education*, 70. (This latter publication is a self-plagiarism of Jokl et al., *Sports in the Cultural Pattern of the World*.)

83. Franche, *Rwanda*, 48. It was de Lacger's *Ruanda* that formed the basis of the first Rwandan-authored history of Rwanda in Kinyarwanda, published in 1943 and reprinted in 1947 by the White Fathers. Ibid.

84. Des Forges, *Leave None to Tell the Story*.

85. Prunier, *The Rwanda Crisis*, 39.

86. Linden, *Church and Revolution in Rwanda*, 211.

87. Lemarchand, *Rwanda and Burundi*, 34.

88. Linden, *Church and Revolution in Rwanda*, 17; Maquet, *The Premise of Inequality in Rwanda*. Maquet used only Tutsi as his respondents, assuming them to have superior knowledge and greater intelligence.

89. Lemarchand, *Rwanda and Burundi*, 32.

90. Chrétien, "Hutu et Tutsi au Rwanda et Burundi," 147.

91. Vidal, *Sociologie des passions*. Quoted in Prunier, *The Rwanda Crisis*, 37. Kagame's great-uncle had commanded a "formidable army" under Rwabugiri. It has been argued that Kagame's "aristocratic representation of pre-colonial Rwanda" was vindicated by Maquet (in *The Premise of Inequality*), one of Kagame's protégés. See Pottier, "Representations of Ethnicity in Post-Genocide Writings," 37.

92. Malkki, *Purity and Exile*, 14.

93. Sibomana, *Hope for Rwanda*, 80. If Sibomana's words are taken literally, Kagame's brief observations about *gusimbuka* (see chapter 2) need to be read with a degree of skepticism, but so, too, must the writings of a number of others.

94. Webster, Ogot, and Chrétien, "The Great Lakes Region, 1500–1800," 804–805.

95. Vansina, *Living with Africa*, 64.

96. Moore, *Anthropology and Africa*, 128.

97. Jefremovas, "Treacherous Waters," 302, and "Contested Identities." The possible "reinvention" of *gusimbuka* is touched on in chapter 2.

98. This draws on E. Schildkrout, "The Spectacle of Africa." Quoted in Mirzoeff, *Bodyscape*, 139.

99. Linden, *Church and Revolution in Rwanda*, 226–27. See also Prunier, *The Rwanda Crisis*, 50.

100. Des Forges, *Leave None to Tell the Story*.

101. Bhatt, "Ethnic Absolutism and Authoritarian Spirit."

102. Taylor, *Sacrifice as Terror*, 28.

103. Banks, *Ethnicity*, 165.

2. Gusimbuka-Urukiramende

1. See, for example, Mangan, *The Games Ethic and Imperialism*; Bale and Sang, *Kenyan Running*; and Deville-Danthu, *Le sport en noir et blanc*.

2. Guttmann, *From Ritual to Record*.

3. Galtung, "Sport and International Understanding."

4. MacAloon, *This Great Symbol*. The world exhibitions shared many of their qualities and characteristics with those of the Olympics. See Gregory, "Power, Knowledge and Geography," 79–83.

5. Hoberman, *Darwin's Athletes*. An interest in this subject continues into the twenty-first century. See Entine, *Taboo*.

6. Deville-Danthu, *Le sport en noir et blanc*, 24. The colonial "machine" and the "processing" of the natives were pervasive metaphors in colonial rhetoric. See Bale and Sang, *Kenyan Running*, 97; and Young, *Colonial Desire*, 166–67. On the use of photographs as "transformation" illustrations, see Maxwell, *Colonial Photography and Exhibitions*, 116–17.

7. The literature is well reviewed in Hoberman, *Darwin's Athletes*.

8. The IAAF maintains records for each affiliated country. In this way, nations can be compared hierarchically. Butler, *Statistics Handbook*, 302, 473.

9. McClelland, "The Numbers of Reason," 59–60.

10. Damkjær, "Innocent Gymnasts in Turbulent Times," 131.

11. Alexandre Massonnet, in conversation, Paris, 15 April 2000; Danielle de Lame (Koninklijk Museum voor Midden-Afrika), in conversation, Tervuren, Belgium, 12 March 1999; Peter Mugisha, in conversation, Oslo, Norway, 23 May 2001. However, some Hutu may have been more familiar with *gusimbuka*

(and perceived it as a Tutsi activity) than these statements suggest. I was informed by Professor Jack Hyatt of the University of Western Ontario that a Canadian investigator into the genocide stated that among the atrocities he encountered was the cutting of the heel tendons of murdered Tutsi. Such an act was said by Hutu to symbolize an end to their high jumping abilities. Jack Hyatt, in conversation, London, Ontario, 30 March 2001.

12. See Watts, "Collective Wish Images," 86. The major source by a Rwandan writer is a doctoral thesis by Ndejuru, "Studien zur Rolle der Leibesübungen in der Traditionellen Gesellschaft Rwanda." I am extremely grateful to Roland Renson of the Katholieke Universiteit, Leuven, Belgium, for alerting me to this study and to Wolfgang Decker, of the Deutsche Sporthochschule, Cologne, for providing me with a copy of it. While born in Rwanda and receiving his early education there, Ndejuru spent thirteen years studying in Germany before submitting his doctoral dissertation. On the significance of place in written work, see Curry, *The Work in the World*.

13. Massonnet, "Rôle et place du sport et du jeu au Rwanda," 48. He states—without citing any evidence—that Europeans had witnessed *gusimbuka* "at the end of the nineteenth century." I am grateful to Jeroen Scheerder of the Katholieke Universiteit, Leuven, for alerting me to this reference.

14. Des Forges, *Defeat Is the Only Bad News*, 64.

15. Burton, *The Lakes Region of Central Africa*, 108.

16. Quoted in Schweitzer, *Emin Pasha*, 111.

17. Decle, "The Watusi," 426. In this quotation, colonial narrative is seen to "contain resistance"; it is as if Tutsi inhospitality was unreasonable. See Barnett, "Impure and Worldly Geography," 245.

18. Cited in *Kreuz und Schwert*, 212. Quoted in Meyer, *Les Barundi*, 93.

19. Quoted in "Letter from Father Joseph," 4. I am grateful to Jeroen Scheerder for translating the latter quotation from the Dutch. Allusions were often made to impressive leaps during dances.

20. There is no mention of any form of high jumping in Burundi in Meyer, *Les Barundi* (which includs a chapter entitled "Jeux—danses—Musique"). Neither is it mentioned in Zuure, "Missie en ontspanning: Sport en spel bij de Burundi" or in "Negervolksspelen," a short, anonymous report on the games of Burundi.

21. Roscoe, *The Northern Bantu*, 141. Roscoe had certainly been in Uganda before 1894. See Ashe, *Chronicles of Uganda*, 165.

22. Des Forges, *Defeat Is the Only Bad News*, 33–34, 126.

23. Ibid., 140.

24. Ibid., 16–17.

25. These included, for example, von Götzen, *Durch Afrika von Ost nach West*; Bauman, *Durch Massailand zur Nilquelle*; Parish "Zwei Reisen durch Ruanda"; Piscicelli, "Nel Ruanda"; Norden, *Fresh Tracks in the Belgian Congo*; and Schebesta, *My Pygmy and Negro Hosts*, 206.

26. Des Forges, *Defeat Is the Only Bad News*, 65.

27. Fabian, *Out of Our Minds*, 8.

28. Mecklenburg, *Ins innerste Afrika* (published in English as *In the Heart of Africa*). It is possible that further research into the archives of missionary organizations in Germany and Belgium, and in the archives of the White Fathers in Rome, would reveal evidence of pre-Mecklenburg contact with *gusimbuka*. Mecklenburg was a pivotal figure in disseminating news of *gusimbuka* to Europe and North America. His life was characterized by colonial exploration and administration and an involvement in sports. The study of anthropology at the University of Dresden enabled him to undertake visits to Africa. He was the first European to visit Lake Chad in 1906 and directed scientific expeditions to central Africa (in 1907–08) and Arabia. From 1912 to 1914 he was governor of the German colony of Togo. His sporting involvement included the introduction of thoroughbred horse racing to Germany. As a golfer, he became president of the Heiligendamm Golf Club, and as a tennis player he assumed the role of president of the Blue-White club—the non-Prussian upper-class club—of Berlin. He was also a board member of the Central German Skeet and Trap Federation and developed an interest in early German motor sports. From 1926 to 1969, Mecklenburg was a member of the board of the German Olympic Committee, and was its president from 1949–69. He was also a member of the International Olympic Committee from 1926–56, and led the constitution of the German Olympic Committee on the day after the formation of the Federal Republic in September 1949. Mecklenburg, who received an honorary doctorate from the University of Rostock, died in 1969. It was alleged by the president of the IOC that during World War II he had a "clean record." I am grateful to Arnd Krüger for much of this information. See also Rürup, *1936: Die Olympischen Spiele*, 223.

29. Honke and Honke, *Le Rwanda et les allemands, 1884–1916*.

30. Mecklenburg, *In the Heart of Africa*, 59.

31. "[D]er Sport des Hochspringens sei bei den Watussi bodenständig ist richtig. Die Watussi solien von jeher ausgezeichnete Springer gewesen sein."

Quoted in Kna, "Die Watussi als Springkünstler," 460. Later, the distinction was clearly made between the European introduction of gymnastics and soccer and a number of native sports, including *gusimbuka-urukiramende*. See Bourgeois, *Banyarwanda et Barundi*, 626. To my knowledge, there is only one documented denial of the indigenous character of *gusimbuka*, which I discuss in chapter 3.

32. Smith, "Aspects de l'esthétique au Ruanda." See also Lestrade, *Notes d'ethnographie du Rwanda*, 8. I am also grateful for a discussion on this subject with Dr. Viviane Baeke of the Koninklijk Museum voor Midden-Afrika, Tervuren, Belgium, 26 January 1998.

33. See Coupez and Kamanzi, *Literature de cour au Rwanda*, 80–81: "[E]lle vit parmi les autres garçons; on vise la cible et elle les bat, on saute et elle les bat." Note also Gasarabwe Laroche, *Le Geste Rwanda*, 41: "Les batusi se vantaient de sauter commes des gazelles, parce que leur ventre ne les gênait pas."

34. Jacob, *Dictionnaire Rwandais-Français*.

35. Interview with Professor André Coupez of the Koninklijk Museum voor Midden-Afrika, Tervuren, Belgium, 26 January 1998. Ndejuru undertakes a lengthy but speculative analysis of the words *gusimbuka-urukiramende* in which he suggests that because *gusimbuka*, unlike spear throwing, archery, or running, had no utilitarian purpose, it must carry deep symbolic significance. See Ndejuru, *Studien zur Rolle der Leibesübungen*. But Ndejuru is surely wrong to assume that high jumping had no utilitarian purpose, especially in times of war. In oral societies such as Rwanda, it is also important to bear in mind whether the oral record of *gusimbuka* became diversified as it was handed down. It is possible, but in my view unlikely, that the words *gusimbuka-urukiramende* described something in 1880 that was very different from what they described in 1940. The extent of that difference provides a potential (though exceedingly problematic) line of inquiry for scholars interested in the history of Rwandan body culture.

36. Jokl, *Physiology of Exercise*, 125 (italics added). See also Avoy, "Physical Endowment of African People," 93. No evidence of a precolonial presence is provided in either case. Maquet's fieldwork in Rwanda took place from 1949–51. Maquet, *The Premise of Inequality in Ruanda*, 21 (italics added). Maquet's respondents were Tutsi people "who had been young when the old regime [i.e., of the precolonial period] was still a working concern," ibid., 1. Like Mecklenburg, Jokl was a major figure in the historiography of *gusimbuka*. Born in Breslau, Germany (today Wrocław, Poland) in 1907, throughout his life he maintained an

interest in sports. He was an athlete whose best events were the sprints and 400-meter hurdles, though the belief, encouraged by some English-language sources, that he represented Germany in the Amsterdam Olympics in 1928 is a myth. In that year he obtained his certificate as a high school teacher of physical education. Soon after, Jokl published his first medical study and subsequently developed a prominent career in sports science. Following medical training at the universities of Breslau and Berlin, he obtained an internship at the University of Breslau's medical school hospital. While there he was introduced to sports medicine through an analysis of the medical assessments of athletes participating in the 1928 Olympics. In 1931, Jokl was appointed as the first director of the Department of Sports Medicine at Breslau, but in 1933 left Germany following enforcement of the "Aryan paragraph" of the Law for the Restoration of the Profesional Civil Service, which mandated the retirement of civil servants of non-Aryan ancestry. He settled in South Africa and became director of physical education at Stellenbosch University as well as physical education consultant to the South African Defense Force. During his time there, he developed a national program in sports science and authored a number of articles on kinesiology, physiology, and sports. Jokl claimed to have visited Rwanda in the late 1930s, and his 1941 paper, "Watussi High Jumping," remains the most detailed scientific treatment of this body cultural practice in the English language. He frequently referred to *gusimbuka-urukiramende* (though not in these words) in later books and articles. In 1952 he took a position at the University of Kentucky, where be worked on rehabilitation, exercise, sports medicine, and physiology. He was a prominent figure in the establishment of the International Committee for Sports Science and Physical Education. Jokl published books and articles on subjects ranging from physical rehabilitation to dance. Following his retirement, he received honorary professorships from the universities of Berlin and Frankfurt, and, in a gesture of reconciliation, a street in Cologne was named after him. In 1993 he received the Distinguished Service Award from the United States Sports Academy for his contributions to sports medicine. Ernst Jokl died in December, 1997. I am grateful to Arnd Krüger and Steve Bailey for much of this information. See also van der Merwe, "Ernst Franz Jokl."

37. Roome, *Tramping through Africa*, 101. Jan Vansina has suggested that certain chiefs (Tutsi, naturally) and Europeans could have collaborated in (re)inventing *gusimbuka*, but this is nothing more than speculation. Jan Vansina, personal communication, 16 February 1998. Additional photographs of *gusimbuka*

by Roome and other English missionaries are held in the archives of the Mid-Africa Mission of the Church Missionary Society, London.

38. Des Forges, *Defeat Is the Only Bad News*, 122.

39. See, for example, Jack, *On the Congo Frontier*, 247.

40. Smith, "A Journey into Belgian Ruanda," 11.

41. Kna, "Die Watussi als Springkünstler," 461.

42. Stanley Smith, letter, 23 November 1920. Ruanda Mission collection, Church Missionary Society Archives, London. I am extremely grateful to Rosemary Keen for alerting me to relevant written and photographic material housed in the CMS Archives.

43. Des Forges, *Defeat Is the Only Bad News*, 275.

44. Ibid., 4.

45. Kanyamachumbi, *Société, culture, et pouvoir politique en afrique interlactustre*, 164.

46. Des Forges, *Defeat Is the Only Bad News*, 290, 313.

47. Linden, *Church and Revolution in Rwanda*, 13 (emphasis added).

48. Prunier, *The Rwanda Crisis*, notes that "all men were part of the intore" (14), while Destexhe, *Rwanda and Genocide in the Twentieth Century*, states that "it would be extremely difficult to find any kind of cultural or folkloric custom that was specifically Hutu or Tutsi" (36). However, Gasarabwe Laroche, in *Le geste Rwanda*, describes Hutu and Twa members of the *intore* as privileged.

49. Massonet, "Rôle et Place du Sport et du Jeu au Rwanda," 55. No evidence is given for this statement, and it is not clear whether "sports" here refers to the training of the *intore* or to a more recreational activity.

50. Ndejuru, *Studien zur Rolle der Leibesübungen*. This avoidance of the word Tutsi may have been the result of a desire to uphold political correctness at a time when it was considered undesirable to distinguish between ethnic groups in Rwanda. That *gusimbuka* was not a typical Tutsi activity was the conclusion reached by Alexandre Massonnet "after many interviews" in Rwanda during the 1990s. Alexandre Massonnet, e-mail communication, 6 December 1999.

51. Des Forges, "The Ideology of Genocide," 45.

52. Linden, *Church and Revolution in Rwanda*, 17. When, in the early twentieth century, members of the *intore* were encouraged to attend mission schools of the White Fathers it was noted that "the boys, accustomed to purely physical training in dancing, jumping, spear throwing, archery, swimming, and

court etiquette, were thoroughly bored by the long classroom lessons, and few attended regularly." Ibid., 80.

53. Kashamura, *Le mœurs et les civilisation des peuples des grand lacs africains*, 128.

54. Codere, *The Biography of an African Country*, 53.

55. Ibid., 54–55.

56. Kagame, *Le code des institutions politiques du Rwanda précolonial*. See also Bourgeois, *Banyarwanda et Barundi*, 276.

57. Schumacher, "Hamitische Wohrsegerei in Ruanda."

58. This may be illustrated by the fact that of 17 photographs taken by Baron Greindl at a festival for the Mwami Musinga, sometime in 1918–19, none include *gusimbuka*. Photographic archives of the Koninklijk Museum voor Midden-Afrika, Tervuren, Belgium.

59. Smith, "Acts XVI," 9; Gunter, *Inside Africa*, 675.

60. Gatti and Gatti, *Here is Africa*, 143.

61. Gatti, *South of the Sahara*, 170.

62. Des Forges, *Defeat Is the Only Bad News*, 16.

63. Maquet, *The Premise of Inequality in Rwanda*, 21.

64. Bourgeois, *Banyarwanda et Barundi*, 627.

65. Pagès, *Un royaume hamite au centre de l'Afrique*, plate VI.

66. Church, "From Dr. Church," 16.

67. Pauwels, "Jeux et divertissements au Rwanda," 241: "Si des enfants de 12 à 13 ans parviennent à sauter à plus d'un mètre de hauter la raison en est que les Nanya-Rwanda ont l'habitude de placer toujours devant l'obstacle une botte de gazon qui leur sert en quelques sorte de tremplin."

68. Ndejuru, *Studien zur Rolle der Leibesübungen*, 156, 187; Massonet, "Rôle et place de sport et du jeu au Rwanda," 54.

69. Ndejuru, *Studien zur Rolle der Leibesübungen*, 244, n. 873. The status of Ndejuru's informants is unknown.

70. Barns, *The Wonderland of the Eastern Congo*, 46.

71. Quoted in Kna, "Die Watussi als Springkünstler," 459.

72. Ibid., 461.

73. Gasarabwe-Laroche, "Meaningful Gestures," 32.

74. I draw here on Malkki, *Purity and Exile*, 92.

75. Ndejuru, *Studien zur Rolle der Leibesbüngen*, 184. Ndejuru was unable to establish from any of his informants the original meaning of the word

urukiramende. The notion that *gusimbuka*—as witnessed by Europeans—formed a rite of passage seems to be a gross simplification, given that rites of passage are generally thought of as events which an individual would not repeat.

76. Ibid., 187. See also Gasarabwe-Laroche, *Le geste Rwanda*, 175.

77. Taylor, *Sacrifice as Terror*, 114, 119.

78. Ibid., 124–25.

79. Taylor, *Milk, Honey, and Money*, 12.

80. Spencer, "Introduction: Interpretations of the Dance in Anthropology," 24 (italics added).

81. This is evident in a photograph of a high jump at a "government Fête Day" at Kiseyi, 1937. Mid-Africa Mission collection (AA1/48/8), Church Missionary Society Archives, London.

82. Roome, *Tramping through Africa*, 103. In the original print from which Figure 3.2 is taken, an athlete is included on the extreme left of the photograph. He seems to be another jumper, following too close for comfort to the athlete clearing the bar.

83. Ndejuru, *Studien zur Rolle der Leibesübungen*, 186–87.

84. This is well described, for example, in Balfour, *Lords of the Equator*, 241. Performing as a group was also typical of German gymnastics. See Mosse, *The Image of Man*, 44.

85. Severn, *Congo Pilgrim*, 196.

86. Bourgeois, *Banyarwanda et Barundi*, 627.

87. Ndejuru, *Studien zur Rolle der Leibesübungen*, 187.

88. Holmes, [untitled article], 6 (exclamation marks as in original).

89. Church, "From Dr. Church," 17. See also Makower, *The Coming of the Rain*, 39–40.

90. Farson, *Behind God's Back*, 390.

91. Ellen Gatti, *Exploring We Would Go*, 78.

92. Joseph Ghesquiere, in conversation, Archennes, Belgium, 12 January, 1996.

93. Jan Vansina, personal correspondence, 16 February 1998.

94. Massonnet, "Rôle et place du sport et du jeu au Rwanda," 55. The Ruanda-Urundi five-franc postage stamp featured spear throwers.

95. The inclusion of Tutsi in the movie reflects a considerable degree of poetic license, given that they are not mentioned by name in Rider Haggard's book on which the film was (loosely) based. In *King Solomon's Mines*, published in

1885, Haggard did, however, allude to the athleticism of the "Kukuana people," who (modeled on Tutsi?) were fantastic runners: "Not one of them was under six feet in height, while many stood six feet three or four" (133, 135).

96. Des Forges, *Defeat Is the Only Bad News*, 284.

97. Linden, *Church and Revolution in Rwanda*, 159.

98. Des Forges, *Defeat Is the Only Bad News*, 290.

99. Linden, *Church and Revolution in Rwanda*, 167.

100. Ibid., 199, 201.

101. Ibid., 159.

102. Ibid., 188.

103. Bourgeois, *Banyarwanda et Barundi*, 296.

104. Gildea and Young, "Rwanda and Burundi," 2. This quotation essentializes Tutsi as an elite group. Most could not have afforded such Western trappings, however.

105. Massonet, "Rôle et place du sport et du jeu au Rwanda," 57.

106. Des Forges, *Defeat Is the Only Bad News*, 247. However, the resulting death in 1921 of two of Musinga's sons from meningitis was seen as the result of enforced swimming lessons. This greatly distressed the court.

107. Sharp, "Letter from Dr. Sharp," 3.

108. *Ruanda-Urundi: Social Achievements*, 66.

109. Codere, *The Biography of an African Society*. See also Dupriez, *Guide de voyageur au Congo Belge*, 448; and Massonet, "Rôle et place du sport et du jeu au Rwanda," 57.

110. Pauwels, "Jeux et divertissements au Rwanda," 377.

111. Codere, *The Biography of an African Society*, 22.

112. In 1950 they were described as "danseurs ou *intore.*" See Rosmant, "Au pays des pages danseurs," 15.

113. Interviews with Marcel d'Hertefeld, Tervuren, Belgium, 13 December, 1996; and André Coupez, Tervuren, 26 January 1996. *Gusimbuka* was unlikely to have been performed after 1960.

114. Personal communication, M. B. Ronaldson, 6 August 1998.

115. Maquet, *Ruanda: Essai photographique.*

116. Interview with Professor Joseph Ghesquiere, Archennes, 12 December 1996.

117. MacCannell, *The Tourist*, 91–107. In the 1990s the privatized Rwandan dance troupe made tours of several European cities.

118. Kirshenblatt-Gimblett, "Objects of Ethnography," 420.

119. Cresswell, *In Place/Out of Place*, 23.

120. For example, limbo dancing has been suggested as a mode of resistance available to the colonial Caribbean as a practice originating in Africa and reinterpreted on the slave ships. See Harris, *History, Fable, and Myth in the Caribbean and Guianas*. Quoted in Parry, "Resistance Theory/Theorising Resistance," 173–74. In late twentieth-century Australia, Aboriginal dance has been read as a potent symbol of resistance and a mode of empowerment. See Gilbert, "Dance, Movement, and Resistance Politics." Modern sport has also been claimed as a vehicle for resistance, as in the examples of West Indian cricket, baseball in the Dominican Republic, and running in Kenya. In each nation, sport has enabled the colonized to defeat the (neo)colonialist master at his own game. See, respectively, James, *Beyond a Boundary*; Klein, *Sugarball*; and Bale and Sang, *Kenyan Running*.

121. Tiffin and Lawson, "The Textuality of Empire," 6.

122. This could be implied from the writing of, for example, Ngugi wa Thiongo. For some applications of Ngugi's work to modern sports, see Bale and Sang, *Kenyan Running*.

123. Tiffin and Lawson, "Introduction: The Textuality of Empire," 6.

124. Conversation with Joseph Ghesquiere, Archennes, 12 December 1996.

125. Bhabha, "Of Mimicry and Man," 153.

126. Ibid.

127. Ibid.

128. Ibid., 157.

129. Ibid.

130. Linden, *Church and Revolution in Rwanda*, 255. The so-called "ethnic" designations are, nevertheless, still widely used.

131. *Ruanda-Urundi: Social Achievements*, 62.

132. Torgovnick, *Gone Primitive*. It might be added that while "the primitive" has been seen as a theme linking seminal work of high modernism such as sculpture, painting, and music, the same cannot be said of sport, also a paradigm of modernity. While sport incorporates "the primitive," it cannot be said to have been influenced by it. See Liveley, *Masks*. L'art nègre was not paralleled by le sport nègre, even if some black sportsmen were the object of negrophilia. See Archer-Straw, *Negrophilia*, 44–49.

133. The notion of the trialectic was introduced by Eichberg, "Kropskulturens Trialektik" and subsequently elaborated in many of his writings. See Eichberg, *Body Cultures*. Gleyse presents a similar three-fold typology of body cultures. In seeking the premises for the archeology of body culture, he recognizes three metaphors (or paradigms) for the dominant movement cultures of the period since the 1600s. These are the factory, the steam engine, and the computer. The first two reflect, in different ways, a concern with the instrumental rationalization of the body. The third reflects goals that are internal to the subject and are nonpublic, thus making sense only to those who do it. See Gleyse, "Instrumental Rationalization of Human Movement," 254–55. Thrift, on the other hand, suggests that a body culture such as running or jumping may center around five overlapping expressive body practices: (1) ritual, as in festive celebrations; (2) work, in cases when it is "sportized" to make it less tedious; (3) community construction, as in representational team sports; (4) leisure and recreation; and (5) formal entertainment. See Thrift, "The Still Point," 143–44.

134. Brownell, *Training the Body for China*, 20.

3. Imagined Olympians

1. See, for example, Barnes and Duncan (eds.), *Writing Worlds*, and Duncan and Ley, *Place/Culture/Representation*. The terms *pictorial* and *literary* are called, respectively, *graphic* and *semantic* (or *metaphorical*) in Gren, *Earth Writing*, 49.

2. Marcus and Fischer, *Anthropology as Cultural Critique*, 9.

3. Olsson, *Lines of Power/Limits of Language*, 167.

4. Gren, *Earth Writing*, 148.

5. Gregory, "Areal Differentiation and Post-Modern Human Geography," 88.

6. Brosseau, "Geography's Literatures," 348.

7. Quigley, "Deconstructing Colonial Fictions," 105–6.

8. Said, *Orientalism*, 55. An elaboration of the distinction between mental maps and imaginative geography is found in the piece by Derek Gregory, "Imaginative Geographies," in Johnston et al., *The Dictionary of Human Geography*, 372–73.

9. Said, *Orientalism*, 71.

10. Ibid., 71–72.

11. Quayson, *Postcolonialism: Theory, Practice, or Process?*, 69. Note also Gregory, "Power, Knowledge, and Geography," 79; and Brown, "The Solitude of Edward Said."

12. Quayson, *Postcolonialism: Theory, Practice, or Process?*, 4.

13. Said, *Orientalism*, 71–72.

14. Boehmer, *Colonial and Postcolonial Literature*, 13. See also Duncan, "Sites of Representation," 40–41.

15. Gregory, "Between the Book and the Lamp," 29. See also Thomas, *Colonialism's Culture*, 37.

16. Miller, *Blank Darkness*, 18.

17. Gikandi, *Maps of Englishness*, 169.

18. Gregory, "Power, Knowledge, and Geography," 78.

19. Gren, *Earth Writing*. It follows that my own images are representations of representations of representations.

20. Gregory, "Between the Book and the Lamp," 34. See also Gregory, "Power, Knowledge, and Geography."

21. Steiner, "Travel Engravings and the Construction of the Primitive," 222. Note also Rony, *The Third Eye*, 65–66.

22. Attilio Gatti, *South of the Sahara*, 169 (emphases added). An African reading of African dance might be quite different, of course. For instance, consider: "La danse! Le chant rythmique et la danse! … Actes de délivrance. Epreuve de vitalité, de virilité et d'harmonie physique et mentale." See Kala-Lobé, "La Vocation africaine de sport," 35.

23. Ryan, *The Cartographic Eye*, 129.

24. Ashcroft, Griffiths, and Tiffin, *The Empire Writes Back*, 127. In addition to the north-south dichotomy, other colonial polarities can be recognized; for example, industrious-indolent, adult-child, clean-dirty, male-female. See Pennycook, *English and the Discourse of Colonialism*, 47–65.

25. Lowe, *Critical Terrains*, 7. Among other critics of Said's *Orientalism* are Clifford, *The Predicament of Culture*, 255–76; Sax, "The Hall of Mirrors"; and Mackenzie, *Orientalism: History, Theory, and the Arts*.

26. Bivona, *Desire and Contradiction*, 37.

27. Boehmer, *Colonial and Postcolonial Literature*, 79 (italics added).

28. Driver, "Geography, Empire, and Visualisation," 6. Driver is here concerned with live subjects at colonial exhibitions, but surely the colonialists' encounters with indigenous people in situ equally involved a display—a "world-as-exhibition." See also Driver, *Geography Militant*, 146–69.

29. Dimeo, "Race, Colonialism, and the Emergence of Football in India," 17. Martial race theory is mainly associated with historical studies of masculinity in South Asia. See, for example, Sinha, *Colonial Masculinity*, notably chapter

2. In an African context, see Mazrui, "Boxer Muhammad Ali and Soldier Idi Amin as International Political Symbols," 191–94.

30. Naylor and Jones, "Writing Orderly Geographies of Distant Lands," 275.

31. See several of the essays in Blunt and Rose (eds.), *Writing Women and Space*.

32. Mills, "Knowledge, Gender, and Empire," 37.

33. Roome, *Tramping through Africa*, v.

34. Ellen Gatti, *Exploring We Would Go*; Gatti and Gatti, *Here Is Africa*.

35. Farson, *Behind God's Back*, ii.

36. Ryan, *The Cartographic Eye*.

37. Rose, *Feminism and Geography*, 70.

38. Phillips, *Mapping Men and Empire*, 45.

39. Boehmer, *Colonial and Postcolonial Literature*, 32.

40. On the role of the Royal Geographical Society in exploration, see, for example, James Ryan, *Picturing Empire*; Simon Ryan, *The Cartographic Eye*; and Barnett, "Impure and Worldly Geography." On the RGS's attitude toward women, see Blunt, *Travel, Gender, and Imperialism*, 148–59.

41. Bivona, *Desire and Contradiction*, 52; and Richards, *The Imperial Archive*, 50. This, Bivona argues, marks Carroll as a critic of the epistemological foundations of cultural imperialism.

42. Spurr, *The Rhetoric of Empire*, 3.

43. Bivona, *Desire and Contradiction*, 52.

44. The term *image world* is taken from Poole, *Vision, Race, and Modernity*, 7. Nor was there only a single colonial reader. For example, those with a background in sports would surely tend to read *gusimbuka* differently from those more interested in exploration or wildlife.

45. Spurr, *The Rhetoric of Empire*. The twelve modes are surveillance, appropriation, aestheticization, classification, debasement, negation, affirmation, idealization, insubstantialization, naturalization, eroticization, and resistance.

46. Ibid., 7. Spurr explains the variety of rhetorical modes by asserting that, as modern civilized human beings, we assert authority over the savage both within us and abroad. But the very energy devoted to such an assertion acknowledges its own incompleteness *as* authority. When we obey or are obeyed, how much of that obedience is mere mimicry? Colonial discourse bears this constant uncertainty, leading to an inherent confusion of identity and difference.

47. Slater, "Situating Geopolitical Representations," 70.

48. Good examples are Driver, "Geography, Empire, and Visualization"; Gregory, "Between the Book and the Lamp"; Jackson, "Constructions Of Culture, Representations of Race"; and Morin, "British Women Travellers and Construction of Racial Difference across the Nineteenth Century American West."

49. Schwartz, "The Geography Book," 124.

50. McClintock, *Imperial Leather*, 124.

51. Ryan, *The Cartographic Eye*, 128.

52. Barnett, "Impure and Worldly Geography," 245.

53. Attilio Gatti, "Jumping Giants of Africa," 25.

54. Attilio Gatti, "The Kingdom of the Giants," 8.

55. Crang, "Picturing Practices," 361.

56. Ryan, *The Cartographic Eye*, 131.

57. Ibid. Recording the height of the athletes and the jumps they achieved was widespread in early twentieth-century manuals on track and field sports. See, for example, Webster, *Why? The Science of Athletics*.

58. See, for example, Bale and Sang, *Kenyan Running*, 75.

59. Mallon, *The 1904 Olympic Games*, 205–6. Mallon quotes extensively from *Spalding's Official Athletic Almanac for 1905: Special Olympic Number Containing the Official Report of the Olympic Games of 1904*, 249–59.

60. Ibid., 208; Schaap, *An Illustrated History of the Olympics*, 77.

61. Mallon, *The 1904 Olympic Games*, 208–9.

62. Eichberg, "Forward Race and the Laughter of Pygmies." It is possible, however, to read such laughter as ironic resistance. See Rony, *The Third Eye*, 40.

63. Quoted in Mallon, *The 1904 Olympic Games*, 209. The rhetoric in the report of the 1904 games strongly suggests that a prevailing view was that Africans, like other peoples, certainly had athletic potential, even if the results were to (temporarily) temper that view. Baron de Coubertin also acknowledged such potential, noting that the "charades" of the "anthropology days" would lose their appeal "when black men, red men and yellow men learn to run, jump and throw, and leave the white men behind them." Quoted in Killanin and Rodda, *The Olympic Games*, 55.

64. Mecklenburg, *In the Heart of Africa*, 59.

65. Diem, *Weltgeschichte des Sports*, 87; Jan Czekanowski, letter to Carl Diem, 22 November 1958 (Mappe 478, Carl und Liselott Diem Archiv, Deutsche Sporthochschule, Cologne.). I am grateful to Jürgen Buschmann for

supplying me with a copy of this letter. It is possible, of course, that Diem's figure of 2.53 is a misreading of Czekanowski's 2.35.

66. Schumacher, "Tanz und Spiel in Rwanda," 391; Pauwels, "Jeux et divertissements au Rwanda," 241; and Gourdinne, "Dans l'est Afrique allemand," 383.

67. Jokl, "High Jump Technique of the Central African Watussis," 146; and Jokl, *The Physiology of Exercise*, 126. There is a suggestion that Jokl's "scientific" observations were, at times, based on highly partial and secondary evidence, despite his claim to have visited Rwanda. His observations that a hemp rope was used in Tutsi high jumping seems to have been based solely on the famous Mecklenburg photograph (shown in chapter 4) which he included in his paper. Every other photograph of Tutsi high jumping that I have seen shows a rigid reed as the crossbar. It is also difficult to reconcile both the absence of Jokl's own photographs of *gusimbuka* and his assertion in "High Jump Technique ..." that Tutsi made up the majority of Rwanda's population with the report of a "scientific" visit to the country.

68. Roome, *Tramping through Africa*, 103.

69. Ndejuru, *Studien zur Rolle der Leibesübungen*, 154–55.

70. Attilio Gatti, *South of the Sahara*, 171 (emphasis added).

71. Birnbaum, "Reception in Ruanda," 306; Balfour, *Lords of the Equator*, 241; Belotti, *Fabulous Congo*, 34.

72. Severn, *Congo Pilgrim*, 22; Roome, *Tramping through Africa*, 103.

73. Catlow, *In Search of the Primitive*, 25; Birnbaum, "Reception in Ruanda," 307; Balfour, *Lords of the Equator*, 242; Roome, *Tramping through Africa*, 103.

74. Kna, "Die Watussi als Springkünstler," 459.

75. Mecklenburg, *In the Heart of Africa*, 59; Attilio Gatti, *South of the Sahara*, 171; Jokl, "High Jump Technique of the Central African Watussis," 147; Birnbaum, "Reception in Ruanda," 307; Severn, *Congo Pilgrim*, 22; Catlow, *In Search of the Primitive*, 25. Arguably the fullest single summary of the mathematics of *gusimbuka* is provided by Bourgeois, who stated that the two vertical rods were placed two meters apart, the athlete's approach run was fifteen to twenty meters long, the termite mound was twenty to thirty centimeters high, and the jumpers jumped on the order of 2.25 meters. This inveterate quantifier also recorded that Tutsi javelin throwers achieved throws between sixty and seventy meters. See Bourgeois, *Banyarwanda et Barundi*, 627. For a critique of this kind of representation, see Barnes, *Logics of Dislocation*, 161–62, 172–73.

76. Jokl, *Physiology of Exercise*, 126.

77. Smith, "A Journey into Belgian Ruanda," 11.

78. Barns, *The Wonderland of the Eastern Congo*, 45.

79. Quoted in Buck-Morss, *The Dialectics of Seeing*, 326.

80. Butchart, *The Anatomy of Power*, 28–29.

81. Said (source not attributed). Quoted in Gregory, "Imaginative Geographies," 458.

82. Ryan, *The Cartographic Eye*, 131.

83. Barnes, *Logics of Dislocation*, 173–76. In a deconstruction of quantification, Barnes draws on the philosopher of science David Bloor. Barnes notes that "[a]nyone claiming a non-ideological viewpoint is adopting an ideology" (175).

84. This is a reading that might be encouraged by applying the ideas of Michael Camille, who reads Léry's seventeenth-century musical notation of a Tupinamba Indian chant in this way. See Greenblatt, *Marvellous Possessions*, 17.

85. Spurr, *The Rhetoric of Empire*, 22.

86. Ibid., 28. Appropriation is also applied to the colonized taking aspects of colonial/imperial culture as a way of articulating their own identities.

87. Boehmer, *Colonial and Postcolonial Literature*, 52.

88. Gregory, *Geographical Imaginations*, 171.

89. Tuan, "Language and the Making of Place," 687.

90. Ashcroft, Griffiths, and Tiffin, *The Empire Writes Back*, 89. See also Buttimer, "Musing on Helicon," 90.

91. Gregory, *Geographical Imaginations*, 171–72.

92. Richards, *The Imperial Archive*, 53.

93. Berg and Kearns, "Naming as Norming," 99. As noted in the introduction, I have tried to overcome this problem by representing the indigenous activity in the language of those who practised it.

94. Boehmer, *Colonial and Postcolonial Literature*, 49.

95. Berg and Kearns, "Naming as Norming," 99.

96. Bergerhoff, *Le Ruanda-Urundi*, 36.

97. Roome, *Through the Lands of Nyanza*, 134 (emphasis added). Holmes's view was that the Tutsi were "keen on sport and games *generally*." Holmes, "Letter from Capt. G. Holmes," 17 (emphasis added).

98. de Ligne, *Africa*, 80.

99. Michiels and Laude, *Notre colonie: Géographie et notice historique*, 64. Contrast this with Jokl's view, cited later in this chapter.

100. Roome, *Through the Lands of Nyanza*, 134.

101. Weule, "Ethnologie des Sports," 14.

102. Roome, *Tramping through Africa*, 102–03 (emphasis added).

103. Jokl, "High Jump Technique," 147. Although Europeans did not view dancing as a sport, it, too, had sometimes to be likened to something from the Occident. The Gattis described Tutsi dancing in Western terms, appropriating it as the precursor of the jitterbug and describing the dancers' dress as "glamorous zoot suits." See Gatti and Gatti, *Here is Africa*, 143.

104. Tirala, *Sport und Rasse*, 49, 165. The U.S. world record holder was referred to as "germanischen" Osborn (165). I am grateful to Henning Eichberg (Idætsførsk, Denmark) for this reference.

105. Roome, *Tramping through Africa*, 102–3; Smith, "A Journey into Belgian Ruanda," 11.

106. Gilbert and Tomkins, *Post-Colonial Drama*, 165.

107. Gatti and Gatti, *Here is Africa*, 143.

108. Mecklenburg, *In the Heart of Africa*, 59. It was, in fact, 1.97 meters by Michael Sweeney. It had been established in 1895, and was not bettered until 1912. See zur Megede and Hymans, *Progression of World Best Performers*, 142.

109. Hoberman, *Darwin's Athletes*, 104. I have already noted that the athletic potential of the African and other peoples was also implicitly recognized in the report of the 1904 Olympics.

110. Caption of a 1939 photograph (HK 2838) by R. P. van Overschelde. Koninklijk Museum voor Midden-Afrika, Tervuren, Belgium.

111. Derkinderen, *Atlas du Congo Belge et du Ruanda-Urundi*, 183. On the typologizing of collectivities into national categories, see Malkki, *Purity and Exile*, 255.

112. See, for example, Chapman, *Lightest Africa*, 161.

113. Rummelt, *Sport im Kolonialismus*, 92.

114. Said, *Orientalism*, 67.

115. Ryan, *The Cartographic Eye*, 7.

116. Quoted in Pratt, *Imperial Eyes*, 202. See also Spurr, *Rhetoric of Empire*, 29–30.

117. Some of this is based on Ryan, *The Cartographic Eye*, 9–10.

118. Gatti, *South of the Sahara*, 169.

119. Birnbaum, "Reception in Rwanda," 298.

120. Balfour, *Lords of the Equator*, 241; "Facts about Ruanda-Urundi," 99, (emphasis added).

121. Ellen Gatti, *Exploring We Would Go*, 79; and Akeley, *Congo Eden*, 59. It is not possible to argue from the evidence presented here that the two women writers I have referred to communicated their views of Tutsi in a form that was different from male writers. Indeed, Gatti's idea of bringing young men back to Europe to compete in Western sports resonates with the well-documented tradition of including natives as objects of display at imperial and other exhibitions in nineteenth- and early twentieth-century Europe and North America. See Coombes, *Reinventing Africa*. Mary Jobe Akeley was the second wife of the well-known American Africanist, explorer, photographer, camera inventor, sculptor, and taxidermist, Carl Akeley. For a brief biographical note on Mary Akeley, see Haraway, *Primate Visions*, 26–58 and 387, n. 27.

122. Jokl, *Physiology of Exercise*, 126.

123. Church, "From Dr. Church," 17. Sheringham is a small seaside town in Norfolk, England.

124. Jokl, *Physiology of Exercise*, 126–27.

125. Quoted in Harri Eljanko collection (6), Sports Archives of Finland, Helsinki. This collection includes manuscripts of speeches, radio lectures, etc., 1931–62. I am grateful to Kenth Sjöblom for calling my attention to this reference and translating it from the Finnish.

126. Willoughby, *The Super-Athletes*, 473.

127. Quercetani, *History of Track and Field Athletics*, 228.

128. Boehmer, *Colonial and Postcolonial Literature*, 55.

129. Said, *Orientalism*, 59.

130. Boehmer, *Colonial and Postcolonial Literature*, 172.

131. Quoted in Hoberman, *Mortal Engines*, 46. Tutsi were also read as being potential record breakers at sprinting. Mecklenburg had "no doubt" that in the running races he witnessed (and possibly organized) "the European records were at least equalled." See Mecklenburg, *In the Heart of Africa*, 61.

132. Quoted in Harri Eljanko collection (6), Sports Archives of Finland (see note 125).

133. Bernatzik, *Afrika*, 896.

134. Smith, "A Journey into Belgian Ruanda," 11.

135. Roome, *Tramping through Africa*, 103.

136. Tirala, *Sport und Rasse*, 50.

137. See Ashcroft et al., *The Empire Writes Back*, 158.

138. Miller, "Theories of Africans," 290.

139. Such spatial designations are discussed in Said, *Orientalism*, 60.

140. Jokl, *Physiology of Exercise*, 126. Sir Arthur Gold, a leading U.K. expert in high-jumping technique, suggested to me that the Tutsi technique was similar to a crude form of the "Eastern cut-off" but that as athletes they would have offered no threat to the best Western high jumpers of the day. (Telephone conversation, 15 January 1997.) Although adopting a Eurocentric perspective, Gold implies that Jokl's claims were exaggerated.

141. Farson, *Behind God's Back*, 389.

142. Gregory, "Imaginative Geographies."

143. McClintock, *Imperial Leather*, 123.

144. Kearns, "The Imperial Subject," 452.

145. Spurr, *Rhetoric of Empire*, 30.

146. Phillips, *Mapping Men and Empire*, 13 (italics added).

147. Pratt, *Imperial Eyes*, 45.

148. Bivona, *Desire and Contradiction*, 60. Bivona's cogent analysis of *Alice in Wonderland* as an allegory of cultural imperialism and his use of Alice's misreading of Wonderland "croquet" and the "caucus-race" are highly illuminating in the context of colonial (mis)readings of indigenous body cultures.

149. Barnes, *Logics of Dislocation*, 149.

150. Czekanowski, *Forschungen im Nil-Congo-Zwischengebiet*, 347.

151. Meeker, *Report on Africa*, 151 (emphasis added).

152. Kna, "Die Watussi als Springkünstler." The use of this and other terms as alternatives to "sport" suggest that travel writers and anthropologists may have been experimenting with language and writing, whether they knew it or not. See Rabinow, "Representations Are Social Facts," 242. It might be possible to view achievement sport as art—some sports do contain strong artistic components—but my feeling is that artistic expression is less intrinsic to serious sport than obtaining a result and the ethic of science, which requires a *quantified* record. Also, art requires an audience whereas sport does not.

153. Borgerhoff, *Le Ruanda-Urundi*, 36 (italics added).

154. Belotti, *Fabulous Congo*, 39.

155. See, for example, Gourdinne, "Dans l'Est Africain allemand," 383.

156. Catlow, *In Search of the Primitive*, 25.

157. Moore, "White Magic in the Belgian Congo," 362. That such a comment could also be read as a form of negation cannot be totally denied.

158. Olsson, *Birds in Egg/Eggs in Bird*, 11e.

159. Gregory, *Geographical Imaginations*, 173n.

160. Mangan, *The Games Ethic and Imperialism*, 191.

161. The same applies to other groups such as the Masai of Kenya, who were often projected as fantastic runners, and the Nuba of the Sudan, who were regarded as superb wrestlers. See Bale and Sang, *Kenyan Running*; and Riefensthal, *The Last of the Nuba*, respectively. On this subject it has also been noted that "the [army] recruitment officers in Uganda came to look at Nilotics and Sudanic communities as being *physically* better 'drill material' than most of the people of the Bantu kingdoms." See Mazrui, "Boxer Muhammad Ali and Soldier Idi Amin as International Political Symbols," 193.

162. Gregory, "Between the Book and the Lamp," 35.

163. Mecklenburg, *In the Heart of Africa*, 59.

164. Czekanowski, *Forschungen im Nil-Congo-Zwischengebeit*, 12.

165. Catlow, *In Search of the Primitive*, 25 (italics added).

166. de Briey, "Musinga," 7.

167. Gatti, *South of the Sahara*, 170 (italics added).

168. Caption of a 1939 photograph (HK2838) by R. P. van Overschelde. Koninklijk Museum voor Midden-Afrika, Tervuren, Belguim. Barns, *The African Eldorado*, 52.

169. Quoted in Ndejuru, *Studien zur Rolle der Leibesübungen*.

170. Bernatzik, *Afrika*, 896.

171. Livingstone, *The Geographical Tradition*, 221–31. Enviornmental determinism was the *leitmotif* of much geographical writing in the early twentieth century. It states that the physical environment controls human behavior. On environmental deterministic explanations of African sports success, see Bale and Sang, *Kenyan Running*, 141–47.

172. Jokl, "African Man-Power" and "Research in Physical Education," 208. Other German scientists in the 1920s also regarded the Tutsi, along with the Finns ("natural" long-distance runners and javelin throwers) as the only groups which fitted the hypothesis that some races were more suited to certain sports than to others. See Hoberman, *Mortal Engines*, 182.

173. Moore-Gilbert, *Postcolonial Theory*, 39.

174. Quoted in Kna, "Die Watussi als Springkünstler." As reported here, Mecklenburg provided a succinct précis of one of the foremost environmentalists of the period, the American geographer Ellen Semple. She wrote: "On the mountains she [i.e., the earth's surface] has given him [i.e., "man"] leg muscles of

iron to climb the slope; along the coast she has left these weak and flabby." See Semple, *Influences of Geographic Environment*, 1.

175. Webster, *Why? The Science of Athletics*, 91.

176. "Die Watussi sind nicht im strengen einne Neger." Tirala, *Sport und Rasse*, 49–50. This reflected the Hamitic hypothesis which argued for the Tutsi being a branch of the Caucasian race (see chapter 2). But, as I will show in the next section of this chapter, the negation of Negro athletes was applied rather differently by Hitler.

177. Ibid.

178. JanMohamed, "The Economy of the Manichean Allegory," 87. See also Spurr, *The Rhetoric of Empire*, 157.

179. Blixen, *Out of Africa*.

180. Jokl, "High Jump Technique of the Central African Watussis," 146 (emphasis added).

181. Sibley, "Creating Geographies of Difference," 125.

182. Low, *White Skins, Black Masks*, 30. See also Rony, *The Third Eye*, 28. On negrophilia, see Archer-Straw, *Negrophilia*. I should also point out that the temporal lens through which these representations were being constructed was a period when the imperial powers of Europe themselves had come to depend on aesthetic and athletic displays and an eagerness to "play up" as well as play the game.

183. Note Broehmer, *Colonial and Postcolonial Literature*, 33, 127. It has been argued that sympathy shown toward black African culture in Rider Haggard's *King Solomon's Mines* may have been as significant to its success as the English taste for adventure. See Bivona, *Desire and Contradictions*, 37.

184. Webster, *Athletes of Today*, 184; and *Why? The Science of Athletics*, 91.

185. Webster, *Athletes of Today*, 184. These antitechnological sentiments are reminiscent of Heideggerian Black Forest "peasant virtues." However, some German observers from the 1930s "looked for inspiration from the people of Papua New Guinea, then a German colony.... Germans could find there, as though by destiny, the primal life force needed to restore their vigor and lead them into a new era." See Wollen, "Tales of Total Art and Dreams of the Total Museum," 175. During the same period, however, virulent racism was present within the Nazi movement. The early twentieth-century body was also compared unfavorably with that of the ancient Greeks, "to whom alcoholism, syphilis, and hereditary diseases were allegedly unknown." See Garb, *Bodies of Modernity*, 56.

186. Mosse, *The Image of Man*, 95.

187. The language here is from Pronger, "Post-Sport: Transgressing Boundaries in Physical Culture," 286. Pronger argues that "techno-scientific culture" is typified by modern sports. Lewis Carroll was uneasy about the loss of innocence that he saw in the growing sports movement of Victorian England, and opposed the installation of cricket pitches on the Oxford University Parks. See Blake, *Play, Games, and Sports,* 149–79.

188. Severn, *Congo Pilgrim,* 195–96.

189. Seltzer, *Bodies and Machines,* 56. See also Lalvani, *Photography, Vision, and the Production of Modern Bodies,* 80.

190. Todorov, *On Human Diversity,* 276–77.

191. Greenblatt, "Resonance and Wonder," 42, 54.

192. Mauss, "Techniques of the Body," 472. On Mauss, see Hunter and Saunders, "Walks of Life."

193. Mauss, "Techniques of the Body," 472.

194. Rail, "Seismography of the Postmodern Condition," 148.

195. Sibley, *Geographies of Exclusion,* 27.

196. Cromwell and Wesson, *Championship Technique in Track and Field,* 6. In a work published in 1905, no mention of black high jumpers was made. See Crowther and Ruhl, *Rowing and Track Athletics.* Likewise, by the mid-1920s the definitive training manual on high jumping give no hint or suggestion that black athletes might be actual or potential high jumpers. See Templeton, *The High Jump.*

197. Cromwell and Wesson, *Championship Technique in Track and Field,* 6.

198. *Athletics World* 64 (1954) reported that this may have been the event in which "the outstanding *natural ability* ... of the African populace first received recognition in international competition.... The winner's *raw spring* is quite breath-taking" (2, 8, emphases added). However, by the mid-1960s an African presence in the world-ranking lists had all but disappeared. On Nigerian track-and-field sports in the late 1940s, see Powell, "The Progress of Athletics in Nigeria."

199. Richards, *Athletic Records and Achievements,* 10–11.

200. Webster, *Why? The Science of Athletics,* 385–86. These opinions could have been encouraged and supported by the successes of black athletes in the pre-Owens era. The African American De Hart Hubbard had won the Olympic long jump in 1924; the Haitian Sylvio Cator had broken the world long-jump record in 1928; and in the 1932 Olympic African Americans Eddie Tolan and Ralph Metcalfe had won the 100- and 200-meter sprints, respectively.

201. "Felan," "An African Causerie," 12.

202. Quoted in Kna, "Die Watussi als Springkünstler," 461.

203. Ibid. On environmental deterministic explanations of African sports success, see Bale and Sang, *Kenyan Running*, 141–47.

204. Ndejuru, *Studien zur Rolle der Leibesübungen*.

205. Attilio Gatti, "Jumping Giants of Africa," 26.

206. Quoted in Kna, "Die Watussi als Springkünstler." This could be a description of the "standing high jump" described in chapter 2.

207. Diem, *Weltgeschichte des Sports*, 86. Given the absence of any written evidence for the kind of training illustrated in Diem's book, it is difficult to ignore the possibility that it was a figment of the Western imagination, especially given the absence of human representation in Banyarwandan art (see chapter 2). The drawing—along with many others in his book—are attributed to Heiner Rotfuchs of Wiesbaden.

208. Schumacher, "De hamitische Wahrsagerei in Ruanda," 195.

209. Ellen Gatti, *Exploring We Would Go*, 79. Classical allusions were not unusual in colonialist writing on Africa. In 1882, for example, W. R. Ludlow had described the Zulus as having "adapted the methods of the Spartans" in the training of warriors. See W. R. Ludlow, *Zululand and Cetewyo*. Quoted in Low, *White Skins, Black Masks*, 30.

210. Seltzer, *Bodies and Machines*, 125.

211. Spurr, *The Rhetoric of Empire*, 132.

212. Sontag, "Fascinating Facism," 316. On this subject, see chapter 4.

213. Rony, *The Third Eye*, 98.

214. Quoted in Phillips, *Mapping Men and Empire*, 116.

215. Lalvani, *Photography, Vision, and the Production of Modern Bodies*, 68.

216. Cagen, *Photography's Contribution to the "Western" Vision of the Colonized Other*. I am grateful to Tamar Rothenberg of Rutgers University for alerting me to this unpublished paper.

217. Pieterse, *White on Black*, 35. See also Jahoda, *Images of Savages*.

218. Spurr, *The Rhetoric of Empire*, 84.

219. Quoted from a Swedish encyclopedia of 1944 by Gøksyr, "One Certainly Expected a Good Deal More from the Savages," 306.

220. Jokl, "High Jump Technique of the Central African Watussis." Typically, Jokl did not seem to find it surprising that Europeans did not engage in African body cultural practices.

221. Spurr, *The Rhetoric of Empire*, 168 (emphasis added).

222. Attilio Gatti, "The Jumping Giants of Rwanda" and 'The Kingdom of the Giants."

223. Mecklenburg, "A Land of Giants and Pygmies," 370; Holmes, [untitled article], 17; Sharpe, *The Backbone of Africa*, 119.

224. Rummelt, *Sport im Kolonialismus*. That Mecklenburg's indication of the height was an estimate is at least questionable, given his reference to "exact measurement" mentioned above but, at the same time, to other measurements (noted above). However, he went on to note that, in addition to the high-jump event, "running races, too, were organised, but owing to the lack of necessary *measuring instruments* I am, unfortunately, not in a position to give the times." It is not clear if the term "measuring instruments" refers to a tape measure (for defining the distance run) or a stopwatch (for measuring the time taken). See Mecklenburg, *In the Heart of Africa*, 61.

225. Note, however, the contents of his 1928 letter to Kna (see chapter 2). Rummelt was apparently unaware of this.

226. Rummelt states that Attilio Gatti could only certify a jump of 2.10 meters and Jokl one of 6 feet 2 inches (1.88 meters). I have shown in this chapter that each of these authors claimed greater heights, though it is likely that the confines of Rummelt's academic and social space excluded his knowledge of their work.

227. Melik-Chaknazarov, *Sport en Afrique*. This is the equivalent of asking people in New York if they are familiar with the nineteenth-century folk games of Québec.

228. Reutler, *Über die Leibesübunbugen in der Primitiven*, 51–52 (emphasis added). The reference to Weule is his article "Ethnologie des Sports."

229. Ndejuru, *Studien zur Rolle der Leibesübungen*, 130.

230. Burleigh and Wippermann, *The Racial State*, 52. During the Nazi period, people of African descent were "normally counted alongside Jews as 'carriers of non-German or related blood'" (50).

231. Ibid., 83. The statement is from a German librarian's journal of 1938. I am grateful to Arnd Krüger of the University of Göttingen and Gertrud Pfister of the University of Copenhagen for additional insights on this subject, e-mail communications, 14 December 1998.

232. I am grateful to Gundolf Krüger of the University of Göttingen for this information, telephone communication, 6 January 1999. Reutler's National Socialist credentials were confirmed in his curriculum vitae, which states that

from 1936 he was sports leader of the Rostock Workers Front. See Reutler, *Über die Leibesübunbugen in der Primitiven*, 63.

233. From Bruno Schultz, "Sport und Rasse," 366–67. Quoted in Hoberman, "Primacy of Performance," 75.

234. Gilroy, *Between Camps*, 174.

235. From Albert Speer, *Inside the Third Reich*, 114. Quoted in Hoberman, "Primacy of Performance," 75.

236. See, for example, Hoberman, *Sport and Political Ideology*, 164–65; and Pieterse, *White on Black*, 219.

237. Rummelt, *Sport im Kolonialismus, Kolonialismus im Sport*, 91. I am grateful to Maren Bischoff for clarification of this from the German original.

238. See Blanchard, *The Anthropology of Sport*; and Blacking, "Games and Sports in Pre-Colonial Africa." Nor is *gusimbuka* mentioned in a shorter review in Omo-Osage, *African Unity through Sports*.

239. The notion of authorial space is taken from Curry, *The Work in the World*.

240. Barnes, *The Logic of Dislocation*, 225.

241. Henning Eichberg, in conversation, Odense, Denmark, 9 March 1998.

242. On writing culture, see Ashcroft et al., *The Empire Writes Back*; and, Marcus and Fischer, *Anthopology as Cultural Critique*.

243. Olsson, *Birds in Egg/Eggs in Bird*, 12e.

244. Pratt, *Imperial Eyes*, 39.

245. Ibid., 34–35.

246. Torgovnick, *Gone Primitive*. Torgovnick does point out, however, that the application of non-art to primitive cultures implies a lack of culture, and hence provides the conditions for colonialism. Is it therefore correct to posit that "any challenge to the designation of [sport] for [precolonial] African, Oceanic and Native American [people] ... flirts dangerously with modes of thought that made the appropriation of land from primitive peoples possible and contributes to their continuing exploitation"? (83). Would this have been overcome if it had been recognized that *gusimbuka* was not high jumping (sport), but accorded much better with the term *spring-artistry* (nonsport)? *Gusimbuka* looked like the jumping seen in the stadiums of Europe rather than the springers of the circus or fairground. But it was the fete and the pantomime, not the arena and the Olympiad, that may have provided the more appropriate metaphors by which Europeans understood the milieu of *gusimbuka*. Words do make a difference. But the application of the term spring-artistry (from the German *Springkünstler)* to

the Rwandan body culture, while more appropriate, is also appropriative. In the final analysis, only *gusimbuka-urukiramende* will do, if Western connotations and colonial stereotyping are to be avoided.

247. Bourdieu, *Sociology in Question*, 119.

248. Torgovnick, *Gone Primitive*, 83.

249. Atkinson and Dodds, "Introduction: Geopolitical Traditions," 10.

250. Hoberman, *Darwin's Athletes*, 240.

251. Jokl et al., *Sports in the Cultural Pattern of the World*, 35-36; *Medical Sociology and Cultural Anthropology of Sport and Physical Education*, 70; and *Physiology of Exercise*, 244.

4. Visual Images and Foreign Bodies

1. The variety of such photographs is well reviewed in Ryan, *Picturing Empire*. While Ryan's book is the most extensive geographical work on colonial photography yet written, he fails to focus on what might be termed 'action photographs' of the body cultural practices of indigenous peoples.

2. Muybridge, *The Human Figure in Motion*. On Marey, see Braun, *Picturing Time*. Note also the contribution of Félix-Louis Regnault; see Rony, *The Third Eye*, 21–43. The contribution of photography to the recording of sports events via the photo-finish camera was first used at the Olympics in 1912. See Killanin and Rodda, *The Olympic Games*, 69.

3. Nochlin, *The Politics of Vision*, 39.

4. For a thorough review, see McQuire, *Visions of Modernity*.

5. Gren, *Earth Writing*, 48–49.

6. Mirzoeff, "What Is Visual Culture?," 9.

7. Rowe, *Sport, Culture, and the Media*, 120–26.

8. These are terms used in Maxwell, *Colonial Photography and Exhibitions*, 7.

9. Berger and Mohr, *Another Way of Telling*, 92.

10. Barthes, *Image, Music, Text*, 1 (emphasis added).

11. Poole, *Vision, Race, and Modernity*, 7. The idea of international flows also encourages the notion of an economic geography of images.

12. Barry, "Reporting and Visualising," 47.

13. Quoted in Driver, "Visualizing Geography," 124. On Mackinder and "visual instruction," see Ryan, *Picturing Empire*, 183–213.

14. Taussig, *Mimesis and Alterity*, 199.

15. Driver, "Visualizing Geography." See also, for example, Duncan, "Sites of Representation"; Jackson, "Constructions of Culture, Representations

of Race"; Rose, "Teaching Visualised Geographies"; Ryan, "Picturing People and Places" and *Picturing Empire*; and Schwartz, "The Geography Lesson." These studies focus on the scalar opposite of a major contemporary photographic concern of many geographers, that of *remote sensing*. The kinds of photographic analyses in the present book are more akin to what has been termed *intimate sensing*. Douglas Porteous describes this as "the appraisal of land and life at the ground level," though he does not seem to appreciate that such an appraisal can also involve the analysis of photographs. See Porteous, "Intimate Sensing," 250.

16. Driver, "Visualizing Geography," 124. For anthropology, see Edwards, "Introduction."

17. Ryan, "Picturing People and Places," 337.

18. Soloman-Godeau, *Photography at the Dock*, 154; Poignant, "Surveying the Field," 42.

19. Nochlin, *The Politics of Vision*, 37. On Gérôme's "realism," see Tawadros, "Foreign Bodies."

20. Pultz, *Photography and the Body*, 21.

21. McClintock, *Imperial Leather*, 123.

22. Sontag, *On Photography*.

23. Haraway, *Primate Visions*, 46.

24. Morphy and Banks, "Introduction: Rethinking Visual Anthropology," 26. On ways of seeing, see Berger, *Ways of Seeing*. The significance of a photograph's content from the perspective of the indigene is part of the field of visual anthropology and, to a large extent, is beyond the scope of the present study.

25. Bourdieu, *Photography*, 6.

26. Faris, "Photography, Power, and the Southern Nuba," 214.

27. Edwards, "Guest Editorial," 1.

28. Sekula, "On the Invention of Photographic Meaning," 91.

29. Tirala, *Sport und Rasse*, 50; Webster, *Why? The Science of Athletics*; and Deutschen Hochschule für Körperkultur, *Körperkultur und Sport*.

30. Quoted in Kna, "Die Watussi als Springkünstler," 460; Birnbaum, "Reception in Ruanda," 306.

31. Barns, *The Wonderland of the Eastern Congo*, vii.

32. Attilio Gatti, *South of the Sahara*, 11.

33. Roome, *Tramping through Africa*, vii.

34. Barns, *The Wonderland of the Eastern Congo*, 268.

35. Pinney, "The Parallel Histories of Anthropology and Photography," 76. Note that "the unique evidential force of the photograph depended equally

on the belief that here, for the first time, representation achieved parity with direct perception." See McQuire, *Visions of Modernity*, 29.

36. Mecklenburg, *In the Heart of Africa*, ix; Attilio Gatti, *South of the Sahara*, 9.

37. Pinney, "The Parallel Histories of Anthropology and Photography," 76.

38. Law and Whittaker, "On the Art of Representation," 181.

39. Nochlin, *The Politics of Vision*, 36–37. This is not to say that orientalist depictions were not Europeanized. The landscapes and peoples depicted in paintings, woodcuts, and etchings often took on the appearance of a classic Europeanness. See, for example, Pinney, *Camera Indica*, 16–19.

40. Pinney, "The Parallel Histories," 92, n. 10.

41. Ryan, "Picturing People and Places," 333.

42. Ryan, *Photography, Geography, and Empire*, 176. See also Slater, "Photography and Modern Vision," 219–20.

43. Pinney, "The Parallel Histories," 76.

44. In the MGM color movie, *King Solomon's Mines* (1950), a number of male Tutsi stereotypes are represented, but no evidence of *gusimbuka* is included.

45. Clarke, *The Photograph*, 23.

46. Mecklenburg, *In the Heart of Africa*, 59.

47. Mecklenburg, "A Land of Giants and Pygmies."

48. Czekanowski, *Forschungen im Nil-Congo-Zwischegebeit*.

49. Mecklenburg, "A Land of Giants and Pygmies"; Hildebrand, "The Geography of Games." As far as I am aware, however, this photograph never became part of the postcard industry.

50. Deford, "Let the Games Begin"; Honke, *Au plus profond de l'Afrique* (as the cover photograph); Guttmann, *Games and Empires*; Bryant, "Major's Mission Seeks Leap of Faith"; Minshull, "First in Flight," 62.

51. Greenblatt, *Marvellous Possessions*, 6.

52. Hintjens, "Through the Looking Glass."

53. Rummelt, *Sport im Kolonialismus*, 88. To my knowledge, no evidence of any alternative arrangements of the contents of the photograph exists. Hence, assertions that it is a montage can be, at best, speculative.

54. See, for example, Jackson, "Constructions of Culture"; and Webb, "Manipulated Images."

55. Pinney, "Classification and Fantasy in the Photographic Construction of Caste and Tribe," 281.

56. Ryan, *Picturing Empire*, 220.

57. Pinney, "The Parallel Histories." See also Foucault, *Discipline and Punish*.

58. Ryan, *The Cartographic Eye*, 200.

59. Rony, *The Third Eye*, 58.

60. Coombes, "The Recalcitrant Self," 96.

61. Barthes, *Camera Lucida*, 23.

62. Burgin, "Art, Common Sense, and photography," 78.

63. These words are based on Clifford's comments on the appearance of the anthropologist Bronislaw Malinowski, photographed with some of his objects of study. See Clifford, *Routes*, 74.

64. Lutz and Collins, *Reading National Geographic*; and Rothenburg, "Voyeurs of Imperialism."

65. Barthes, in *Camera Lucida*, describes such a point as a "photograph's *punctum* … that accident which pricks me (but also bruises me, is poignant to me)" (27).

66. These terms are taken from Pinney, *Camera Indica*, 46. The question of which of these should be represented often led orientalist photographers to construct a different reality for the camera.

67. "Die Watussi sollen von jeher ausgezeichnete Springer gewesen sein, und da wir ihnen die Beliebtheit dieses Sportes wahrnahmen, veranstalteten wir […] das Hochspringen." Quoted in Ndejuru, "Studien zur Rolle der Leibesübungen in der traditionellen Gesellschaft Rwanda," 130. This statement implies that *gusimbuka* was an indigenous body culture.

68. Vansina, "Photographs of the Sankunu." On staging, posing, and re-enactment in photography in colonial Africa, see Geary, "Photographing Practice in Africa."

69. Taussig, *Mimesis and Alterity*, 21.

70. Pauwels, "Jeux et divertessements au Rwanda," 241.

71. Taussig, *Mimesis and Alterity*, 21.

72. Willis, "Photography and Film," 77.

73. Czekanowski, *Forschungen im Nil-Congo-Zwischengebeit*, 12. Askari were German-employed African soldiers.

74. Faris, "Photography, Power, and the Nuba," 214.

75. Lalvani, *Photography, Vision, and the Production of Modern Bodies*, 87–137. Such anthropometric photography was far from absent in early twentieth-century photography of Tutsi and Hutu types. See, for example, Schumacher, "Das Eherecht in Ruanda."

76. Thomas, *Colonialism's Culture*, 36.

77. Greenblatt, *Marvelous Possessions*, 4.

78. Mecklenburg, *In the Heart of Africa*, 378; and "A Land of Giants and Pygmies," 387. This photograph is reproduced in Bale and Sang, *Kenyan Running*, 60.

79. Gregory, "Scripting Egypt," 116.

80. Mirzoeff, *Bodyscapes*, 139.

81. Ellen Gatti, *Exploring We Would Go*, 79.

82. Crang, "Picturing Practices," 361.

83. Barns, *The Wonderland of the Eastern Congo*.

84. De Ligne, *Africa*, facing 76. I am grateful to Patricia van Schuylenbergh of the Koninklijk Museum voor Midden-Afrika, Tervuren, Belgium, for this reference.

85. Cagen, "Photography's Contribution to the 'Western' Vision of the Colonized Other," 26.

86. It was published by Éditions Jos. Dardenne. See Elias and Helbig, "Deux mille collines pour les 'petits' et les 'grandes,'" 94. I am grateful to Bambi Ceupens of Keele University for alerting me to this reference.

87. Edwards, "Beyond the Boundary," 61–62.

88. Attilio Gatti, "The Kingdom of the Giants," 9.

89. Balfour, *Lords of the Equator*, 241; Birnbaum, "Reception in Ruanda," 298.

90. These ideas are based on suggestions by Henning Eichberg, personal communication, 9 March 1999.

91. Mudimbe, *The Idea of Africa*, 157–58.

92. Mid-Africa Mission collection (AA1/15/14), Church Missionary Society Archives, London.

93. Smith, *An African Nebuchadnezzar*. The caption to the photograph described the young boy standing at the upright on the right as a "pygmy."

94. See Pinney, "The Parallel Histories of Anthropology and Photography," 76.

95. van Overschelde, *Bij de reuzen en dwergen van Rwanda*, 177.

96. Collection of Professor Joseph Ghesquiere.

97. Moore, "White Magic in the Belgian Congo," 362.

98. Lutz and Collins, *Reading National Geographic*, 40.

99. Dupriez, *Guide du voyageur au Congo Belge*.

100. Sontag, "Fascinating Fascism," 316. It has been argued that "logically,

the fascist celebration of the primitive would invoke a blond-haired, blue-eyed" Aryan, not a black African and that the "aesthetic idealization of an 'inferior' race" is incompatible with the idea of fascism, *sensu stricto*. Instead, such images might be read as a reminder that "fascism and popular ethnography share in the eroticization of power and domination." See Gates, "Of Seeing and Otherness," 239–40. The view that a fascist aesthetic is not bounded by race is forcefully put in Gilroy, *Between Camps*, 173–74.

101. Ball and Smith, *Analyzing Visual Data*, 9.

102. Pultz, *Photography and the Body*, 24.

103. Lutz and Collins, *Reading National Geographic*, 206.

104. Gregory, "Imaginative Geographies," 453.

105. Ryan, *Picturing Empire*, 102.

106. Ibid., 159.

107. See, for example, Webb, "Manipulated Images."

108. Chrétien, "Hutu et Tutsi au Rwanda et au Burundi," 146.

109. Edwards, "Science Visualized," 116.

110. Farnell, "Ethno-Graphics of the Moving Body," 736.

111. Edwards, "Science Visualized," 116.

112. Barringer, "Fabricating Africa," 72.

113. Augé, *A Sense for the Other*, 84.

114. Farnell, "Ethno-Graphics of the Moving Body," 936.

115. Bate, "Photography and the Colonial Vision." Orientalists would dress in native costume to facilitate participant observation, but Bate also notes that being photographed in Eastern dress enabled orientalism to "devour" the oriental—or, ambivalently, the colonizing vision was threatened by its double (90).

116. Pratt, *Imperial Eyes*, 7.

117. Lutz and Collins, *Reading National Geographic*, 203.

118. Ibid., 206.

119. This is analogous to the term *environmental portraiture*. See Pinney, *Camera Indica*, 26.

120. Riefenstahl, *The Last of the Nuba*.

121. Guttmann, *The Erotic in Sports*, 113.

122. Sontag, "Fascinating Facism," 318. See also McFee and Tomlinson, "Riefenstahl's *Olympia*"; and Gilroy, *Between Camps*, 170–76.

123. Ibid., 316.

124. Schiarini, "Spoglie di un imperso coloniale," 64; Barns, *Across the*

Great Crater World to the Congo, 161–62. It has been suggested that African men were less easily feminized than other indigenous people, possibly because of their "robust" physical appearance. See Bleys, *The Geography of Perversion*, 46. However, robustness is hardly a word that could be applied to the Tutsi stereotype, and the fluidity in the meaning inferred by "the feminized male" is exemplified in an early 1920s statement that, while once warlike, Tutsi men were now "effeminate." See Sharpe, *The Backbone of Africa*, 119. Note also the comments and illustrations in McClintock, *Imperial Leather*, 56.

125. Young, *Colonial Desire*, 110–11; and McClintock, *Imperial Leather*, 56. French black male athletes from Africa were said to have "always presented feline attitudes" or to have been "terribly feline." Quoted from the French sports newspapers, *L'Équipe* (29 January 1958) and *L'Auto* (24 September 1922), respectively. See Deville-Danthu, *Le sport en noir et blanc*, 121, 316.

126. Sinha, *Colonial Masculinity*.

127. Rigby, *African Images*, 69.

128. This contrast between the high jumpers as part of a countryside idyll and as images of power was paralleled by exactly the same contrast in artistic representations of the body during the National Socialist period in Germany. See van der Will, "The Body and the Body Politic as Symptom and Metaphor," 46–50.

129. Lutz and Collins, *Reading National Geographic*, 204.

130. Ibid., 197.

131. Smith, "A Journey into Belgian Ruanda," 10. The caption accompanying the original print in the Mid-Africa Mission collection (AA1/8/8), Church Missionary Society Archives, London, reads: "Batutsi youth. Champion high jumper of the world, 7 ft."

132. Lutz and Collins, *Reading National Geographic*, 202.

133. Ibid., 200.

134. Ibid., 203.

135. Ibid., 197.

136. Ibid.

137. Ryan, *The Cartographic Eye*, 193.

138. Gordon, *Picturing Bushmen*, 72.

139. Ibid., 69.

140. Tomas, *Transcultural Space and Transcultural Beings*, 77.

141. I am extremely grateful to Professor Ghesquiere for allowing me to take copies of his photographs and for several discussions with him about his time in Rwanda. One of Ghesquiere's photographs of *gusimbuka* was, in fact,

published in a Danish newspaper on the occasion of a visit by him to Copenhagen in 1950, where he gave a lecture on the subject. I have been unable to establish the precise bibliographical details.

142. Gregory, "Imaginative Geographies," 458.

143. Morphy and Banks, "Introduction: Rethinking Visual Anthropology," 15–16.

144. See Braun, *Picturing Time*; and Muybridge, *The Human Figure in Motion*.

145. Doane, "Temporality, Storage, Legibility: Freud, Marey, and the Cinema," 316.

146. Jokl, *South African Reminiscences*, 13.

147. Jokl, "High Jump Technique," 148. This paper was reprinted in Jokl, *Research in Physical Education*.

148. Ibid., 147. The acknowledgments of whose films Jokl analyzed are contradictory. In the original publication he cites Professor J. H. Wellington (149), but in his memoirs he names Ernest Ullman as having made the films from which his drawings were made. See Jokl, *South African Reminiscences*, 13. I am grateful to Floris van der Merwe of Stellenbosch University for alerting me to the latter reference. Despite Jokl's claim that he visited Rwanda, he illustrated his published writings on Rwanda with the 1907 Mecklenburg photograph and included a number of factually incorrect statements. The paper is based entirely on secondary sources.

149. Law and Whittaker, "On the Art of Representation," 161.

150. Gregory, *Geographical Imaginations*, 249. The quotation in this sentence is from Gregory's description of Allan Pred's "time-geography" line diagram (modeled on an idea introduced by Torsten Hägerstrand for representing time-space activities). Jokl's diagrams seem to me to be analogous to those of time-geography because of their impression of the *technical* high jump or, indeed, of modern sport, as "an endless repetition of time-space routines"—which, I think, it actually is (251).

151. Seltzer, *Bodies and Machines*, 156. This also brings to mind the theory of biomechanics adumbrated by the Russian theater director, Vsevolad Meirhold. Seeing the body as an "automotive mechanism," he compiled a vocabulary consisting of twenty-two movements which was recorded on film to assist in the training of actors. It is suggested that this was inspired by F. W. Taylor's time-and-motion studies. See Clark, "The 'New Man's Body," 38–39.

152. Lalvani, *Photography, Vision, and the Production of Modern Bodies*, 159–60.

153. Seltzer, *Bodies and Machines*, 160. Seltzer also sees such images as "a resemblance between the mechanisms of scientific management and the invention of sado-masochism," a quote of Deleuze, who saw in both "a naturalistic and mechanistic approach imbued with the mathematical spirit." See also, Law and Whittaker, "On the Art of Representation," 76.

154. Mecklenburg, *In the Heart of Africa*.

155. Gourdinne, "Dans l'Est Afrique allemand."

156. Barns, *The Wonderland of the Eastern Congo*, 258.

157. Sharp, "The Medical Work Reviewed by Dr. Sharp," 13.

158. Marcus and Fischer, *Anthropology as Cultural Critique*, 76. For a critical view of ethnographic film as a representation of bodily movement, see Farnell, "Ethno-Graphics of the Moving Body," 964–66. Note also Loizos, *Innovation in Ethnographic Film*, 5–9.

159. On Belgian propaganda material on the Congo (and, by implication, on Ruanda-Urundi), see Vints, *Kongo Made in Belgium*. The movies referred to in this section were screened for me at the Koninklijk Museum voor Midden-Afrika, Tervuren, Belgium, and at the Catholic Documentation Center (KADOC) of the Katholieke Universiteit, Leuven, Belgium.

160. Ramirez and Rolot, *Histoire du cinéma au Zaïre au Ruanda et a Burundi*, 236.

161. The movie was first shown in Paris in 1935 and arrived in Belgian cinemas in 1936. I am grateful to Luc Vints of KADOC, Katholieke Universiteit, Leuven, Belgium, for this information and for showing me various promotional material.

162. The inclusion of pole-vaulting among the body-cultural practices encouraged in missionary education surprised me until I learned that it was central to the Swedish gymnastic tradition (following from the inspiration of Victor Balck) that was diffused and adopted as part of the Belgian gymnastic model. I am grateful to Roland Renson of the Katholieke Universitiet, Leuven, Belgium, and Verner Møller of Odense Universitet, Odense, Denmark, for this information.

163. Edwards, "Introduction," 11.

164. Gren, *Earth Writing*, 49.

165. Barthes, *Image, Music, Text*, 26.

166. Attilio Gatti, "Jumping Giants of Africa," 9.

167. Birnbaum, "Reception in Ruanda," 298.

168. Gilbert, "Dance, Movement, and Resistance Politics," 342. Note also

Mirzoeff, *Bodyscapes*, 136; and Sekula, "On the Invention of Photographic Meaning," 104.

169. Gordon, *Picturing Bushmen*, 69.

170. Ndejuru, "Studien zur Rolle der Leibesübungen in der traditionellen Gesellschaft Rwanda," 187. Of the travel writing about Ruanda-Urundi that I have encountered, Roome is the only author to have actually used the name of a Rwandan high jumper. See Roome, *Tramping through Africa*, 103.

171. Lutz and Collins, *Reading National Geographic*, 79.

172. See, respectively, Mecklenburg, *Ins innerste Afrika*, 114, and "A Land of Giants and Pygmies," 388; and Guttmann, *Games and Empires*. The term *champion* is also used in the caption to the same photograph in Deford, "Let the Games Begin," 54.

173. Webster, *Why? The Science of Athletics*, facing 376.

174. Elias and Helbig, "Deux mille collines pour les 'petits' et les 'grandes'," 94; Pagès, *Une royaume hamite au centre de l'Afrique*.

175. Kanyamachumbi, *Société, culture, et pouvoir politique en Afrique Inter-lacustre*, 124.

176. Curry, *The Work in the World*, 13.

177. Olsson, *Birds in Egg/Eggs in Bird*, 11e. Olsson also points out that neither the scientist nor the artist can avoid categorization: "This presents a most serious dilemma, for to categorize is to fetter and not to categorize is to tear the world asunder. . . . We are damned if we do and damned if we don't."

178. See Kohn, *The Race Gallery*; and especially Hoberman, *Darwin's Athletes*. Note also Miller, "The anatomy of scientific racism"; and Entine, *Taboo*.

179. Kirshenblatt-Gimblett, "Objects of Ethnography," 413.

180. Gilbert and Tomkins, *Post-Colonial Drama*, 207.

181. Edwards, "Science Visualized," 116.

182. Faris, "Photography, Power, and the Southern Nuba," 216.

Epilogue

1. Mirzoeff, *Bodyscape*, 153.

2. Livingstone, "Reproduction, Representation, and Authenticity," 15.

3. Ibid.

4. Gren, *Earth Writing*, 293.

5. Tuan, *Passing Strange and Wonderful*, 19.

6. The "bleed" metaphor (tragically appropriate in this context) is taken from Gregory, "Imaginative Geographies," 453.

7. Squire, "Accounting for Cultural Meanings," 6–7; Crang, "Picturing Practices."

8. Gren, *Earth Writing*, 145.

9. Mitchell, *Cultural Geography*, 123.

10. This section is based on Foucaultian ideas in Towadros, "Foreign Bodies," 54–56.

11. Law and Whittaker, "On the Art of Represenation."

12. Destexhe, *Rwanda and Genocide in the Twentieth Century*, 47. The continuing need for, and use of, stereotypes is still found in an electronic age. Technical improvements in communication do not necessarily lead to progressive tendencies in representation, and may, in fact, reinforce stereotypes. See Morley and Robins, *Spaces of Identity*, 133. In the Rwanda context, see Chrétien, *Rwanda: Les médias du génocide*.

13. Prunier, *The Rwanda Crisis*, 39.

14. Foucault, *The Archaeology of Knowledge*.

15. Hintjens, "Through the Looking Glass."

16. Hobsbawm, "Introduction: Inventing Traditions," 1.

17. Ranger, "The Invention of Tradition in Colonial Africa."

18. Fisiy, "Of Journeys and Border Crossings," 18; Kesby, *The Cultural Regions of East Africa*, 136.

19. Destexhe, *Rwanda and Genocide in the Twentieth Century*, 54 (parentheses added).

20. This point has been drawn from the absence of Jews in National Socialist art of 1930s Germany. See van der Will, "The Body and the Body Politic," 46.

21. The details of the events leading up to the 1994 genocide are discussed in detail in, for example, Destexhe, *Rwanda and Genocide in the Twentieth Century*; Taylor, *Sacrifice As Terror*; and Des Forges, *Leave None to Tell the Story*.

22. Mirzoeff, *Bodyscapes*, 151.

23. Hopkins, "The Ethnography of Conquest," 142–43.

24. Gilman, *Difference and Pathology*, 21.

25. Sibomana, *Hope for Rwanda*, 80.

26. Avoy, "Physical Endowment of African People," 93; and Tirala, *Sport und Rasse*, who talked about the Tutsi having practiced high jumping "for centuries."

27. Guttmann, *Games and Empires*, 188.

28. Des Forges, "The Ideology of Genocide," 45.

29. Kagame, *Le code des institutions*, 23–24.

30. Webster, Ogot, and Chrétien, "The Great Lakes Region, 1500–1800," 805.

31. Positive images created to impress foreigners are exemplified by Hitler's attempts to "normalize" Berlin during the 1936 Olympic Games and Leni Riefenstahl's normalization of Hitler in her film *Olympia*.

32. For an exploration of the range of possible causes of the Rwanda genocide, see Hintjens, "Explaining the 1994 Genocide in Rwanda"; and Mamdami, *When Victims Become Killers*.

33. Taylor, *Sacrifice As Terror*, 184.

34. Uvin, "Prejudice, Crisis, and Genocide in Rwanda," 91.

35. Bernault and Spear, "Guest Editors' Introduction," 3–4.

36. See Chrétien, *Rwanda: Les médias de génocide*; and Taylor, *Sacrifice as Genocide*.

37. This idea is usually attributed to Gayatri Chakravorty Spivak. It describes the situation when essentialism (e.g., negritude) is used tactically "in the emergence from the process of 'assimilation' imposed by colonial regimes to a fully decolonized national culture." See Moore-Gilbert, *Postcolonial Theory*, 179.

38. McFee and Tomlinson, "Riefenstahl's *Olympia*." See also Richardson, "The Nazification of Women in Art"; and Mosse, *The Image of Man*.

39. On these astonishing films, see Downing, *Olympia*; and, for example, Guttmann, *The Erotic in Sports*, 111–15.

40. McFee and Tomlinson, "Riefenstahl's *Olympia*," 104.

Appendix

1. Shearman, *Athletics and Football*, 143. I am grateful to Bob Phillips for making a copy of this book available to me.

2. Williams, "High jumping," 50.

3. Ibid.

4. Shearman, *Athletics and Football*, 143.

5. This is according to zur Megede and Hymans (eds.), *Progression of World Best Performers*. This publication is typical of the quantitative nature of the recording of athletic performance, both over time and between places. I am presenting the measurements in this chapter to three or four decimal places, and to various fractions of an inch, following the style of the IAAF publications in

which these statistics are recorded. This attempt at precision is typical of the achievement sport mind-set.

6. Quoted in Webster, *Olympian Field Events*, 49.

7. Each of these forms of high jumping was reported, for example, in the *Sporting Chronicle Annual* for 1898. I am grateful to Gerhardo Bonini (European University Institute, Florence) for this reference.

8. Templeton, *The High Jump*, 205. An arguably less authoritative source, Robert Ripley (author of the somewhat sensationalist *Believe It Or Not* books) noted that in 1905 R. P. Williams made a running high-kick of 10 feet 3 inches. See Ripley, *The New Believe It Or Not*, 9.

9. The statistical information in this paragraph is taken from zur Megede and Hymans, *Progression of World Best Performers*.

10. Reported in *Athletics World*, 2, no. 1 (1954): 16.

11. Quercetani, *Athletics: A History of Modern Track and Field Athletics*; Butler (ed.), *Statistics Handbook*, 9.

12. zur Megede and Hymans, *Progression of World Best Performers*.

13. Dyer, *Catching up the Men*, 148.

14. Stokvis, "Sports and Civilisation," 122.

15. Gibson, *Performance versus Results*, 28.

16. Bale, *Landscapes of Modern Sport*. The term *placelessness* is derived from Relph, *Place and Placelessness*.

17. Brohm, *Sport: A Prison of Measured Time*, 74.

18. Quoted in Braun, *Picturing Time*, 212.

19. Pronger, "Post-Sport: Transgressing Boundaries in Physical Culture," 284. Note also Rail, "Seismography of the Postmodern Condition," 148–49.

20. In figure skating, it has been found that jumps are perfected and found to be higher through the help of music as a guide to motion. Especially with the curved run in the "Fosbury flop," a musical piece could help the jumper control the speed of the approach. How might the IAAF standardize possible musical assistance in the future? This intriguing question and the accompanying observations have been posed by Joe Faust, e-mail communication, 12 August 1999.

21. Tuccaro, *Trois dialogues de l'exercise de sauter et voltiger au l'air*. I am grateful to Arnd Krüger of the University of Göttingen for alerting me to this.

22. Castiglione, *The Book of the Courtier*, 20. I am grateful to Anthony

Bale of Oxford University for this reference. Other early gymnastic treatises are alluded to in Glyse, "Instrumental Rationalization of Human Movement."

23. Quoted in Vigarello, "The Upward Training of the Body," 180.

24. Ueberhorst, *Friedrich Ludwig Jahn 1778/1978*, 64.

25. K. A. Knudsen, *Om sport–Indtryk fra en Rejse i England* (1895). Quoted in Korsgaard, *Kampen om Kroppen*, 167. I am very grateful to Jørn Møller (Gerlev Sports Academy, Slagelse, Denmark) for alerting me to this quotation and for translating it into English.

26. Lindhard, *The Theory of Gymnastics*, 345.

27. Eichberg, *Body Cultures*.

28. Braun, *Picturing Time*, 108.

29. Eichberg, *Body Cultures*, 111–27.

30. Clark, "The 'New Man's' Body."

31. See, for example, Bernett, *Leichtatletik in Historischen Bilddokumenten*, 105. Here, a photograph from 1911 shows the German gym master, Hans Liesche demonstrating the turner technique by clearing two grown men, but in the absence of rope or bar. He is shown taking off from a wooden ramp. This photograph is followed by the widely published image of Mecklenburg and the so-called Tutsi high jumper.

32. Guttmann, *Games and Empires*, notes: "Gymnastics became such an important element in Swiss culture that the development of soccer football [*sic*] was long delayed," (146). See also Ueberhorst, "Turnen."

33. Quoted in Webster, *Olympian Field Events*, 48. Similar stories are reported from Germany. See Tirala, *Sport und Rasse*.

34. I am grateful to Peter Mewett of Deakin University, Geelong, Australia, for this information.

35. This kind of high jumping remains as an oral record among people still living today. I am grateful to Steve Bailey of Winchester College for this information.

36. I am grateful to Roger Ruth of the University of Victoria, British Columbia, for this information.

37. See Holland, *Strange Facts and Clever Turns*, 65–73. Originally published as Oswald North, "The Champion Jumper of the World," *The Strand Magazine* (1897) 15.

38. For overviews and bibliographies of the variety of "traditional" body cultures in South America and Africa, see, van Mele and Renson, *Traditional*

Games in South America; and Scheerder and Renson, *Annotated Bibliography of Traditional Play and Games in Africa*.

39. Bull, *From Rattlesnake Hunt to Hockey*. Quoted in Vennum, *American Indian Lacrosse*, 123. But note that no record of vertical jumping is found in the monumental record of indigenous North American games and "sports" by Culin, *Games of the North American Indians*.

40. I am grateful to Bruce Kidd of the University of Toronto, Ontario, for reminding me of Inuit jumping. See "Inuit Jumping Games" at http://www.ahs.uwaterloo.ca/~museum/vexhibit/inuit/english/jump.html. Consulted 18 July 2001.

41. Quoted in Damm, "The So-Called Sport Activities of Primitive People," 54.

42. See Renson, "Save Our Sports," 44. This event is covered in more detail in Marschall, *Der Berg des Herrn der Erde*. I am grateful to Henning Eichberg of Idrætsforsk, Denmark, for this reference.

43. Guttmann, *A Whole New Ball Game*.

44. Eichberg, *Body Cultures*, 128–48.

Bibliography

Admiralty Naval Staff. *The Belgian Congo*. London: Naval Intelligence Division, 1944.

Akeley, Mary. *Congo Eden*. London: Gollancz, 1951.

Archer-Straw, Petrine. *Negrophilia: Avant-Garde Paris and Black Culture in the 1920s*. London: Thames and Hudson, 2000.

Ashcroft, Bill. "Constructing the Post-Colonial Male Body." In *The Body in the Library*, edited by Leigh Dale and Simon Ryan, 207–24. Amsterdam: Rodopi, 1998.

Ashcroft, Bill, Gareth Griffiths, and Helen Tiffin. *The Empire Writes Back: Theory and Practice in Post-Colonial Literature*. London: Routledge, 1989.

———. *Key Concepts in Post-Colonial Studies*. London: Routledge, 1998.

Ashe, R. P. *Chronicles of Uganda*. London: Hodder and Stoughton, 1894.

Atkinson, David, and Klaus Dodds. "Introduction: Geopolitical Traditions." In *Geopolitical Traditions: A Century of Geopolitical Thought*, edited by Klaus Dodds and David Atkinson, 1–24. London: Routledge, 2000.

Augé, Marc. *A Sense for the Other: The Timeliness and Relevance of Anthropology*. Stanford: Stanford University Press, 1998.

Avoy, Mark. "Physical Endowment of African People." *Insight and Opinion* 4, no. 3 (1969): 93–97.

Bale, John. *Landscapes of Modern Sport*, London: Leicester University Press, 1994.

———. "The Rhetoric of Running: The Representation of Kenyan Body Culture in the Early Twentieth Century." In *Sports, Body, and Health*, edited by Jørn Hansen and Niels Kayser Nielsen, 123–32. Odense: Odense University Press, 2000.

Bale, John, and Joe Sang. *Kenyan Running: Movement Culture, Geography, and Global Change*. London: Frank Cass, 1996.

Balfour, Patrick. *Lords of the Equator: An African Journey*. London: Hutchinson, 1937.

Ball, Michael, and Gregory Smith. *Analyzing Visual Data*. London: Sage, 1992.

Banks, Marcus. *Ethnicity*. London: Routledge, 1996.

Barnes, Trevor. *Logics of Dislocation: Models, Metaphors, and Meanings of Economic Space*. New York: Guilford, 1996.

Barnes, Trevor, and James Duncan, eds. *Writing Worlds: Discourse, Text, and Metaphor in the Representation of Landscape*. London: Routledge, 1992.

Barnes, Trevor, and Derek Gregory, eds. *Reading Human Geography*. London: Arnold, 1996.

Barnett, Clive. "Awakening the Dead: Who Needs the History of Geography?" *Transactions of the Institute of British Geographers*, n.s., 20, no. 4 (1995): 417–19.

———. "The Cultural Turn: Fashion or Progress in Human Geography?" *Antipode* 30, no. 4 (1998): 379–94.

———. "Impure and Worldly Geography: The Africanist Discourse of the Royal Geographical Society." *Transactions of the Institute of British Geographers*, n.s., 23, no. 2 (1998): 239–52.

Barns, Alexander. *The Wonderland of the Eastern Congo*. London: Putnam, 1922.

———. *Across the Great Craterland to the Congo*. London: Ernest Benn, 1923.

———. *The African Eldorado*. London: Methuen, 1926.

Barringer, Tim. "Fabricating Africa: Livingstone and The Visual Image." In *David Livingstone and the Victorian Encounter with Africa*, edited by J. Mackenzie, 169–200. London: National Portrait Gallery, 1996.

Barry, Andrew. "Reporting and Visualising." In *Visual Culture*, edited by Clive Jenks, 42–57. London: Routledge, 1995.

Barthes, Roland. *Mythologies*. London: Paladin, 1973.

———. *Image, Music, Text*. London: Fontana, 1977.

———. *Camera Lucida*. London: Vintage, 1993.

Bate, David. "Photography and the Colonial Vision." *Third Text* 22 (1993): 81–91.

Baucom, Ian. *Out of Place: Englishness, Empire, and the Locations of Identity*. Princeton: Princeton University Press, 1996.

Bauman, Oscar. *Durch Massailand zur Nilquelle*. Berlin: Dietrich Reimer, 1894.

Beckles, Hilary, and Brian Stoddart, eds. *Liberation Cricket*. Manchester: Manchester University Press, 1995.

Belotti, Felice. *Fabulous Congo*. London: Andre Deutsch, 1957.

Berg, Lawrence, and Robin Kearns. "Naming as Norming: Race, Gender, and Identity Politics of Naming Places in Aotearoa/New Zealand." *Society and Space* 14, no. 1 (1996): 99–122.

Berger, John. *Ways of Seeing*. London: Penguin, 1977.

Berger, John, and Jean Mohr. *Another Way of Telling*. Cambridge, England: Granta, 1989.

Bernatzik, Hugo. *Afrika: Handbuch der Angewandten Völkerunde*. Innsbruck: Schüsselverlag, 1947.

Bernault, Florence, and Thomas Spear. "Guest Editors' Introduction." *Africa Today* 45, no. 1 (1998): 3–6.

Bernett, Hajo. *Leichtatletik in Historischen Bilddokumenten*. Munich: Copress Verlag, 1986.

Bhabha, Homi. "Of Mimicry and Man: The Ambivalence of Colonial Discourse." In *Tensions of Empire*, edited by Frederick Cooper and Ann Stoler, 152–60. Berkeley: University of California Press, 1997. Originally published in *October 28* (1984), 125–33.

Bhatt, Chetan. "Ethnic Absolutism and Authoritarian Spirit." *Theory, Culture, and Society* 16, no. 2 (1999): 65–85.

Birnbaum, Martin. "Reception in Ruanda." *Natural History* 44 (1939): 298–307.

Bivona, Daniel. *Desire and Contradiction: Imperial Vision and Domestic Debates in Victorian Literature*. Manchester: Manchester University Press, 1990.

Blacking, John. "Games and Sports in Pre-Colonial African Societies." In *Sport in Africa*, edited by William Baker and James Mangan, 3–22. New York: Africana, 1987.

Blake, Andrew. *Body Language: The Meaning of Modern Sport*. London: Lawrence and Wishart, 1996.

Blake, Katherine. *Play, Games, and Sport: The Literary Works of Lewis Carroll*. Ithaca: Cornell University Press, 1974.

Blanchard, Kendall. *The Anthropology of Sport*. Westport, Conn.: Bergin and Garvey, 1995.

Bleys, Rudi. *The Geography of Perversion*. London: Cassell, 1996.

Blixen, Karen [Isaac Dinesen]. *Out of Africa*. Harmondsworth, England: Penguin, 1954.

Blunt, Allison. *Travel, Gender, and Imperialism: Mary Kingley and West Africa*. New York: Guilford, 1994.

Blunt, Allison, and Gillian Rose, eds. *Writing Women and Space*. New York: Guilford, 1994.

Boehmer, Elleke. *Colonial and Postcolonial Literature*. Oxford: Oxford University Press, 1995.

Borgerhoff, Robert. *Le Ruanda-Urundi*. Brussels: Dewit, 1928.

Bourdieu, Pierre. *Photography: A Middle-Brow Art*. Stanford: Stanford University Press, 1990.

————. *Sociology in Question*. London: Sage, 1993.

Bourgeois, R. *Banyarwanda et Barundi*. Vol. 1. Brussels: Académie Royale des Sciences Coloniales, 1957.

Braun, Marta. *Picturing Time: The work of Etienne-Jules Marey, 1830–1904*. Chicago: University of Chicago Press, 1992.

Briey, Comte de. "Musinga." *Congo* 1 (1920): 1–13.

Brohm, Jean-Marie. *Sport: A Prison of Measured Time*. London: Ink Links, 1978.

Brosseau, Marc. "Geography's Literature." *Progress in Human Geography* 18, no. 3 (1994): 333–53.

Brown, James. "The Solitude of Edward Said: The Fate of Gibb, Lane, and Massignon in *Orientalism*." *Economy and Society* 28, no. 4 (1999): 550–69.

Brownell, Susan. *Training the Body for China*. Chicago: University of Chicago Press, 1995.

————. "Thinking Dangerously: The Person and His Ideas." In Henning Eichberg, *Body Cultures: Essays on Sport, Space, and Identity*, edited by John Bale and Chris Philo, 22–44. London: Routledge, 1998.

Bruce, Toni. "Postmodernism and the Possibilities of Writing 'Vital' Sports Texts." In *Sport and Postmodern Times*, edited by Geneviève Rail, 3–19. Albany: State University of New York Press, 1998.

Bryant, John. "Major's Mission Seeks Leap of Faith." *The Times* (London). 30 November 1995, 46.

Buck-Morss, Susan. *The Dialectics of Space: Walter Benjamin and the Arcades Project*, Cambridge: MIT Press, 1991.

Burgin, Victor. "Art, Common Sense, and Photography." In *The Camerawork Essays: Context and Meaning in Photography*, edited by Jessica Evans, 74–85. London: Rivers Oram, 1997.

Burleigh, Michael, and Wolfgang Wiermann. *The Racial State: Germany 1933–1945*. London: Routledge, 1991.

Burton, Richard. *The Lakes Region of Central Africa.* Vol. 2. 1860. Reprint, London: Sidgewick and Johnson, 1961.

Butchart, Alexander. *The Anatomy of Power: European Constructions of the African Body.* London: Zed Books, 1998.

Butler, Mark. *Statistics Handbook.* Monaco: International Amateur Athletics Federation, 1995.

Cagen, Steve. "Photography's Contribution to the 'Western' Vision of the Colonized 'Other.'" Seminar paper, Rutgers University, 1990.

Camus, C. "Le Ruanda et l'Urundi." *Bulletin de la Societé Royale Belge de Géographie* 47 (1923): 112–20.

Castiglione, Baltasar. *The Book of the Courtier.* Translated by Friench Simpson. 1528. Reprint, New York: Frederick Unger, 1959.

Catlow, Lewis. *In Search of the Primitive.* New York: Little, Brown, 1966.

Chapman, F. Spencer. *Lightest Africa.* London: Chatto and Windus, 1955.

Childs, Peter, and Patrick Williams. *An Introduction to Postcolonial Theory.* London: Prentice-Hall, 1997.

Chrétien, Jean-Pierre. "Hutu et Tutsi au Rwanda et au Burundi." In *Au Cœur l'Éthnie,* edited by Jean-Loup Amrelle and Elika M'Bokolo, 129–85. Paris: Éditions la Découverte, 1995.

———. *Rwanda: Les médias du génocide.* Paris: Éditions Karthala, 1995.

Church, J. E. "From Dr. Church." *Ruanda Notes* 32 (April 1930): 17–20.

Clark, Toby. "The 'New Man's' Body: A Motif in Early Soviet Culture." In *Art of the Soviets,* edited by Matthew Brown and Brandon Taylor, 33–50. Manchester: Manchester University Press, 1993.

Clarke, Graham. *The Photograph.* Oxford: Oxford University Press, 1997.

Clifford, James. *The Predicament of Culture.* Cambridge: Harvard University Press, 1988.

———. *Routes: Travel and Translation in the Late Twentieth Century.* Cambridge: Harvard University Press, 1997.

Clifford, James, and George Marcus, eds. *Writing Culture: The Poetics and Politics of Ethnography.* Berkeley: University of California Press, 1986.

Codere, Helene. *The Biography of an African Country.* Tervuren, Belgium: Koninklijk Museum voor Midden-Afrika, 1973.

Coombes, Annie. "The Recalcitrant Self: Colonial Contact and the Question of Hybridity." In *Colonial Discourse/Postcolonial Theory,* edited by Frances Baker, Peter Hulme, and Margaret Iversen, 89–114. Manchester: Manchester University Press, 1994.

————. *Reinventing Africa: Museums, Material Culture, and Popular Imagination in Late Victorian and Edwardian England.* New Haven: Yale University Press, 1995.

Coupez, André and Thomas Kamanzi. *Littérature de cour de Rwanda.* Oxford: Clarendon, 1970.

Crang, Mike. "Picturing Pictures: Research through the Tourist Gaze." *Progress in Human Geography* 21, no. 3 (1997): 359–73.

Cresswell, Tim. *In Place/Out of Place: Geography, Ideology, and Transgression.* Minneapolis: University of Minnesota Press, 1996.

Cromwell, Dean, and Al Wesson. *Championship Techniques in Track and Field.* New York: McGraw-Hill, 1941.

Crowther, Samuel, and Arthur Ruhl. *Rowing and Track Athletics.* New York: Macmillan, 1905.

Crush, Jonathon. "Postcolonialism, De-colonisation, and Geography." In *Geography and Empire*, edited by Anne Godlewska and Neil Smith, 333–50. Oxford: Blackwell, 1994.

Culin, Stuart. *Games of the North American Indians.* 1907. Reprint, New York: Dover, 1975.

Curry, Michael. *The Work in the World: Geographical Practice and the Written Word.* Minneapolis: University of Minnesota Press, 1996.

Czekanowski, Jan. *Forschungen im Nil-Congo-Zwischengebeit.* Vol 3. Leipzig: Klinkhardt und Bierman, 1911.

Damkjær, Søren. "Innocent Gymnastics in Turbulent Times: Reciprocal Images of Gymnastics in Denmark and the Soviet Union." *Culture and History* 14 (1997): 114–28.

Damm, Hans. "The So-Called Sport Activities of Primitive People: A Contribution Towards the Genesis of Sport." In *The Cross-Cultural Analysis of Sport and Games*, edited by Günther Lüschen, 52–69. Champaign, Ill.: Stipes, 1970.

Darby, H. C. "The Problem of Geographical Description." *Transactions of the Institute of British Geographers* 30 (1962): 1–14.

Decle, Lionel. "The Watussi." *Journal of the Anthropological Institute* 23 (1892): 423–26.

Deford, Frank. "Let the Games Begin." *National Geographic* 190 (1996): 42–69.

de Ligne, Prince Eugène. *Africa: L'évolution d'un continent vue des volcans du Kivu.* Brussels: Librairie Générale, 1961.

Denzin, Norman. *Interpretive Ethnography: Ethnographic Practices for the Twenty-First Century*. Thousand Oaks, Calif.: Sage, 1997.

Derkinderen, Gaston. *Atlas du Congo Belge et du Ruanda-Urundi*. Brussels: Elsevier, 1955.

Des Forges, Alison. 1972. *Defeat Is the Only Bad News: Ruanda under Musinga 1896–1931*. Ann Arbor, Mich.: University Microfilms, 1972.

———. "The Ideology of Genocide."*Issue: A Journal of Opinion* 23, no. 2 (1995): 44–47.

———. *Leave None to Tell the Story: Genocide in Rwanda*. New York: Human Rights Watch, 1999. Web site: http://www.hrw.org/reports/1999/rwanda/.

Destexhe, Alain. *Rwanda and Genocide in the Twentieth Century*. London: Pluto, 1995.

Deuchen Hochschule für Körperkultur. *Körperkultur und Sport*. Leipzig: Verlag Enzyklopädie, 1960.

Deville-Danthu, Bernadette. *Le sport en noir et blanc*, Paris: L'Harmattan, 1997.

d'Hertefelt, Marcel. "Mythes et idéologies dans le Rwanda ancien et contemporain." In *The Historian and Tropical Africa*, edited by J. Vansina, R. Murray, and L. Thomas, 219–38, Oxford: Oxford University Press, 1964.

d'Hertefelt, Marcel, and D. de Lame, eds. *Societé, culture, et histoire du Rwanda*. Tervuren, Belgium: Koninklijk Museum voor Midden-Afrika, 1987.

Diem, Carl. *Weltgeschichte des Sports und der Leibeserziehung*. Stuttgart: Cotta Verlag, 1960.

Dimco, Paul. "Race, Colonialism, and the Emergence of Football in India." *Scottish Centre Research Papers in Sport, Leisure, and Society*, 3 (1998–99): 15–30.

Doane, Mary Ann. "Temporality, Storage, Legibility: Freud, Marey, and the Cinema," *Critical Inquiry*, 22, no. 2 (1996): 312–43.

Downing, Taylor. *Olympia*. London: British Film Institute, 1992.

Driver, Felix. "Geography's Empire: Histories of Geographical Knowledge." *Society and Space* 10, no. 1 (1992): 23–40.

———. "Geography, Empire, and Visualisation: Making Representations." *Research Papers, gen. series*, no. 1. London: University of London, Royal Holloway, and Bedford New College, 1994.

———. "Sub-merged Identities: Familiar and Unfamiliar Histories," *Transactions of the Institute of British Geographers*, n.s. 20, no. 4 (1995): 410–13.

———. "Visualizing Geography: A Journey to the Heart of the Discipline." *Progress in Human Geography* 19, no. 1 (1995): 123–34.

————. "Histories of the Present: The History of the Philosophy of Geography, Part III." *Progress in Human Geography*, 20, no. 1 (1996): 100–109.

————. *Geography Militant: Cultures of Exploration and Empire*, Oxford: Blackwell, 2000.

Duncan, James. "Sites of Representation: Place, Time, and the Discourse of the Other." In *Place/Culture/Representation*, edited by James Duncan and David Ley, 39–56. London: Routledge, 1993.

————. "After the Civil War: Reconstructing Cultural Geography as Heterotopia." In *Re-reading Cultural Geography*, edited by Kenneth Foote et al., 401–8. Austin: University of Texas Press, 1994.

Duncan, James, and Derek Gregory, eds. *Writes of Passage: Reading Travel Writing*. London: Routledge, 1999.

Duncan, James, and David Ley, eds. *Place/Culture/Representation*. London: Routledge, 1993.

Dupriez, R., ed. *Guide du voyageur au Congo Belge et au Ruanda-Urundi*. Brussels: L'Office du Congo Belge et de Ruanda-Urundi, 1949.

During, Simon. "Postmodernism, or Post-colonialism Today." In *The Post-Colonial Studies Reader*, edited by Bill Ashcroft, Gareth Griffiths, and Helen Tiffin, 125–29. London: Routledge, 1995. Originally published in *Textual Practice* 1, (1987), n.p.

Dyer, Kenneth. *Catching up the Men*. London: Junction Books, 1982.

Eagleton, Terry. "Postcolonialism and 'Postcolonialism.'" *Interpretations* 1, no. 1 (1998): 24–26.

Edwards, Elizabeth. "Introduction." In *Anthropology and Photography 1860–1920*, edited by Elizabeth Edwards, 3–17. New Haven: Yale University Press, 1992.

————. "Science Visualized: E. H. Man in the Andaman Islands." In *Anthropology and Photography 1860–1920*, edited by Elizabeth Edwards, 108–21. New Haven: Yale University Press, 1992.

————. "Beyond the Boundary: A Consideration of the expressive in Recent Photography and Anthropology." In *Rethinking Visual Anthropology*, edited by Marcus Banks and Howard Morphy, 53–80. New Haven: Yale University Press, 1997.

————. "Guest editorial." *History of Photography* 21, no. 1 (1997): 1–2.

Eichberg, Henning. "Kropskuturens trialektik." *Centring* 4, no. 3 (1983): 129–39.

————. "Forward Race and the Laughter of Pygmies." In *Fin de Siècle and its*

Legacy, edited by Mikulàs Tiech and Roy Porter, 115–31. Cambridge: Cambridge University Press, 1990.

———. *Body Cultures: Essays on Sport, Space, and Identity*. Edited by John Bale and Chris Philo. London: Routledge, 1998.

Elias, Michel, and Danielle Helbig. "Deux mille colines pour les 'petits' et les 'grands.'" In *Racisme du continent obscur*, edited by Jean-Pierre Jacquemin, 94–111. Brussels: Coopération par l'Éducation et la Culture-Le Noir du Blanc, 1991.

Entine, Jon. *Taboo: Why Black Athletes Dominate Sports, and Why We're Afraid to Talk About It*. New York: Public Affairs, 2000.

Fabian, Johannes. *Out of Our Minds: Reason and Madness in the Exploration of Central Africa*. Berkeley: University of California Press, 2000.

"Facts about Ruanda-Urundi." *The Belgian Congo Today* 2, no. 3 (1953): 98–102.

Faris, James. "Photography, Power, and the Nuba." In *Anthropology and Photography 1860–1920*, edited by Elizabeth Edwards, 211–17. New Haven: Yale University Press, 1992.

Farnell, Brenda. "Ethno-Graphics and the Moving Body." *Man* 29, no. 4 (1994): 929–74.

Farred, Grant. "The Maple Man: How Cricket Made a Postcolonial Intellectual." In *Rethinking C. L. R. James*, edited by Grant Farred, 165–86. Oxford: Blackwell, 1996.

Farson, Negley. *Behind God's Back*. New York: Harcourt, Brace, 1941.

"Felan." "An African Causerie." *African World* (August 1948): 12.

Fisiy, Cyprian. "Of Journeys and Border Crossings: Return of Refugees, Identity, and Reconstruction in Rwanda." *African Studies Review* 41, no. 1 (1998): 17–28.

Foucault, Michel. *The Archaeology of Knowledge*. London: Tavistock, 1972.

———. *Discipline and Punish*, Harmondsworth, England: Penguin, 1979.

Franche, Dominique. *Rwanda: Généalogie d'un génocide*, Paris. Éditions Mille et Une Nuits, 1997.

Fyfe, Gordon, and John Law. "Introduction: On the Invisibility of the Visual." In *Picturing Power: Visual Depictions and Social Relations*. Sociological Review Monograph Series, no. 35, ed. Gordon Fyfe and John Law, 1–14. London: Routledge, 1988.

Galtung, Johann. "Sport and International Understanding: Sport as a Carrier of Deep Culture and Structure." In *Sport and International Understanding*, edited by I. Ilmarinen, 12–19. Bern: Springer-Verlag, 1984.

Gandhi, Leela. *Postcolonial Theory: A Critical Introduction*. Edinburgh: Edinburgh University Press, 1998.

Garb, Tamar. *Bodies of Modernity: Figure and Flesh in Fin-de-Siècle France*. London: Thames and Hudson, 1998.

Gasarabwe-Laroche, Edouard. *Le geste Rwanda*. Paris: Union Générale d'Éditions, 1978.

———. "Meaningful Gestures," *The UNESCO Courier* 46, no. 9 (1993): 31–33.

Gatti, Attilio. "The Kingdom of the Giants," *Travel*, 77, nos. 7–11 (1941): 42.

———. "Jumping Giants of Africa." *The Negro Digest* (December 1945): 25–7.

———. *South of the Sahara*. London: Hodder and Stoughton, 1946.

Gatti, Ellen. *Exploring We Would Go*. London: Robert Hale, 1950.

Gatti, Ellen, and Attilio Gatti. *Here Is Africa*. New York: Charles Scribner's Sons, 1943.

Gates, Lisa. "Of Seeing and Otherness: Leni Riefenstal's African Photographs." In *The Imperial Imagination: German Colonialism and Its Legacy*, edited by Sara Friedrichsmeyer, Sara Lennox, and Susanne Zantop, 233–46. Ann Arbor: University of Michigan Press, 1998.

Geary, Christraud. "Photographic Practice in Africa and Its Implications for the Use of Historical Photographs as Contextual Evidence." In *Fotografia e storia dell'Africa*, edited by Alessandro Triulzi, 103–30. Naples: Instituto Universitario Orientale, 1995.

Gibson, John. *Performance versus Results: A Critique of Values in Contemporary Sport*. Albany: State University of New York Press, 1993.

Gidley, Mick. *Edward S. Curtis and the North American Indian, Incorporated*. Cambridge: Cambridge University Press, 1998.

Gikandi, Simon. *Maps of Englishness*. New York: Columbia University Press, 1996.

Gilbert, Helen. "Dance, Movement, and Resistance Politics." In *The Post-Colonial Studies Reader,* edited by Bill Ashcroft, Gareth Griffiths, and Helen Tiffin, 341–45. London: Routledge, 1995.

Gilbert, Helen, and Joanne Tompkins. *Post-Colonial Drama: Theory, Practice, and Politics*. London: Routledge, 1996.

Gildea, Roy, and Alice Young. "Ruanda and Burundi." *Focus* 13, no. 6 (1963): 1–6.

Gilman, Sander. *Difference and Pathology: Stereotypes of Sexuality, Race, and Madness,* Ithaca: Cornell University Press, 1985.

Gilroy, Paul. *Between Camps: Nations, Cultures, and the Allure of Race*. London: Allen Lane, 2000.

Gleyse, Jacques. "Instrumental Rationalization of Human Movement: An

Archeological Approach." In *Sport and Postmodern Times*, edited by Geneviève Rail, 239–60. Albany: State University of New York Press, 1998.

Godlewska, Anne, and Neil Smith. *Geography and Empire*. Oxford: Blackwell, 1994.

Gøksyr [misspelling of Goksøyr], Matti. "'One Certainly Expected a Great Deal More from the Savages': The Anthropology Days at St. Louis, 1904, and Their Aftermath." *International Journal of the History of Sport* 7, no. 2 (1990): 297-306.

Gordon, Robert. *Picturing Bushmen: The Denver Expedition of 1925*. Athens: Ohio University Press, 1997.

Götzen, G. A. von. *Durch Afrika von Ost nach West*. Berlin: Dietrich Reimer, 1895.

Gourdinne E. "Dans l'Est-africain allemand occupé par les belges." *Bulletin de la Société Belge d'Études Colonials* 26 (1919): 378–86.

Greenblatt, Stephen. "Resonance and Wonder." In *Exhibiting Cultures: the Poetics and Politics of Museum Display*, edited by Ivan Karp and Steven Levine, 42–56. Washington, D.C.: Smithsonian Institution, 1991.

—— *Marvelous Possessions: The Wonder of the New World*. Oxford: Clarendon, 1992.

Gregory, Derek. "Areal Differentiation and Post-Modern Human Geography." In *Horizons in Human Geography*, edited by Derek Gregory and Rex Walford, 67–96. London: Macmillan, 1989.

———. *Geographical Imaginations*. Oxford: Blackwell, 1994.

———. "Social Theory and Human Geography." In *Human Geography: Society, Space, and Social Science*, edited by Derek Gregory, Ron Martin, and Graham Smith, 78–112. London: Macmillan, 1994.

———. "Between the Book and the Lamp: Imaginative Geographies of Egypt, 1849–50." *Transactions of the Institute of British Geographers*, n.s. 20, no. 12 (1995): 29–57.

———. "Imaginative Geographies." *Progress in Human Geography*, 19 (1995): 447–85.

———. "Power, Knowledge, and Geography," *Geographische Zeitschrift*, 86, no. 2, (1998): 70–93.

Gren, Martin. *Earth Writing*. Publications Series B. Göteborg: Department of Geography, University of Göteborg, 1994.

Grogan, Ewart, and Arthur Sharp. *From the Congo to the Cape*. London: Hurst and Brackett, 1900.

Gunther, John. *Inside Africa*. London: Hamish Hamilton, 1955.

Guttmann, Allen. *From Ritual to Record: the Nature of Modern Sports*. New York: Columbia University Press, 1978.

———. *A Whole New Ball Game: An Interpretation of American Sports*. Chapel Hill: University of North Carolina Press, 1988.

———. *Games and Empires*. New York: Columbia University Press, 1994.

———. *The Erotic in Sports*. New York: Columbia University Press, 1996.

Haggard, Rider. *King Solomon's Mines*. London: Cassell, 1885.

Hall, Stuart. "The Spectacle of the Other." In *Representations*, edited by Stuart Hall, 223–90. London: Sage, 1997.

Haraway, Donna. *Primate Visions*. New York: Routledge, 1989.

Hildebrand, J. "The Geography of Games." *National Geographic* 36 (1919): 139–50.

Hintjens, Helen. "Explaining the 1994 Genocide in Rwanda." *The Journal of Modern African Studies*, 37, no. 2 (1999): 241–86.

———. "Through the Looking Glass: Belgians's Images of Rwanda," Paper presented at "Belgium's Africa," a conference at the University of Ghent, Belgium. 1999.

Hoberman, John. *Sport and Political Ideology*. London: Heinemann, 1984.

———. *Mortal Engines: The Science of Performance and the Dehumanization of Sport*. New York: Free Press, 1992.

———. *Darwin's Athletes: How Sport Has Damaged Black America and Preserved the Myth of Race*. Boston: Houghton Mifflin, 1997.

———. "Primacy of Performance: Superman, not Superathlete." In *Shaping the Superman: Fascist Body As Political Icon—Aryan Fascism*, edited by J. A. Mangan, 69–85. London: Frank Cass, 1999.

Hobsbawm, Eric. "Introduction: Inventing Traditions." In *The Invention of Tradition*, edited by Eric Hobsbawm and Terence Ranger, 1–14. Cambridge: Cambridge University Press, 1993.

Holland, Charles. *Strange Feats and Clever Turns*. London: Holland and Palmer, 1998.

Holmes, Geoffrey. [Untitled article.] *Ruanda Notes* 14 (1925), 6.

———. "Letter from Captain G. Holmes." *Ruanda Notes*, 15, no. 1 (1926): 20.

Honke, Gudrun. *Au plus profond de l'Afrique: Le Rwanda et la colonisation allemande 1885–1919*. Wuppertal: Peter Hammer Verlag, 1990.

Honke, Gudrun, and Otto Honke. *Le Rwanda et les allemands 1884–1916.* Notes accompanying an exhibition. Kigali, Rwanda: 1985.

Hopkins, Elizabeth. "The Ethnography of Conquest." In *Dialectical Anthropology: Essays in Honor of Stanley Diamond,* vol. 1, edited by Christine Ward Gailey, 137–65. Gainesville: University of Florida Press, 1992.

Hunter, Ian, and David Saunders. "Walks of Life," *Body and Society* 1, no. 2, (1995): 65–81.

Jack, E. M. *On the Congo Frontier: Exploration and Sport.* London: Fisher Unwin, 1914.

Jackson, Peter. "Constructions of Culture, Representations of Race: Edward Curtis's 'Way of Seeing.'" In *Inventing Places: Studies in Cultural Geography,* edited by Kay Anderson and Fay Gale, 90–106. Melbourne: Longman Cheshire, 1992.

Jackson, Peter, and Jane Jacobs. "Editorial." *Society and Space* 14, no. 1 (1996): 1–3.

Jacob, Irénée. *Dictionnaire Rwandais-Français.* 3 vols. Kigali: L'Institute National de Recherche Scientifique, 1984.

Jahoda, Gustav. *Images of Savages: Ancient Roots of Modern Prejudice in Western Culture.* London: Routledge, 1999.

James, Allison, Jenny Hockey, and Andrew Dawson. "Introduction: The Road from Santa Fe." In *After Writing Culture,* edited by Allison James, Jenny Hockey, and Andrew Dawson, 1–15. London: Routledge, 1997.

James, C. L. R. *Beyond a Boundary.* London: Stanley Paul, 1963.

Jamoule, M. "Notre mandat sur Ruanda-Urundi." *Congo,* 7, no. 1 (1927): 477–96.

JanMohamed, Abdul R. "The Economy of the Manichean Allegory: The Function of Racial Difference in Colonial Literature." In *"Race," Writing, and Difference,* edited by Henry Louis Gates, 78–106. Chicago: University of Chicago Press, 1986.

Jarvie, Grant, and Joseph Maguire. *Sport and Leisure in Social Thought.* London: Routledge, 1995.

Jefremovas, Villia. "Contested Identites: Power and the Fictions of Ethnicity, Ethnography, and History in Rwanda." *Anthropoligica* 39, (1997): 91–104.

———. "Treacherous Waters: The Politics of History and the Politics of Genocide in Rwanda and Burundi." *Africa,* 20, no. 2, (2000): 298–308.

Johnston, R. J., et al., eds. *The Dictionary of Human Geography.* Oxford: Blackwell, 2000.

Jokl, Ernst. "High Jump Technique of the Central African Watussis." *Journal of Physical Education and School Hygiene* 33 (1941): 145–9.

———. "African Man-Power." *Race Relations* 11, no. 2 (1944): 504–14.

———. *Research in Physical Education.* Lexington: University of Kentucky, 1960.

———. *Medical Sociology and Cultural Anthropology of Sport and Physical Education.* Springfield, Ill.: Thomas, 1964.

———. *The Physiology of Exercise.* Springfield, Ill.: Thomas, 1964.

———. *South African Reminiscences.* Lexington, Ky.: 1988. Self-published.

Jokl, Ernst, et al. *Sport in the Cultural Pattern of the World.* Helsinki: Institute of Occupational Health, 1956.

Kabagewa, Innocent. *Ruanda unter deutscher Kolonialherrschaft 1899–1916.* Frankfurt am Main: Peter Lang, 1993.

Kagame, Alexis. *Le code des institutions politiques du Rwanda précolonial.* Brussels: Institut Royal Colonial Belge, 1952.

Kala-Lobe, Iwiyé. "La vocation africaine du sport." *Présence Africaine* 41 (1962): 34–57.

Kandt, Richard. *Caput Nili: Eine empfindsame Reise den Quellen des Nils.* Berlin: Deitrich Reimer, 1914.

Kanyamachumbi, Msgr. P. *Société, culture, et pouvoir politique en Afrique Interlacustrine.* Kinshasa: Éditions Select, 1995.

Kashamuru, A. *Les mœurs et les civilisations des peuples des grand lacs africains.* Bibliothèque Publique Beaubourg, Paris, n.d. Mimeographed.

Keane, Fergal. *Season of Blood: A Rwandan Journey.* Penguin: London, 1996.

Kearns, Gerry. "The Imperial Subject: Geography and Travel in the Work of Mary Kingsley and Halford Mackinder." *Transactions of the Institute of British Geographers*, n.s. 22, no. 4 (1997): 450–72.

Kesby, John. *The Cultural Regions of East Africa.* London: Academic, 1979.

Killanin, Lord, and John Rodda. *The Olympic Games.* London: Macdonald and Janes, 1976.

Kirby, Andrew. "The Construction of Geographical Images: The World According to Biggles (and Other Fictional Characters)." In *Geopolitical Traditions: A Century of Geopolitical Thought*, edited by Klaus Dodds and David Atkinson, 52–71. London: Routledge, 2000.

Kirshenblatt-Gimblett, Barbara. "Objects of Ethnography." In *Exhibiting Cultures: The Poetics and Politics of Museum Display*, edited by Ivan Karp and Steven Levine, 386–443. Washington, D.C.: Smithsonian Institute, 1991.

Klein, Allan. *Sugarball: The American Game, the Dominican Dream.* New Haven: Yale University Press, 1991.

Kna, H. "Die Watussi als Springkünstler." *Erdball* 12 (1929): 459–62.

Kohn, Marek. *The Race Gallery: The Return of Racial Science.* London: Jonathan Cape, 1995.

Korsgaard, Ove. *Kampen om Kroppen.* Copenhagen: Gyldendal, 1982.

Lalvani, Suren. *Photography, Vision, and the Production of Modern Bodies.* Albany: State University of New York Press, 1996.

Law, John, and John Whittaker. "On the Art of Representation." In *Picturing Power: Visual Depictions and Social Relations.* Sociological Review Monograph Series no. 35, ed. Gordon Fyfe and John Law, 160–83. London: Routledge, 1988.

Lemarchand, René. *Rwanda and Burundi.* London: Pall Mall, 1970.

———. "Rwanda: The Rationality of Genocide." In *Ethnic Hatred: Genocide in Rwanda*, edited by Obi Igwanu, 59–70. London: ASEN Publications, 1995.

———. *Burundi: Ethnic Conflict and Genocide.* New York: Woodrow Wilson Center, 1996.

Lestrade, Arthur. *Notes d'ethnographie du Rwanda.* Tervuren, Belgium: Koninklijk Museum voor Midden-Afrika, 1972.

"Letter from Father Joseph." *Annalen der Afrikaansche Missiën* 4 (1905): 66.

Linden, Ian. *Church and Revolution in Rwanda.* Manchester: Manchester University Press, 1977.

Lindhard, J. *The Theory of Gymnastics.* London: Methuen, 1934.

Lively, Adam. *Masks: Blackness, Race, and the Imagination.* London: Chatto and Windus, 1998.

Livingstone, David. *The Geographical Tradition.* Oxford: Blackwell, 1992.

———. "Reproduction, Representation, and Authenticity: A Rereading." *Transactions of the Institute of British Geographers*, n.s., 23, no. 1 (1998): 13–20.

Loizos, Peter. *Innovation in Ethnographic Film.* Chicago: University of Chicago Press, 1993.

Loomba, Ania. *Colonialism/Postcolonialism.* London: Routledge, 1998.

Louis, William. *Ruanda-Urundi: 1884–1919.* Oxford: Clarendon, 1963.

Low, Gail Ching-Liang. *White Skins, Black Masks: Representation and Colonisation.* London: Routledge, 1996.

Lowe, Lisa. *Critical Terrains: French and British Orientalisms.* Ithaca: Cornell University Press, 1991.

Lutz, Catherine, and Jane Collins. *Reading National Geographic*. Chicago: University of Chicago Press, 1993.

MacAloon, John. *This Great Symbol: Pierre de Coubertin and the Origins of the Modern Olympic Games*. Chicago: University of Chicago Press, 1981.

MacCannell, Dean. *The Tourist: A New Theory of the Leisure Class*. New York: Schocken, 1989.

Mackenzie, John. *Orientalism: History, Theory, and the Arts*. Manchester: Manchester University Press, 1995.

McClelland, John. "The Numbers of Reason: Luck, Logic, and Art in Renaissance Concepts of Sport." In *Ritual and Record*, edited by John M. Carter and Arnd Krüger, 53–64. New York: Greenwood, 1990.

McClintock, Anne. *Imperial Leather: Race, Gender, and Sexuality in the Colonial Contest*. London: Routledge, 1995.

McDonal, G., et al. *Area Handbook for Burundi*. Washington, D.C.: U.S. Government Printing Office, 1969.

McFee, Graham, and Alan Tomlinson. "Riefenstahl's Olympia: Ideology and Aesthetics in the Shaping of the Aryan Athletic Body." *The International Journal of the History of Sport* 16 (1999): 86–106.

McQuire, Scott. *Visions of Modernity: Representations, Memory, Time, and Space in the Age of the Camera*. London: Sage, 1998.

Mair, Lucy. *African Kingdoms*. Oxford: Oxford University Press, 1977.

Makower, Katherine. *The Coming of the Rain: The Life of Joe Church*. Carlisle, England: Paternoster Press, 1999.

Malkki, Liisa. *Purity and Exile*. Chicago: University of Chicago Press, 1995.

Mallon, Bill. *The 1904 Olympic Games: Results for All Competitors in All Events, with Commentary*. Jefferson, N.C.: McFarland, 1999.

Mamdami, Mahmood. "From Conquest to Consent as a Basis of State Formation: Reflections on Rwanda." *New Left Review* 316 (1996): 3–36.

———. *When Victims Become Killers: Colonialism, Nativism, and the Genocide in Rwanda*. Princeton: Princeton University Press, 2001.

Mangan, James. *The Games Ethic and Imperialism*. London: Viking, 1986.

Maquet, Jacques. *Ruanda: Essai photographique sur une société africaine en transition*. Brussels: Elsevier, 1957.

———. *The Premise of Inequality in Ruanda*. London: Oxford University Press, 1961.

Marcus, George, and Michael Fischer. *Anthropology as Cultural Critique*. Chicago: University of Chicago Press, 1986.

Massonnet, Alexandre. "Rôle et place du sport et du jeu au Rwanda." Master's thesis, Université Panthéon-Sorbonne, Paris, 1996.

Mauss, Marcel. "Techniques of the Body." In *Incorporations*, edited by Jonathan Crary and Sanford Kwinter, 455–77. New York: Zone, 1993. Originally published in 1934.

Maxwell, Anne. *Colonial Photography and Exhibitions*. London: Leicester University Press, 1999.

Mazrui, Ali. "Boxer Muhammad Ali and Soldier Idi Amin as International Political Symbols: The Bioeconomics of Sport and War." *Comparative Studies in Society and History*, 19, no. 2 (1977): 189–215.

Mecklenburg, Adolf Friedrich Herzog zu. *In the Heart of Africa*. London: Cassell, 1910. Originally published as *Ins innerste Afrika* (Leipzig: Klinkhardt und Biermann, 1909).

———. "A Land of Giants and Pygmies" *National Geographic* 23 (1912): 366–88.

Meeker, Oden. *Report on Africa*. London: Chatto and Windus, 1955.

Megede, Ekkehard zur, and Richard Hymans. *Progression of World Best Performers*. Monaco: International Amateur Athletics Federation, 1995.

Melik-Chakhnazarov, Achôt. *Le sport en Afrique*. Paris: Présence Africaine, 1971.

Mentore, George. "Society, Body, and Style: An Archery Contest in an Amerindian Society." In *Games, Sports, and Cultures*, edited by Noel Dyke, 65–80. Oxford: Berg, 2000.

Meyer, Hans. *Les Burundi: Une étude ethnologique en Afrique Orientale*. 1916. French reprint of original German edition. Paris: Société Français d'Histoire d'Outre Mer, 1984.

Michaels, Anne. *Fugitive Pieces*. London: Bloomsbury, 1997.

Michiels, A., and N. Laude. *Notre colonie: Géographie et notice historique*. Brussels: A. Dewit, 1924.

Miller, Christopher. *Blank Darkness: Africanist Discourse in French*. Chicago: University of Chicago Press, 1985.

———. "Theories of Africans: The Question of Literacy and Anthropology." In *"Race," Writing, and Difference*, edited by Henry Louis Gates, 281–300. Chicago: University of Chicago Press, 1985.

Miller, Patrick. "The Anatomy of Scientific Racism: Racialist Responses to Black Athletic Achievement." *Journal of Sport History* 25, no. 1 (1998): 119–51.

Mills, Sara. "Knowledge, Gender, and Empire." In *Writing Women and Space: Colonial and Postcolonial Geographies*, edited by Alison Blunt and Gillian Rose, 29–50. New York: Guilford, 1994.

Minshull, Phil. "First in Flight." *IAAF Magazine* 11, no. 2 (1996): 62–5.

Mirzoeff, Nicholas. *Bodyscape: Art, Modernity, and the Ideal Figure*, London: Routledge, 1995.

———. "What is *Visual Culture?*" In *The Visual Culture Reader*, edited by Nicholas Mirzoeff, 3–13. London: Routledge, 1999.

Mitchell, Don. *Cultural Geography: A Critical Introduction*. Oxford: Blackwell, 2000.

Morgan, William. "Hassiba Boulmerka and Islamic Green: International Sports, Cultural Differences, and Their Postmodern Interpretation." In *Sport and Postmodern Times*, edited by Geneviève Rail, 345–66. Albany: State University of New York Press, 1998.

Montefiore, Janet. "Latin, Arithmetic, and Mastery: A Reading of Two Kipling Fictions." In *Modernism and Empire*, edited by Howard Booth and Nigel Rigby, 112–36. Manchester: Manchester University Press, 2000.

Moore, Sally Falk. *Anthropology and Africa: Changing Perspectives on a Changing Scene*. Charlottesville: University of Virginia Press, 1994.

Moore, W. R. "White Magic in the Belgian Congo." *National Geographic* 63 (1952): 323–62.

Moore-Gilbert, Bart. *Postcolonial Theory: Contexts, Practices, Politics*. London: Verso, 1997.

Morin, Karen. "British Women Travellers and Constructions of Racial Difference across the Nineteenth Century American West." *Transactions of the Institute of British Geographers*, n.s., 23, no. 4 (1998): 311–30.

Morley, David, and Kevin Robins. *Spaces of Identity: Global Media, Electronic Landscapes, and Cultural Boundaries*. London: Routledge, 1995.

Morphy, Howard, and Marcus Banks. "Introduction: Rethinking Visual Anthropology." In *Rethinking Visual Anthropology*, edited by Marcus Banks and Howard Morphy, 1–35. New Haven: Yale University Press, 1997.

Mudimbe, V. Y. *The Idea of Africa*. Indianapolis: Indiana University Press, 1993.

Muybridge, Eadweard. *The Human Figure in Motion*. 1901. Reprint, New York: Dover, 1955.

Naylor, Simon, and Gareth Jones. "Writing Orderly Geographies of Distant Places: The Regional Survey Movement and Latin America." *Ecumeme* 4, no. 3 (1997): 273–299.

Ndejuru, Aimable. "Studien zur Rolle der Leibesübungen in der traditionellen Gesellschaft Rwanda." Ph.D. diss., University of Cologne, 1983.

"Negervolksspelen." *Annalen der Afrikaansche Missiën*, 4 (1905): 102.

Newbury, Catharine. *The Cohesion of Oppression: Clientship and Ethnicity in Rwanda 1860–1960*. New York: Columbia University Press, 1988.

———. "Ethnicity and the Politics of History in Rwanda." *Africa Today* 45, no. 1 (1998): 45–58.

Newbury, David. "The Clans of Rwanda: An Historical Hypothesis." *Africa* 50, no. 4 (1989): 389–403.

———. "Understanding Genocide." *African Studies Review*, 41, no. 1 (1998): 73–79.

Nochlin, Linda. *The Politics of Vision: Essays on Nineteenth-Century Art and Society*. London: Thames and Hudson, 1991.

Norden, Herman. *Fresh Tracks in the Belgian Congo*. London: Witherby, 1924.

Olsson, Gunnar. *Birds in Egg/Eggs in Bird*. London: Pion, 1980.

———. *Lines of Power/Limits of Language*. Minneapolis: University of Minnesota Press, 1991.

Omo-Osage, Anthony. *African Unity through Sports*. Benin City, Nigeria: Ambik Press, [1965?].

Oriard, Michael. *Reading Football: How the Popular Press Created an American Spectacle*. Chapel Hill: University of North Carolina Press, 1993.

Owusu, Maxwell. "Ethnography of Africa: The Usefulness of the Useless," *Amercian Anthropologist* 80, no. 1 (1978): 310–34.

Pagès, Albert. *Un royaume hamite au centre de l'Afrique*. Brussels: Librairie Falk Fils, 1933.

Parish, Oscar von. "Zwei Reisen durch Ruanda, 1902 bis 1903." *Globus* 85, no. 1 (1904): 5–13, 73–79.

Parry, Benita. "Resistance Theory/Theorising Resistance, or Two Cheers for Nativism." In *Colonial Discourse/Postcolonial Theory*, edited by Francis Barker, Peter Hulme, and Margaret Iversen, 172–96. Manchester: Manchester University Press, 1994.

Pauwels, Marcel. "Jeux et divertissements au Rwanda." *Annali Lateranensi* 24 (1960): 219–363.

Pennycook, Alastair. *English and the Discourses of Colonialism*. London: Routledge, 1998.

Phillips, Richard. *Mapping Men and Empire: A Geography of Adventure*. London: Routledge, 1997.

Pieterse, Jan. *White on Black: Images of Africa and Blacks in Western Popular Culture*. New Haven: Yale University Press, 1992.

Pinney, Christopher. "Classification and Fantasy in the Photographic Construction of Caste and Tribe." *Visual Anthropology*, 3 (1990): 259–88.

———. "The Parallel Histories of Anthropology and Photography." In *Anthropology and Photography 1860–1920*, edited by Elizabeth Edwards, 74–96. New Haven: Yale University Press, 1992.

———. *Camera Indica: The Social Life of Indian Photographs*. London: Reaktion 1997.

Piscicelli, Maurizio. "Nel Ruanda." *Bolletino della Società Geografica Italiana* 4, no. 12 (1911): 197–205.

Poignant, Rosalind. "Surveying the Field: The Making of the RAI Photographic Collection." In *Anthropology and Photography 1860–1920*, edited by Elizabeth Edwards, 42–73. New Haven: Yale University Press, 1992.

Poole, Deborah. *Vision, Race, and Modernity: A Visual Economy of the Andean Image World*. Princeton: Princeton University Press, 1997.

Porteous, Douglas. "Intimate Sensing." *Area* 18, no. 2 (1986): 250–1.

Pottier, Johann. "Representations of Ethnicity in Post-Genocide Rwanda." In *Ethnic Hatred: Genocide in Rwanda*, edited by Obi Igwara, 35–57. London: ASEN Publications, 1995.

Powell, V. B. V. "The Progress of Athletics in Nigeria." *African World* (August 1948): 16–17.

Pratt, Mary Louise. "Scratches on the Face of the Country; or, What Mr. Barrow Saw in the Land of the Bushmen." In *"Race," Writing, and Difference*, edited by Henry Louis Gates, 238–62. Chicago: University of Chicago Press, 1986.

———. *Imperial Eyes: Travel Writing and Transculturation*. London: Routledge, 1992.

Pronger, Brian. "Post-Sport: Transgressing Boundaries in Physical Culture." In *Sport and Postmodern Times*, edited by Geneviève Rail, 278–98. Albany: State Univ. of New York Press, 1998.

Prunier, Gérard. *The Rwanda Crisis: History of a Genocide, 1959–1994*. London: Hurst, 1995.

Pultz, John. *Photography and the Body*. London: Weidenfeld and Nicholson, 1995.

Quayson, Ato. *Postcolonialism: Theory, Practice, or Process?* Cambridge: Polity, 2000.

Quercetani, Roberto. *Athletics: A History of Modern Track and Field Athletics*. London: Oxford University Press, 1964.

Rabinow, Paul. "Representations Are Social Facts: Modernity and Post-Modernity in Anthropology." In *Writing Culture: The Poetics and Politics of Ethnography*, edited by James Clifford and George Marcus, 234–61. Berkeley: University of California Press, 1986.

Rail, Geneviève. "Seismography of the Postmodern Condition: Three Theses on the Implosion of Sport." In *Sport and Postmodern Times*, edited by Geneviève Rail, 143–62. Albany: State University of New York Press, 1998.

Ramirez, Francis, and Christian Rolot. *Histoire du cinéma au Zaïre, au Ruanda, et au Burundi*. Tervuren, Belgium: Koninklijk Museum voor Midden-Afrika, 1985.

Ranger, Terrence. "The Invention of Tradition in Africa." In *The Invention of Tradition*, edited by Eric Hobsbawm and Terence Ranger, 211–62. Cambridge: Cambridge University Press, 1983.

Relph, Edward. *Place and Placelessness*. London: Pion, 1976.

Renson, Roland. "Save Our Sports," *UNESCO Courier*, (December 1993): 41–45.

Reutler, Karl. *Über die Leibesübungen der Primitiven*. Rostock: Carl Kinstorffs Buchdruckerei, 1940.

Riefenstahl, Leni. *The Last of the Nuba*. 1975. Reprint, London: Harvill, 1995.

Richards, D. J. P. "Athletic Records and Achievements in Relation to Climate, Social, and Environmental Factors." Master's thesis, University of Wales, 1953.

Richards, Thomas. *The Imperial Archive: Knowledge and Fantasy of Empire*. London: Verso, 1993.

Richardson, Annie. "The Nazification of Women in Art." In *The Nazification of Art*, edited by Brandon Taylor and Wilfried van der Will, 53–79. Winchester, England: Winchester Press, 1990.

Rigby, Peter. *African Images: Racism and the end of Anthropology*. Oxford: Berg, 1996.

Ripley, Robert. *The New Believe It or Not*. London: Stanley Paul, 1931.

Rony, Fatimah Tobing. *The Third Eye: Race, Cinema, and Ethnographic Spectacle*. Durham: Duke University Press, 1991.

Roome, J. W. *Tramping through Africa: A Dozen Crossings of the Continent*. London: A. and C. Black, 1930.

————. *Through the Lands of Nyanza*. London: Marshall, Morgan, and Scott, 1931.

Roscoe, John. *The Northern Bantu*. Cambridge: Cambridge University Press, 1915.

Rose, Gillian. *Feminism and Geography*. London: Polity, 1993.

————. "Geography and Gender, Cartographies and Corporealities." *Progress in Human Geography* 19, no. 4 (1995): 544–48.

————. "Teaching Visualised Geographies: Towards a Methodology for the Interpretation of Visual Materials." *Journal of Geography in Higher Education* 20, no. 3 (1996): 281–94.

Rosmant, M. "Au pays des pages danseurs." *Touring Club du Congo Belge* 1 (1950): 13–23.

Rothenberg, Tamar. "Voyeurs of Imperialism: *The National Geographic Magazine* before World War II." In *Geography and Empire*, edited by Anne Godlewska and Neil Smith, 155–72. Blackwell: Oxford, 1994.

Rowe, David. *Sport, Culture, and the Media*. Buckingham, England: Open University Press, 1999.

Ruanda-Urundi: Social Achievements. Translated by Goldie Blankoff-Scarr. Brussels: Belgian Congo and Ruanda-Urundi Information and Public Relations Office, 1960.

Rummelt, Peter. *Sport im Kolonialismus—Kolonialismus im Sport*. Cologne: Pahl-Rugenstein, 1986.

Ryan, James. "Photography, Geography, and Empire, 1840–1914." Ph.D. diss., University of London, 1994.

————. "Picturing People and Places." Review of *Anthropology and Photography 1860–1920*, by Elizabeth Edwards. *Journal of Historical Geography* 20 (1994): 332–37.

————. *Picturing Empire: Photography and the Visualization of the British Empire*. London: Reaktion, 1997.

Ryan, Simon. *The Cartographic Eye*. Cambridge: Cambridge University Press, 1996.

Rürup, Reinhard. *1936: Die Olympischen Spiele und der Nationalsozialismus*. Berlin: Stiftung Topographie des Terrors, 1999.

Said, Edward. *Culture and Imperialism*. London: Vintage, 1994.

————. *Orientalism: Western Conceptions of the Orient*. 1978. Reprint, London: Penguin, 1995.

————. "John McEnroe plus Anyone." *London Review of Books*, 1 July 1999, 34–5.

Sander, L. *Die Deutschen Kolonien in Wort und Bild*. Leipzig: Verlag für Allgemeines Missen, 1907.

Sanders, Edith. "The Hamitic Hypothesis: Its Origin and Functions in Time Perspective." *Journal of African History* 10, no. 4 (1969): 521–32.

Saunders, D. "Walks of Life: Mauss on the Human Gymnasium." *Body and Society*, 1, no. 2 (1995): 65–81.

Sax, William. "Hall of Mirrors: Orientalism, Anthropology, and the Other." *American Anthropologist*, 100, no. 2 (1998): 292–301.

Schaap, Richard. *An Illustrated History of the Olympics*. New York: Knopf, 1963.

Schantz, H. "Urundi, Territory and People." *The Geographical Review* 12 (1922): 329–57.

Schebesta, Paul. *My Pygmy and Negro Hosts*. Translated by Gerald Griffin. London: Hutchinson, 1936.

Scheerder, Jeroen, and Roland Renson. *Annotated Bibliography of Traditional Play and Games in Africa*. Berlin: International Council of Sport Science and Physical Education, 1998.

Schiarini, Pompilio. "Spoglie di un impero coloniale: Il Ruanda e l'Urundi." *La Terra e la Vita* 1 (1922): 63–69.

Schultz, Bruno. "Sport und Rasse." *Leibesübungen und Körperliche Erziehung*, (1939): 366–67.

Schumacher, Peter. "Der Eherecht in Ruanda." *Anthropos* 12 (1912): 1–32.

———. "Tanz und Spiel in Ruanda." *Comptes Rendus Semaines de Missiologie* 16 (1938): 381–407.

———. "De hamitische Wahrsagerei in Ruanda." *Anthropos*, 34 (1939): 130–206.

Schwartz, Joan. "The Geography Lesson: Photographs and the Construction of Imaginative Geographies," *Journal of Historical Geography*, 22 (1996): 16–45.

Schweitzer, Georg. *Emin Pasha: His Life and Work*. Vol. 2. Westminster: Archibald Constable, 1898.

Sekula, Allan. "On the Invention of Photographic Meaning." In *Thinking Photography*, edited by Victor Burgin, 84–109. London: Macmillan, 1982.

Sellström, Tor, and Lennart Wohlgemuth. "The International Response to Conflict and Genocide: Lessons from the Rwanda Experience." Copenhagen: Steering Committee of the Joint Evaluation Team of Emergency Assistance to Rwanda, 1996.

Seltzer, Mark. *Bodies and Machines*. New York: Routledge, 1992.

Semple, Ellen. "Influences of Geographic Environment." In *Human Geography: An Essential Introduction*, edited by John Agnew, David Livingstone, and

Alisdair Rogers. New York: Henry Holt, 1911. Reprint, 252–67. Oxford: Blackwell, 1996.

Severn, Merlyn. *Congo Pilgrim*. London: Travel Book Club, 1952.

Sharp, Leonard. "Letter from Dr. Sharp." *Ruanda Notes* 4 (1922): 3–4.

———. "The Medical Work Reviewed by Dr. Sharp." *Ruanda Notes*, 22 (1927): 11–13.

Sharpe, Sir Alfred. *The Backbone of Africa*. London: Witherby, 1921.

Shearman, Montague. *Athletics and Football*. London: Longmans Green, 1894.

Sibley, David. *Geographies of Exclusion: Society and Difference in the West*. London: Routledge, 1995.

———. "Creating Geographies of Difference." In *Human Geography Today*, edited by Doreen Massey, John Allen, and Philip Sarre, 116–28. Cambridge, England: Polity, 1999.

Sibomana, André. *Hope for Rwanda: Conversations with Laure Guilbert and Hervé Deguine*. Translated by Carina Tertsakian. London: Pluto, 1999.

Sidaway, James. "The (Re)Making of the Western Geographical Tradition: Some Missing Links." *Area* 29, no. 1 (1997): 72–80.

———. "Postcolonial Geographies: An Exploratory Essay." *Progress in Human Geography* 24, no. 4 (2000): 591–612.

Sinha, Mrinalini. *Colonial Masculinity: The "Manly Englishman" and the "Effeminate Bengali" in the Late Nineteenth Century*. Manchester: Manchester University Press, 1995.

Slater, David. "Geopolitics and the Postmodern: Issues of Knowledge, Difference, and North-South Relations." In *Space and Social Theory: Interpreting Modernity and Postmodernity*, edited by Georges Benko and Ulf Strohmayer, 324–35. Oxford: Blackwell, 1997.

———. "Situating Geopolitical Representations: Inside/Outside and the Power of National Development." In *Human Geography Today*, edited by Doreen Massey, John Allen, and Philip Sarre, 62–84. Cambridge, England: Polity, 1999.

Slater, Don. "Photography and Modern Vision: The Spectacle of 'Natural Magic.'" In *Visual Culture*, edited by Charles Jenks, 218–37. London: Routledge, 1995.

Smith, Pierre. "Aspects de l'esthétique au Ruanda." *L'Homme* 25 (1985): 7–22.

Smith, Stanley. "A Journey into Belgian Ruanda." *Ruanda Notes* 21 (1927): 9–13.

———. "Acts XVI, 7 and the Story of a Broken Bridge." *Ruanda Notes* 25 (1928): 9–11.

————. *An African Nebuchadnezzar: The Story of a Ruandan Chief.* Croydon, England: Ruanda General and Medical Mission, [1948?].

Soloman-Godeau, Abigail. *Photography in the Dock: Essays on Photographic History, Institutions, and Practices.* Minneapolis: University of Minnesota Press, 1991.

Sontag, Susan. *On Photography.* Harmondsworth, England: Penguin, 1978.

————. "Fascinating Fascism." In *A Susan Sontag Reader*, 305–25. London: Penguin, 1982.

Speer, Albert. *Inside the Third Reich.* New York: Avon, 1971.

Spencer, Paul. "Introduction: Interpretations of the Dance in Anthropology." In *Society and the Dance*, edited by Paul Spencer, 1–46. Cambridge: Cambridge University Press, 1995.

Spurr, David. *The Rhetoric of Empire: Colonial Discourse in Journalism, Travel Writing, and Imperial Administration.* Durham: Duke University Press, 1993.

Squire, Shelagh. "Accounting for Cultural Meanings: The Interface Between Geography and Tourism Studies Re-Examined." *Progress in Human Geography* 18, no. 1 (1994): 1–16.

Steiner, Christopher. "Travel Engravings and the Construction of the Primitive." In *Prehistories of the Future: The Primitivist Project and the Culture of Modernism*, edited by Elazar Barkan and Robert Bush, 202–25. Stanford: Stanford University Press, 1995.

Stokvis, Ruud. "Sports and Civilization: Is Violence a Central Theme?" In *Sport and Leisure in the Civilizing Process: Critique and Counter-Critique*, edited by Eric Dunning and Chris Rojek, 121–36. Toronto: University of Toronto Press, 1992.

Symanski, Richard. "The Manipulation of Ordinary Language." *Annals of the Association of American Geographers*, 66, no. 4 (1976): 605–14.

Tamplin, Ron. "Noblemen and Noble Savages." In *Representing Others: White Views on Indigenous Peoples*, edited by Mick Gidley, 60–83. Exeter: Exeter University Press, 1992.

Taussig, Michael. *Mimesis and Alterity: A Particular History of the Senses.* New York: Routledge, 1991.

Taylor, Christopher. *Milk, Honey, and Money: Changing Concepts of Rwandan Healing.* Washington, D.C.: Smithsonian Institution, 1992.

————. *Sacrifice as Terror: The Rwandan Genocide of 1994.* Oxford: Berg, 1999.

Templeton, Robert. *The High Jump.* New York: American Sports Publishing, 1926.

Thomas, Nicholas. *Colonialism's Culture: Anthropology, Travel, and Government.* Cambridge, England: Polity, 1994.

Thrift, Nigel. "The Still Point: Resistance, Expressive Embodiment and Dance." In *Geographies of Resistance*, edited by Steve Pile and Michael Keith, 124–51. London: Routledge, 1997.

Tiffin, Chris, and Alan Lawson. "The Textuality of Empire." In *De-Scribing Empire*, edited by Chris Tiffin and Alan Lawson, 1–11. London: Routledge, 1994.

Tirala, Lothar Gottlieb. *Sport und Rasse*. Frankfurt-am-Main: Bechhold Verlagsbuchhandlung, 1936.

Todorov, Tzvetan. *On Human Diversity: Nationalism, Racism, and Exoticism in French Thought*. Cambridge: Harvard University Press, 1993.

Tomas, David. *Transcultural Spaces and Transcultural Beings*. Boulder: Westview, 1996.

Torgovnick, Mariana. *Gone Primitive: Savage Intellects, Modern Lives*. Chicago: University of Chicago Press, 1990.

Towadros, Çeylan. "Foreign Bodies: Art History and the Discourse of Nineteenth-Century Orientalist Art." *Third Text* 3/4 (1988): 51–67.

Tuan, Yi-Fu. "Use of Simile and Metaphor in Geographical Descriptions." *The Professional Geographer* 9 (1957): 9–11.

———. *Dominance and Affection: The Making of Pets*. New Haven: Yale University Press, 1984.

———. "Language and the Making of Place: A Narrative Descriptive Approach." *Annals of the Association of American Geographers* 81, no. 4 (1991): 684–96.

———. *Passing Strange and Wonderful: Aesthetics, Nature, and Culture*. Washington, D.C.: Island, 1993.

Tuccaro, Archange. *Trois dialogues de l'exercise de sauter et voliger en l'air*. Paris: Claude de Monstroel, 1599.

Tyler, Stephen. "Post-Modern Anthropology: From Document of the Occult to Occult Document." In *Writing Culture*, edited by James Clifford and George Marcus, 122–40. Berkeley: University of California Press, 1986.

Ueberhorst, Horst. *Friedrich Ludwig Jahn 1778/1978*. Munich: Heinz Moos Verlag, 1978.

———. "Turnen." In *Encyclopedia of World Sports*, vol. 3, edited by David Levinson and Karen Christensen, 1110–14. Santa Barbara: ABC Clio, 1996.

Uvin, Peter. "Prejudice, Crisis, and Genocide in Rwanda." *African Studies Review* 40, no. 2 (1997): 91–115.

van der Merwe, Floris. "Ernst Franz Jokl as the Father of Physical Education in Southern Africa." Paper presented at the Annual Meeting of the North American Society for Sports History, Banff, Canada, May 1990.

van der Will, Wilfried. "The Body and the Body Politic as Symptom and Metaphor in the Transition of German Culture to National Socialism." In *The Nazification of Art*, edited by Brandon Taylor and Wilfried van der Will, 14–52. Winchester, England: Winchester Press, 1990.

van Overschelde, G. *Bij de reuzen en dwergen van Rwanda*. Tielt, Belgium: Lannoo, 1947.

Vansina, Jan. "Photographs of the Sankuna and Kasai River Basin Expedition Undertaken by Emil Torday 1876–1931 and M. W. Hilton Simpson 1881–1936." In *Anthropology and Photography 1860–1920*, edited by Elizabeth Edwards, 193–205. New Haven: Yale University Press, 1992.

———. *Living with Africa*. Madison: University of Wisconsin Press, 1994.

———. "The Politics of History and the Crisis in the Great Lakes." *Africa Today* 45, no. 1 (1998): 37–44.

van Ween, Veerle, and Roland Renson. *Traditional Games in South America*. Schorndorf, Germany: Verlag Paul Hoffmann, 1992.

Vennum, Thomas. *American Indian Lacrosse: Little Brother of War*. Washington, D.C.: Smithsonian Institution, 1994.

Vigarello, Georges. "The Upward Training of the Body from the Age of Chivalry to Courtly Civility." In *Fragments for a History of the Human Body*, part 2, edited by Michael Fehr, Ramona Naddaff, and Nadra Tazi, 148–99. New York: Zone, 1989.

Vints, Luc. *Kongo Made in Belgium*. Leuven, Belgium: Kritak, 1984.

Waal, Alex de. "Genocide in Rwanda." *Anthropology Today* 10, no. 3 (1994): 1–2.

Walder, Dennis. *Post-Colonial Literatures in English: History, Language, Theory*. Oxford: Blackwell, 1998.

Watts, Michael. "Collective Wish Images: Geographical Imaginaries and the Crisis of National Development." In *Human Geography Today*, edited by Doreen Massey, John Allen, and Philip Sarre, 85–107. Cambridge, England: Polity, 1999.

Webb, Virginia-Lee. "Manipulated Images: European Photographs of Pacific People." In *Prehistories of the Future: The Primitivist Project and the Culture of Modernism*, edited by E. Baran and R. Bush, 175–201. Stanford: Stanford University Press, 1995.

Webster, F. A. M. *Olympian Field Events: Their History and Practice*. London: George Newnes, 1914.

———. *Athletes of Today: History, Development, and Training*. London: Frederick Warne, 1929.

———. *Why? The Science of Athletics*. London: John G. Shaw, [1937?].

Webster, J. B., B. A. Ogot, and J. P. Chrétien. "The Great Lakes Region, 1500–1800. In *UNESCO General History of Africa*, vol. 5, edited by B. A. Ogot, 776–827. Paris: UNESCO, 1992.

Weule, Karl. "Ethnologie des Sports." In *Geschichtes des Sports aller Völker und Zeten*, vol. 1, edited by G. A. E. Bogeng, 1–75. Leipzig: Seeman, 1926.

Williams, Reginald. "High jumping." In *The Encyclopædia of Sport*, vol. 1, edited by the Earl of Suffolk and F. G. Aflalo, 50–51. London: Lawrence and Wishart, 1897.

Willis, Anne-Marie. "Photography and Film: Figures in/of History." In *Fields of Vision: Essays in Film Studies, Visual Anthropology, and Photography*, edited by Leslie Devereaux and Roger Hillman, 77–93. Berkeley: University of California Press, 1995.

Willoughby, David. *The Super-Athletes*. South Brunswick, N.Y.: Barnes, 1970.

Wollen, Peter. "Tales of Total Art and Dream of the Total Museum." In *Virtual Display: Culture Beyond Appearances*, edited by Lynne Cooke and Peter Wollen, 154–77. Seattle: Bay Press, 1995.

Young, Robert. *Colonial Desire: Hybridity in Theory, Culture, and Race*. London: Routledge, 1995.

Zuure, Bern. "Missie en ontspanning: Sport en spel bij de Barundi." *Comptes rendus semaines de missiologie*, 13 (1935): 224–51.

Permissions

The University of Minnesota Press is grateful for permission to reprint the photographs and other art in this book. We have tried to contact all copyright holders or original sources of these images; if any proper acknowledgment has not been made, we encourage copyright holders to notify us.

Frontispiece: From *South of the Sahara*, by Attilio Gatti (London: Hodder and Stoughton Publishers, 1946). Reproduced by permission of Hodder and Stoughton Limited.

Figure 2.1: From *Tramping through Africa*, by William John Waterman Roome (London: A & C Black, 1930). Reprinted by permission of A & C Black (Publishers) Limited.

Figure 2.2: Courtesy of the collection of Africa Museum Tervuren (Belgium).

Figure 2.3: Courtesy of Sabena.

Figure 2.4: Courtesy of Joseph Ghesquiere.

Figure 2.5: Courtesy of Joseph Ghesquiere.

Figure 2.6: Courtesy of Joseph Ghesquiere.

Figure 4.1: From *In the Heart of Africa*, by Duke Adolphus Frederick of Mecklenburg, translated by G. E. Maberly-Oppler (Cassell, 1910).

Figure 4.2: From *Forschungen im Nil-Kongo-Zwischengebiet*, by Jan Czekanowski (Leipzig: Klinkhardt & Biermann, 1911).

Figure 4.3: From *The Wonderland of the Eastern Congo: The Region of the Snow-Crowned Volcanoes, the Pygmies, the Giant Gorilla, and the Okapi*, by Thomas Alexander Barns (London: G. P. Putnam's Sons, 1922).

Figure 4.4: Courtesy of the collection of Africa Museum Tervuren (Belgium).

Figure 4.5: Courtesy of the collection of Africa Museum Tervuren (Belgium).

Figure 4.6: From "The Kingdom of the Giants," by Attilio Gatti, in *Travel* 77 (1942).

Figure 4.7: From *Lords of the Equator: An African Journey*, by Patrick Balfour (London: Hutchinson, 1937).

Figure 4.8: Courtesy of the Mid-Africa Ministry (Rwanda Mission), Church Missionary Society, London.

Figure 4.9: W. Robert Moore/NGS Image Collection. Used by permission of the National Geographic Society.

Figure 4.10: Courtesy of Joseph Ghesquiere.

Figure 4.11: From *Guide du Voyageur au Congo Belge et au Ruanda-Urundi*, R. Dupriez, ed. (Brussels: L'Office du Congo Belge et au Ruanda-Urundi, 1949).

Figure 4.12: Courtesy of the collection of Africa Museum Tervuren (Belgium).

Figure 4.13: Courtesy of the Mid-Africa Ministry (Rwanda Mission), Church Missionary Society, London.

Figure 4.14: From *Histoire du cinéma au Zaïre au Ruanda et au Burundi*, by Francis Ramirez and Christian Rolot. Courtesy of the collection of Africa Museum Tervuren (Belgium).

Figure 4.15: From *South of the Sahara*, by Attilio Gatti (London: Hodder and Stoughton Publishers, 1946). Reproduced by permission of Hodder and Stoughton Limited.

Figure 4.16: Courtesy of the Mid-Africa Ministry (Rwanda Mission), Church Missionary Society.

Figure 4.17: Courtesy of the collection of Africa Museum Tervuren (Belgium).

Figure 4.18: Courtesy of Joseph Ghesquiere.

Figure 4.19: Courtesy of Joseph Ghesquiere.

Figure 4.20: From "High Jump Technique of the Central African Watussis," by Ernst Jokl, in *Journal of Physical Education and School Hygiene* (1941).

Figure 4.21: Courtesy KADOC, Leuven, Belgium (Film collection White Fathers).

Figure 4.22: Courtesy KADOC, Leuven, Belgium (Film collection White Fathers).

Figure A.1: Courtesy of Jan Agertz.

Figure A.2: From *Om sport—Indtryk fra en Rejse i England,* by K. A. Knudsen (1895).

Figure A.3: Photograph of Schenkel (1886), by Étienne-Jules Marey (1830–1904).

Index

John Bale is professor of sports geography at Keele University, U.K., and visiting professor of sports studies at Aarhus University, Denmark. Among his books are *The Brawn Drain: Foreign Student Athletes in American Universities*; *Sport, Space, and the City*; *Landscapes of Modern Sports*; and, with Joe Sang, *Kenyan Running: Movement Culture, Geography, and Global Change*. His articles have been published in journals related to human geography, sports history, sports sociology, and physical education.